P9-ARY-509

Development of the Industrial U.S.

Primary Sources

Development of
the Industrial U.S.
Primary
Sources

Sonia G. Benson
Jennifer York Stock,
Project Editor

U·X·L
An imprint of Thomson Gale,
a part of The Thomson Corporation

THOMSON
───★───
GALE

Detroit • New York • San Francisco • San Diego • New Haven, Conn. • Waterville, Maine • London • Munich

Development of the Industrial U.S: Primary Sources

Sonia G. Benson

Project Editor
Jennifer York Stock

Editorial
Sarah Hermsen

Rights Acquisitions and Management
Shalice Shah-Caldwell, Kim Smilay

Imaging and Multimedia
Randy Bassett, Lezlie Light,
Daniel Newell, Denay Wilding

Product Design
Pamela A. E. Galbreath

Composition
Evi Seoud

Manufacturing
Rita Wimberly

LIBRARY OF CONGRESS CATALOGING-IN-PUBLICATION DATA

Benson, Sonia.
    Development of the industrial U.S. Almanac / Sonia G. Benson ; Jennifer York Stock,
project editor.
        p. cm.
    Includes bibliographical references and index.
    ISBN 1-4144-0179-5 (hardcover : alk. paper)
        1. Industries–United States–History–Juvenile literature. 2. Industrial revolution–
United States–History–Juvenile literature. [1. United States–Economic conditions–To
1865–Juvenile literature.] I. Stock, Jennifer York, 1974- II. Title.

HC105.B4543 2006
330.973'05–dc22   2005016349

Printed in the United States of America
10 9 8 7 6 5 4 3 2 1

Table of Contents

Introduction

Industrialization is the widespread development of profit-making businesses that manufacture products on a large scale, using labor-saving machinery. Understanding the history of the development of industrialization in the United States, which took place over two centuries, involves learning about some of its technical elements, such as technology and the economy. But the history of U.S. industrialism is also a dramatic story of people rising and falling from power or struggling desperately to make the world a better place. Industrialization fueled the national culture, economy, daily life, and politics, creating such tremendous social changes that it is impossible to imagine what life in the United States would be like without it.

Though the Industrial Revolution, a period of rapid industrial growth causing a shift in focus from agriculture to industry, first began in England and Europe in the middle of the eighteenth century, industrialization did not begin to take root in the United States until after the American Revolution (1775–83). Even then American industrialization had a slow start, due to overwhelming obstacles. At the time, the vast majority of

Americans lived independent lives as farmers in remote areas. For the most part, they had little connection with anyone but neighboring farmers, since there were few good roads or systems of communication. Most people did not even own clocks; time was determined by the seasons and the rising and setting of the sun. Few people worked for wages, and those manufactured goods Americans could afford generally came from Europe. The new nation had vast natural resources, such as land, timber, metals, minerals, water power, and ports, but without transportation or manufacturing it was nearly impossible to make industrial use of them.

Once begun, the American Industrial Revolution took on its own character, differing from that of other countries. This was primarily because Americans themselves had been shaped and selected by a unique set of forces. After fighting hard to gain independence from England, most Americans were passionate about the ideals of liberty and equality for all (although to many Americans at the time this meant only white males), and they were determined to create a society in which any individual could rise and prosper through his or her own efforts. They were also driven by the desire for wealth. Though many Europeans immigrated to America to find religious or social freedom, the majority came seeking riches. Many had faced bitter hardships and were prepared to take major risks to obtain wealth. Another key trait of Americans was a spirit of innovation; it had been a necessary attribute for emigrants who left Europe in the seventeenth century, for they would have to reinvent the most basic aspects of their daily lives in the New World. The combined spirit of individualism, greed, and innovation came to characterize U.S. industrialism.

In the years between the American Revolution and the American Civil War (1861–65), innovation and invention were highly esteemed by the American public. Most industrial designs and ideas came initially from Europe, but once they reached the machine makers, or "mechanicians," of American shops, they were improved until they became distinctly American, suited to the land and its people. The times produced an extremely talented group of inventors and innovators, and from their workshops, which were mainly located in the northeastern United States, the "American System," or mass production and the use of interchangeable parts, emerged. It would forever change the nature of manufacturing worldwide.

With new advances in technology, some enterprising business people built the first U.S. factories, and most of them flourished. However, from the start the stark division in wealth and position between industry owners and their workers was at odds with the popular belief in American liberty and equality. Despite early factory owners' efforts to humanize factory work, workers faced low wages and poor working conditions. Many claimed they were slaves to wage labor. It was not long after the first industrial workforces were hired that the first labor strikes took place. The conflict between employers and employees continued, and the factory owners' early attempts to create ideal circumstances for workers were abandoned. Professional managers were hired to get as much work from the workforce as possible. A huge influx of immigrants from Europe and Asia from the 1840s until the 1920s supplied inexpensive labor, but labor strikes continued.

After a slow beginning in the Northeast industrialization began to spread at a rapid pace with the nationwide building of transportation and communications systems. The construction of the transcontinental railroad spanning the nation from one coast to the other—a mammoth undertaking—signaled the start of a new way of life for all Americans. Where railroads went, towns and cities with bustling new commerce arose. The construction of the railroads spawned giant new industries in steel, iron, and coal. Railroads brought farmers' crops to distant markets and were instrumental in bringing the industrial society to the West.

For the railroads to be built and industry to advance, capital, or vast quantities of money, was required. The art of raising large amounts of capital and applying it to industry was mainly accomplished by a generation of extremely capable industrialists who built the gigantic industries that dominated the nation and ruled its economy. These legendary men, admired as the "captains of industry" by some and loathed as ruthless crooks, or "robber barons," by others, included railroad owner Cornelius Vanderbilt, steel empire founder Andrew Carnegie, Standard Oil tycoon John D. Rockefeller, investment banker J. P. Morgan, and many others. Though some of them came from wealthy backgrounds, many were born in humble circumstances and rose to wealth and power through their own efforts. These industrialists created new systems of doing business that are still in place today. Their tactics almost always included creating monopolies, huge corporations that dominated their industry nationwide and limited attempts at competition by others. As the industrialists prospered, most of the wealth of the nation fell into their hands. This period became known as the Gilded Age, the era of industrialization from the early 1860s to the turn of the century in which a few wealthy individuals gained tremendous power and influence. During the Gilded Age the power of industrialists and their corporations seemed unstoppable.

The number of U.S. companies dwindled from thousands to hundreds as the most powerful industrialists bought out or crushed their competitors. Once again, the national spirit of liberty and equality was aroused. Farmers, laborers, poor immigrants, and labor unions as well as middle class reformers sought relief from the power of the corporations, giving rise to the Progressive Era, or the period of the American Industrial Revolution that spanned roughly from the 1890s to about 1920, in which reformers worked together in the interest of distributing political power and wealth more equally. It was during this time that the strong hand of the federal government was finally felt in American industry, as it began to leave behind its laissez-faire, or non-interference, policies in order to regulate businesses, curb monopolies, and protect workers.

By the twentieth century, the United States was the richest and most powerful industrial nation in the world, but the process of industrialization continued. During the twentieth century industry was shaped by scientists like Frederick Winslow Taylor, who devised measurable methods of business management designed to produce top levels of efficiency. The best-known follower of "Taylorism" was Henry Ford, who began to mass produce affordable automobiles in 1909. The Great Depression (1929–41) and World War II (1939–45) both had profound effects on American industrialism, causing government controls and assistance to individuals to increase even more. In recent decades, computers and globalism have been the active agents of change in U.S. industrialism.

Finally, it is worthwhile to note that the development of U.S. industrialization is not finished. It took more than one hundred years for the United States to transform from a farming society to an industrial world power. Adjusting to industrialism has already taken up another century and will continue for many years to come.

Sonia G. Benson

Reader's Guide

The United States began as a nation of farmers living in remote areas, but over a period of two hundred years the country became the wealthiest and most powerful industrial nation of the world. During the American Industrial Revolution inventors and innovators created new and improved machines for manufacturing, while a new breed of American businessmen created revolutionary methods of conducting business and managing labor. The road to industrialization was not always heroic. Ruthlessness and greed were often key ingredients in advancing industry. While a few found wealth and power, multitudes of workers and farmers suffered, and small businesses were crushed by the powerful new corporations. Reformers, unions, and protestors against big business played a crucial role in the industrialization process as they pressed for the rights of workers and regulations on business to help farmers and consumers. The diverse people and events that forever changed the nation from a rural farming economy to an industrialized urban nation create a dramatic story that lies at the heart of U.S. history.

Coverage and features

Development of the Industrial U.S.: Primary Sources presents eighteen full or excerpted written works, speeches, and other documents that were influential during American industrialization. The volume includes excerpts from the writings of Thomas Jefferson and Alexander Hamilton reflecting their debate on industrialization; excerpts from legislation regarding industrialization, such as the Interstate Commerce Act and the Sherman Antitrust Act; segments of popular novels by Horatio Alger and William Dean Howells depicting the effects of industrialization on American society; political cartoons; a popular labor song; an excerpt from an essay by William Graham Sumner presenting the concept of social Darwinian, and much more.

Each excerpt presented in *Development of the Industrial U.S.: Primary Sources* includes the following additional material:

- An **introduction** places the document and its author in historical context.

- **"Things to remember while reading ..."** offers readers important background information and directs them to central ideas in the text.

- **"What happened next ..."** provides and account of the subsequent events, but in U.S. industrialization and in the life of the author.

- **"Did you know ..."** provides significant and interesting facts about the document, the author, or the events discussed.

- **"Consider the following ..."** gives students and teachers research and activity ideas that pertain to the subject of the excerpt.

- **"For more information"** lists sources for further reading on the author, the topic, or the document.

Nearly fifty photographs and illustrations, a timeline, sources for further reading, and an index supplement the volume.

U•X•L Development of the Industrial U.S. Reference Library

Development of the Industrial U.S.: Primary Sources is only one component of the three-part U•X•L Development of the

Industrial U.S. Reference Library. The other two titles in this set are:

- *Development of the Industrial U.S.: Almanac* presents an overview of the history of American industrialization. Its fourteen chapters cover the first American factories, inventors, the rise of big business and railroads, urbanism, labor unions, industrial influences in places such as the South or the Great Plains, the Gilded Age, the Progressive Era, the post-industrial era, and much more. Each chapter of the *Almanac* features informative sidebar boxes highlighting glossary terms and issues discussed in the text and concludes with a list of further readings. Also included are more than sixty photographs and illustrations, a timeline, a glossary, a list of suggested research and activity ideas, and an index providing easy access to subjects discussed throughout the volume.

- *Development of the Industrial U.S.: Biographies* profiles twenty-six significant figures who participated in American industrialization. The biographies cover a wide spectrum of people, from the creators of the first factories, such as Samuel Slater and Francis Cabot Lowell, to inventors and innovators, including John Fitch, Elijah McCoy, and Thomas Edison. Industrialists Andrew Carnegie, J. P. Morgan, and John D. Rockefeller are profiled, as are reformers and educators such as Jane Addams, Florence Kelley, and Booker T. Washington. *Biographies* also includes labor advocates such as Eugene Debs and A. Philip Randolph. The volume features more than fifty photographs and illustrations, a timeline, a glossary, and sources for further reading.

A cumulative index of all three volumes in the U•X•L Development of the Industrial U.S. Reference Library is also available.

Comments and suggestions

We welcome your comments on *Development of the Industrial U.S.: Primary Sources* and suggestions for other topics in history to consider. Please write: Editors, *Development of the Industrial U.S.: Primary Sources,* U•X•L, 27500 Drake Rd., Farmington Hills, Michigan, 48331-3535; call toll-free: 1-800-877-4253; fax to: 248-699-8097; or send e-mail via http://www.gale.com.

Timeline of Events

1780: American mechanics in the Northeast begin to apply principles learned from the English Industrial Revolution in their innovations on tools and machines.

1781: Oliver Evans invents machines to replace human labor in flour mills.

1785: Thomas Jefferson argues against U.S. industrialization in *Notes on the State of Virginia.*

1790: Eighty percent of the nation's population is made up of farmers and ninety-five percent of the population lives in rural areas.

1776
Adam Smith
publishes *Wealth
of Nations*

1775–83
American
Revolution

1789
French
Revolution
begins

1775   1780   1785   1790

1790: Congress passes the first patent law.

1791: Alexander Hamilton presents to Congress his famous *Report on Manufactures*, advocating industrialization of the United States.

1793: Eli Whitney submits his **Cotton Pin Petition** to the U.S. secretary of state. He is granted a patent one year later.

1798: Eli Whitney proposes to make 4,000 muskets for the U.S. government, using new machine-making tools and interchangeable parts.

1807: Robert Fulton's steamboat, the *Clermont,* makes its maiden voyage from New York City to Albany, New York.

1807: Eli Terry builds four thousand clockworks on a tight schedule using the latest principles of mass production.

1817: Congress authorizes the construction of the National Road, the first road to run west across the Appalachian Mountains.

1817–1825: The Erie Canal is built, connecting Albany and Buffalo, New York.

1825: The New York Stock Exchange opens its new headquarters at 11 Wall Street.

1826: The first U.S. railway, the Baltimore and Ohio (B & O) is launched.

1831: Cyrus McCormick invents the first workable reaper.

1834: Ten-year-old Harriet Hanson Robinson goes to work in the Lowell textile mills, an experience she will later write about in her memoirs, ***Loom and Spindle: or, Life among the Early Mill Girls*** (1898).

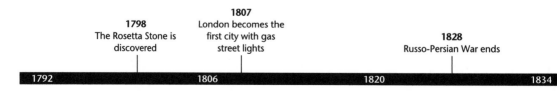

1798
The Rosetta Stone is discovered

1807
London becomes the first city with gas street lights

1828
Russo-Persian War ends

| 1792 | 1806 | 1820 | 1834 |

1835: Nathaniel Hawthorne writes about his trip along the Erie Canal in **"The Canal Boat,"** published in *New England Magazine.*

1836: Two thousand women workers go on strike for better wages and conditions at the Lowell textile mills.

1837: John Deere invents the steel plow.

1840: The *Lowell Offering,* a journal written by the women workers of the Lowell mills, is launched.

1840s: Immigration to the United States from Europe increases significantly. Between 1840 and 1920 37 million immigrants will arrive in the country.

1844: Samuel F. B. Morse sends the first official telegraph message from Washington, D.C., to Baltimore, Maryland.

1846: Elias Howe patents his sewing machine. Isaac M. Singer will market a more practical sewing machine within four years.

1851: U.S. technology exhibits impress visitors at the Crystal Palace Exhibition of London, the first world's fair.

1852: Samuel Colt opens a large arms manufacturing factory, using advanced mass-production techniques.

1859: The first successful effort to drill for oil gives rise to the oil industry.

1860: Shoemakers in Lynn, Massachusetts, launch a massive strike for better wages and working conditions. The strike will spread to factories over a wide area and include as many as twenty thousand men and women workers.

1838
Northern abolitionists
organize the
Underground Railroad

1847
Marx and Engels publish
the *Communist Manifesto*

1859
John Brown leads a
raid on Harper's Ferry

1835   1843   1851   1859

1862: The Pacific Railroad Act calls for building a transcontinental railroad from Omaha, Nebraska, to Sacramento, California.

1862: Congress enacts the Homestead Act, which provides small pieces of public land to settlers in the West for farming; industry soon expands into the new territories.

1864: The first Bessemer converter, a new process for making steel, is introduced in the United States.

1866: The National Labor Union (NLU) is formed to promote the eight-hour workday.

1867: In the first cattle drive, organized by James G. McCoy, cattle are driven from Texas to Abilene, Kansas, where they are shipped by railroad to Chicago, Illinois.

1867: The National Grange of the Patrons of Husbandry (usually called the Grange) is founded to advance the interests of farmers.

1868: Writer Henry Adams returns to the United States after a long stay in Europe to find his native land so changed by industry and big business he does not recognize it. He will later write about the experience in *The Education of Henry Adams,* originally printed in 1907.

1868: Writer Horatio Alger publishes his popular rags-to-riches novel, *Ragged Dick, or, Street Life in New York with the Boot-Blacks.*

1869: The two railroad companies, the Union Pacific and the Central Pacific, commissioned to build the transcontinental railroad meet at Promontory Point, Utah, marking the completion of the first transcontinental railroad.

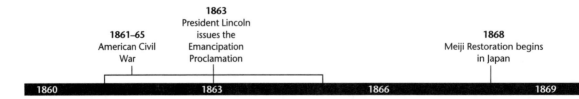

1861–65
American Civil
War

1863
President Lincoln
issues the
Emancipation
Proclamation

1868
Meiji Restoration begins
in Japan

1860   1863   1866   1869

1869: The Knights of Labor, one of the early national labor unions, is founded.

1869: On September 24 or "Black Friday," the price of gold fell due to the speculations of James Fisk and Jay Gould, creating a financial panic.

1869: A fire in the Avondale coal mine in Pennsylvania kills 108 men and boys.

1872: Hunters and railroad workers have killed millions of buffalo on the Great Plains, reducing their numbers from 15 million to 7 million. The extermination will continue until less than one thousand buffalo remain in the 1890s.

1873: One of the nation's largest banks, owned by Jay Cooke, fails, causing business failures and unemployment. A nationwide depression follows.

1875: The National Farmers' Alliance is founded. It quickly divides into two groups, the Northern Alliance and the Southern Alliance.

1876: The **"Memorial of the Chinese Six Company"** petitions President Ulysses S. Grant to end unfair discrimination against Chinese immigrants, particularly in regard to immigration laws.

1877: A large railroad strike begins in West Virginia to protest wage reductions. Within a few weeks, it spreads throughout the nation with about ten thousand participating workers. More than one hundred are killed by federal troops and about one thousand are jailed before the Great Strike is suppressed.

1880s: William Graham Sumner writes **"The Concentration of Wealth: Its Economic Justification,"** one of his many essays that advocate the theories of social

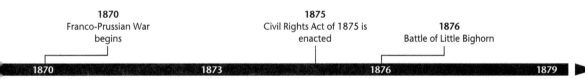

1870
Franco-Prussian War
begins

1875
Civil Rights Act of 1875 is
enacted

1876
Battle of Little Bighorn

1870   1873   1876   1879

Darwinism, arguing that the rich have become so because of their abilities, and the government should not interfere in their businesses.

1885: Writer William Dean Howells publishes his most famous book, ***The Rise of Silas Lapham,*** which describes the social changes that occur when the "new rich"—people from humble backgrounds who had made a fortune in the industrial era—enter the once-exclusive circles of Boston's old ruling class.

1886: The Haymarket Riots erupt in Chicago, pitting striking workers against police.

1886: The American Federation of Labor (AFL) reorganizes under the leadership of Samuel Gompers as a federation of trade unions formed to improve wages and working conditions, shorten working hours, abolish child labor, and provide for collective bargaining.

1886: The Colored Farmers' Alliance is founded.

1887: Congress passes the **Interstate Commerce Act** to regulate the railroads. It is the first regulatory act designed to establish government supervision over a major industry.

1880s: Political cartoons become a popular means of expression. The giant trusts run by John D. Rockefeller and Andrew Carnegie are frequent targets of their humor.

1880s: "Eight Hours" becomes the official song of the eight hours working day movement.

1889: James Buchanan Duke merges his tobacco company with four others to create the American Tobacco Company, controlling 90 percent of the U.S. tobacco industry.

1881	**1883**	**1886**	
Clara Barton founds the Red Cross	American railroads adopt standard time zones	Statue of Liberty is dedicated in New York Harbor	
1880	1883	1886	1889

1890: Congress enacts the **Sherman Antitrust Act** to prohibit companies from restricting competition or creating monopolies.

1890: The People's Party, better known as the Populists, is formed to combine the interests of farmers in the South and West and laborers nationwide to combat the powers of the Eastern industrialists.

1890: Jacob Riis publishes his book *How the Other Half Lives: Studies Among the Tenements of New York,* portraying the miserable conditions of the New York slums.

1892: In the Homestead Strike, the workers at Andrew Carnegie's steel mills strike to protest low wages and the hiring of nonunion workers. A violent battle ensues, and the union in the steel mills is crushed.

1893: A financial panic, mainly due to the collapse of hundreds of railroad companies, results in a nationwide depression.

1894: When the workers at the Pullman factory go on strike for better wages, 125,000 railroad workers in the American Railway Union (ARU) join the strike to support the Pullman workers.

1900: New York City becomes grossly overpopulated, with about 1.2 million people, or about 75 percent of its population living in overcrowded tenement buildings without adequate water, air, sewage, or garbage removal.

1900: About 1.7 million children under the age of sixteen are working in factories.

1900: Industrial accidents kill about 35,000 workers each year and disable 500,000 others.

1890 Battle of Wounded Knee	**1893** Lizzie Borden trial	**1896** Supreme Court rules on *Plessy v. Ferguson*	
1890	1893	1896	1899

1900: African Americans begin to migrate from the South to Northern industrial cities. By 1910, 366,880 African Americans will migrate to Northern cities from the South. From 1910 to 1920 between five hundred thousand and one million African Americans will make the trip north.

1900: Several U.S. magazines present a new form of journalism called muckraking, which investigates corruption in big business and government.

1903: President Theodore Roosevelt creates a federal Department of Commerce and Labor to investigate the operations and conduct of corporations.

1903: Frederick Winslow Taylor publishes an essay about making the workplace more efficient that will quickly become the basis of a new movement of scientific business management, or Taylorism.

1904: Ida M. Tarbell publishes her classic muckraking work, ***History of the Standard Oil Company,*** which probes the questionable tactics of the dominant oil-refining company and its owner, John D. Rockefeller.

1904: The U.S. Supreme Court rules that the Northern Securities Trust, a combination of several railroads owned in a trust under the management of James J. Hill, Edward H. Harriman, and J. P. Morgan, is in violation of the Sherman Antitrust Act. It is the first major trust to be dissolved under the act.

1907: A federal law against child labor is introduced to Congress, but it is defeated. Three years later, an estimated 2 million American children are still employed by industries.

1900
Boxer Rebellion
begins in China

1903
Wright brothers make
historic flight

1906
San Francisco earthquake

| 1900 | 1903 | 1906 | 1909 |

1909: John D. Rockefeller published his memoirs, *Random Reminiscences of Men and Events.*

1910: In the South, 80 percent of African American farmers and 40 percent of white farmers are either sharecroppers or tenant farmers struggling to survive.

1911: The U.S. Supreme Court rules that the Standard Oil Trust and the American Tobacco Company are in violation of the Sherman Antitrust Act and order them to dissolve.

1911: A fire at the Triangle Shirtwaist Company, a garment factory, kills 146 workers, mostly poor immigrant women and girls.

1914: Congress enacts the Clayton Antitrust Act, which updates the Sherman Antitrust Act and includes an important provision allowing workers to unionize and strike.

1920: For the first time in the United States, more people live in the city than in the country.

1927: Charles A. Lindbergh makes his famous 2,610-mile transatlantic (spanning the Atlantic Ocean) solo flight from Long Island, New York, to Paris, France, launching the aviation industry.

1932: Franklin Delano Roosevelt initiates his New Deal reforms, creating federal jobs, assisting farmers, protecting citizens from losing their homes to mortgage foreclosures, and enacting the Social Security Act to create an old-age pension system and paying benefits to the disabled and widows with children.

1938: Congress passes the Fair Labor Standards Act (FLSA), which sets a minimum wage for all workers, sets a maximum workweek of forty-four hours, and prohibits

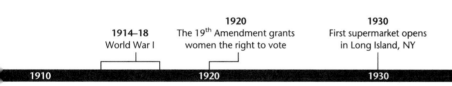

1914–18
World War I

1920
The 19th Amendment grants women the right to vote

1930
First supermarket opens in Long Island, NY

1910   1920   1930   1940

interstate shipment of goods produced by children under the age of sixteen.

1945: During American participation in World War II, the number of workingwomen rises to 18.6 million, a 50 percent increase from the 11.9 million workingwomen of 1940.

1946: The first real computer, the Electronic Numerical Integrator and Computer (ENIAC), is introduced to the public, starting the computer age.

1951: Former Triangle Shirtwaist Factory employee P. M. Newman writes **Letters to Michael and Hugh [Owens]** in which she describes the working conditions at the factory in the early 1900s.

1969: The first personal computers are introduced.

1980s: Companies begin scale back production and staffs, and American factories begin to deteriorate as investors build factories in other countries to benefit from lower labor costs.

1990s: The U.S. workforce experiences a widespread shift from industrial labor to service labor, marking the start of the postindustrial era.

2000: Multinational corporations account for about 20 percent of the world's production.

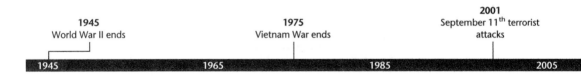

Words to Know

A

anarchist: An individual who advocates the use of force to overthrow all government.

antitrust laws: Laws opposing or regulating trusts or similar business monopolies.

apprentice: Someone who is bound to work for someone else for a specific term in order to learn a trade.

aristocracy: A government controlled by a wealthy, privileged social class.

artisan: A person who is skilled at a particular trade or craft.

assimilation: The social process of being absorbed, or blending into the dominant culture.

aviation: The operation and manufacture of aircraft.

B

bankruptcy: A state of financial ruin in which an individual or corporation cannot pay its debts.

boiler: A tube (or several connected tubes) in which water is heated to steam.

bond: A certificate of debt issued by a government or corporation that guarantees repayment of the original investment with interest by a specified date.

boycott: Consumer refusal to buy a company's goods in order to express disapproval.

bureaucratic structure: An organization with many levels of authority, in which people specialize in their jobs and follow set rules of operation.

C

capital: Accumulated wealth or goods devoted to the production of other goods.

capitalism: An economic system in which the means of production and distribution are privately owned by individuals or groups and competition for business establishes the price of goods and services.

capitalist: A person who invests his or her wealth in business and industry.

compulsory attendance: Mandatory obligation to go to school.

Confederate states: The eleven Southern states that withdrew from the United States in 1860 and 1861.

conservation: Planned management of natural resources to prevent their misuse or loss.

consolidation: A process in which companies purchase other companies and fold them into one large corporation.

conveyor belt: A moving belt that carries materials from one place to another.

corporation: A company, or organization of employers and employees that is permitted by law, usually owned by a group of shareholders and established to carry out a business or industry as a body. Corporations have legal rights usually reserved for individuals, such as the right to sue and be sued and to borrow or loan money.

cylinder: A tube-shaped chamber or tank.

D

depression: A period of drastic decline in the economy.

directorates: Boards of directors of different companies that have at least one director in common.

E

entrepreneur: A person who organizes a new business.

evolution: Evolution is the process by which all plant and animal species of plant and animal change over time because of variations that are passed from one generation to the next. The theory of evolution was first proposed by naturalist Charles Darwin (1809–1882).

F

factory: A building or group of buildings in which manufactured goods are made from raw materials on a large scale.

feudalism: A system in which most people live and work on farms owned by a noble who grants it to them in exchange for their loyalty.

foreclosure: A legal process in which a borrower who does not make payments on a mortgage or loan is deprived of the mortgaged property.

G

gauge: Distance between the rails of a railroad track.

Gilded Age: The era of industrialization from the early 1860s to the turn of the century in which a few wealthy individuals gained tremendous power and influence.

grain elevators: Huge storage bins built next to railroad tracks to hold grain until it is loaded into train cars.

grant: A transfer or property by deed or writing.

Great Plains: An area of grassland that stretches across the central part of North America eastward from the Rocky Mountains, from Canada in the north down to Texas in the south.

gross national product (GNP): The total of all goods and services produced each year.

H

holding company: A company that is formed to own stocks and bonds in other companies, usually for the purpose of controlling them.

horizontal expansion: Growth occurring when a company purchases rival companies in the same industry in an effort to eliminate competition.

hydroelectric power plants: Plants that produce electricity from waterpower.

I

industrialism: The social system that results from an economy based on large-scale industries.

industrialists: People who engage in profit-making enterprises that manufacture a certain product, such as textiles or steel.

industrialization: The development of industry.

Industrial Revolution: A period of rapid industrial growth causing a shift in focus from agriculture to industry beginning in the late eighteenth century and continuing through the nineteenth century. During this time new manufacturing technologies and improved transportation gave rise to the modern factory system and a massive movement of the population from the countryside to the cities. The Industrial Revolution began in England around 1760 and spread to the United States around 1780.

industry: A distinct group of profit-making enterprises that manufacture a certain product, such as the textile or steel industry.

infant mortality: The percentage of babies born in a year that die before they reach the age of one.

intellectual: A person devoted to study, analysis, and reflection, using rational intellect rather than emotions in pursuit of enlightenment.

interchangeable parts: Standardized units of a machine that could be used in any machine of that model.

interstate commerce: Trade that crosses the borders between states.

L

labor union: An organization of workers formed to protect and further their mutual interests by bargaining as a group with their employers over wages, working conditions, and benefits.

laissez-faire: An economic doctrine that opposes government regulation of commerce and industry beyond the minimum necessary.

loom: A frame or machine used to weave thread or yarns into cloth.

M

machine tool: A machine that shapes solid materials.

machinist: A worker skilled in operating machine tools.

magnate: A powerful and influential person in an industry.

manufacture: To make something from raw materials, usually as part of a large-scale system of production using machinery.

mass production: The manufacture of goods in quantity by using machines and standardized designs and parts.

mechanize: To equip with mechanical power.

mediation: Intervention to help two opposing sides of a dispute reach an agreement.

monopoly: The exclusive possession or right to produce a particular good or service.

muckrakers: Journalists who search for and expose corruption in public affairs.

N

New Deal: A set of legislative programs and policies for economic recovery and social reform initiated in the 1930s during the presidency of Franklin Delano Roosevelt.

O

omnibus: A horse-drawn coach for hire.

overhead expenses: The costs of running a business not directly related to producing the goods, such as rent or heating and lighting the workspace.

overproduction: An economic condition that occurs when there are more goods on the market than there are consumers to purchase them, usually leading to lower prices.

P

patent: A legal document issued by a government granting exclusive authority to an inventor for making, using, and selling an invention.

pension: A fixed sum paid regularly, usually as a retirement benefit.

philanthropy: The desire or effort to help humankind, as by making charitable donations.

pools: Agreements among rival companies to share their profits or divide up territories to avoid destructive competition and maintain higher prices.

postindustrial era: A time marked by the lessened importance of manufacturing and increased importance of service industries.

productivity: The amount of work someone can do in a set amount of time.

Progressive Era: The period of the Industrial Revolution that spanned roughly from the 1890s to about 1920, in which reformers worked together in the interest of distributing political power and wealth more equally.

public domain: Land held by the federal government.

pulley: Simple machine consisting of a wheel with a groove through which a rope passes. The pulley is used to move things up, down, or across, such as a flagpole or a curtain rod.

R

refinery: A building in which a raw material is processed to free it from impurities.

reservations: Land set aside by the U.S. government for use by Native Americans.

robots: Machines that automatically perform routine, often complex, tasks.

S

settlement houses: Places established and run by educated, and often wealthy, reformers to provide social and educational services to the residents of poor urban immigrant communities.

sharecropper: A tenant farmer who works the land for an agreed share of the value of the crop, minus the deductions taken out of his share for his rent, supplies, and living costs.

shuttle: A device that carries threads across a loom in the weaving process.

slums: Severely overcrowded urban areas characterized by the most extreme conditions of poverty, run-down housing, and crime.

speculator: A person who takes a business risk in the hope of making a profit, particularly when buying or selling stocks or commodities (economic goods) in order to profit from shifts in the market.

socialism: An economic system in which the means of production and distribution is owned collectively by all the workers and there is no private property or social classes.

solidarity: Unity based on common interests.

steam engine: An engine that burns fuel to heat water into steam, which becomes the power that turns the parts of the engine.

stock: An element of ownership of a corporation that has been divided up into shares that can be bought and sold.

stock market: A system for trade in companies, ventures, and other investments through the buying and selling of stocks, bonds, mutual funds, limited partnerships, and other securities.

strike: A work stoppage by employees to protest conditions or make demands of their employer.

sweatshop: A factory in which workers work long hours in poor conditions for very low wages.

T

tariffs: Government-imposed fees on imported goods.

telegraph: Any system that transmits encoded information by signal across a distance.

tenant farmer: Someone who farms land owned by someone else and pays rent or a share of the crop for the use of the land.

tenement: Urban dwellings rented by impoverished families that barely meet or fail to meet the minimum standards of safety, sanitation, and comfort.

textile: Cloth.

transcontinental: Spanning the continent from one coast to the other.

transcontinental railroad: A railroad that spans a continent, from coast to coast.

trusts: A group of companies, joined for the purpose of reducing competition and controlling prices..

turnover: Employees quitting their jobs and others being hired to take their place.

turnpike: A road which people have to pay to use.

V

ventilation: Air circulation or access to fresh air.

vertical expansion: Growth that occurs when a primary company purchases other companies that provide services or products needed for the company's business, in order to avoid paying competitive prices.

W

wage worker: A person who works for others for pay.

Wall Street: Financial district and home of the nation's major stock exchanges in New York, New York.

warp yarn: The threads that run lengthwise on a loom.

waterwheel: A wheel that rotates due to the force of moving water; the rotation of the wheel is then used to power a factory or machine.

woof: The threads that run crosswise on a loom.

work ethic: A belief in the moral good of work.

workers' compensation: Payments made to an employee who is injured at work.

Y

Yankee: A Southern word for Northerners.

Text Credits

The following is a list of the copyright holders who have granted us permission to reproduce excerpts from primary source documents in *Development of the Industrial U.S.: Primary Sources*. Every effort has been made to trace copyright; if omissions have been made, please contact us.

Copyrighted excerpts reproduced from the following books:

Sumner, William Graham. From "The Concentration of Wealth: Its Economic Justification," in *Social Darwinism: Selected Essays by William Graham Sumner*. Edited by Stow Persons. Prentice-Hall Inc., 1963. Copyright © 1963 by Prentice-Hall, Inc., copyright renewed © 1991 by Stow Persons. All rights reserved. Reprinted with permission of Simon & Schuster Adult Publishing Group.

Development of the Industrial U.S.

Primary Sources

Notes on the State of Virginia

"Query XIX: The present state of manufactures, commerce, interior and exterior trade?" Excerpt from Notes on the State of Virginia

First written in 1780 as a set of responses to questions from French diplomat François de Barbé Marbois. Published in book form in 1785 Reprinted in *The Life and Writings of Thomas Jefferson* Published in 1944

American statesman Thomas Jefferson (1743–1826) was one of the founding fathers of the United States. The founding fathers are the members of the Constitutional Convention that drafted the U.S. Constitution in 1787. A man of many interests, Jefferson played a central role in shaping the new nation. He strongly supported the movement toward republicanism, or rule by an elected government that represented a population of citizens all seen as fairly equal in the eyes of the law. (This equality, however, was limited to white males). His goal was to eliminate the kind of class structure that existed in England, where the wealthy upper class ruled the poor lower class. For Jefferson, an economy based on agriculture was important to the new American republicanism. He did not believe the promise of freedom and liberty in the new nation would be fulfilled if industrialization (the development of industry) became widespread. He feared the abuse of workers by industrialists (people who engage in profit-making enterprises that manufacture a certain product, such as textiles or steel) and the urban misery and corruption that had accompanied the Industrial Revolution in England (a period between 1750

"While we have land to labor then, let us never wish to see our citizens occupied at a workbench...."

Jefferson feared the abuse of workers by industrialists. *(Courtesy of The Library of Congress.)*

and 1850 in which rapid advances in technology significantly altered the way people lived). Instead, Jefferson had a strong vision of the United States as a rural land of independent farmers.

Jefferson's father had been a prominent leader and landowner and one of the earliest settlers of the wilderness country around Albemarle County, Virginia, where Jefferson was born.

Jefferson was an eager student from an early age, and he believed he had been destined by nature to be a scientist. At the age of seventeen he entered the College of William and Mary. Since there was little use for a scientist in Virginia at the time, he studied law and began a successful law practice in 1767.

As the American Revolution (1775–83; the American colonists' fight for independence from England) began, Jefferson joined the Continental Congress, a committee of representatives formed to lead the American colonies in the war for independence from England. The Congress appointed Jefferson to a committee charged with writing the Declaration of Independence. Though other members of the colonial congress made changes to the document, Jefferson is generally credited with its authorship. The document presented commonly held beliefs of the time and a summary of Jefferson's personal political beliefs: that all men, a term that included white males only, are created equal; that they possess inalienable (not able to be taken away or sold) rights granted by God; that governments exist to uphold these rights; and that governments get their authority from the consent of the people they govern.

During the American Revolution, Jefferson served as a member of the Virginia legislature, and in 1779 he was elected governor of the colony. As governor Jefferson composed the first version of his only full-length book, *Notes on the State of Virginia*. Written in response to a series of questions posed to him by a French minister visiting the United States, the work outlines the geography and natural history of Virginia, then adds a description of the region's social, economic, and political structure. When published in 1785, the book established Jefferson's reputation as a scholar and a pioneering American scientist.

One of the questions posed in *Notes on the State of Virginia* was about the state of industry in the nation. Jefferson responded that industry should be left to Europe. He had been to England and witnessed the miserable conditions of the industrial working people there. The workers were generally very poor, lived in slums (severely overcrowded urban areas characterized by run-down housing and crime), and were entirely dependent upon their employers for their survival. Most had no hope of a better life. Jefferson believed the

Jefferson had seen the miserable living conditions of the industrial workers in England. *(© Bettmann/Corbis.)*

revolution had been fought so that Americans would be free from slavery and no one would rule over others simply because they had more power and money. (It is worth noting that despite his devotion to the principle of personal liberty, Jefferson was a slave owner with mixed feelings about the South's African slave system.) Since the newly formed United States had what seemed to be unlimited land available for farming, he argued that there was no need for industry. He saw the new country as a strictly farming economy, in which each family had their own land and answered only to the seasons and the soil for their income. Jefferson firmly believed that farming was noble work—the work human beings were meant to do—while trade and manufacturing brought out greedy ambitions and corrupt behavior in which human beings used one another for selfish gain.

Things to remember while reading "Query XIX" from *Notes on the State of Virginia*:

- American colonists had long been receiving most of their manufactured goods, such as textiles (cloth), kitchenware, and tools, from England, but during the American Revolution trade between the warring nations ceased, and the colonists were forced to make their own goods. After the war England was eager to return to the profitable trade it had established with America, but a growing section of the U.S. population believed that Americans should not allow themselves to be economically dependent on Britain. This group, unlike Jefferson, wanted the United States to start its own Industrial Revolution, like the one that had already swept England earlier in the century.

- At the time of the American Revolution, all farmland in England was owned by the nobility (people from England's long-ruling families; the upper classes). England had experienced a population explosion in the seventeenth century and there was not enough land to support the people. Some 25 to 50 percent of the population lived in poverty. A portion of the rural poor migrated to cities seeking jobs. London's population, for example, grew from about 200,000 in 1600 to 575,000 in 1700. Jefferson argued against similar industrialization since, unlike Europe, the United States could support all its people on its available lands.

"Query XIX: The present state of manufactures, commerce, interior and exterior trade?" Excerpt from Notes on the State of Virginia

*We never had an **interior trade** of any importance. Our **exterior commerce** has suffered very much from the beginning of the **present contest**. During this time we have manufactured within our families the most necessary articles of clothing. Those of cotton will bear some comparison with the same kinds of manufacture in Europe; but those of wool, **flax**, and **hemp** are very coarse, unsightly, and unpleasant: and such is our attachment to agriculture, and such our preference for foreign manufactures, that be it wise or unwise, our people will certainly return as soon as they can, to the raising raw materials, and exchanging them for finer manufactures than they are able to execute themselves.*

*The political economists of Europe have established it as a principle that every state should endeavour to manufacture for itself: and this principle, like many others, we transfer to America, without calculating the difference of circumstance which should often produce a difference of result. In Europe the lands are either **cultivated**, or locked up against the cultivator. Manufacture must therefore be resorted to of necessity not of choice, to support the surplus of their people. But we have an immensity of land courting the industry of the husbandman [farmer]. Is it best then that all our citizens should be employed in its improvement,*

Interior trade: Trade within the nation.

Exterior commerce: Trade with other nations.

Present contest: The American Revolution.

Flax: Fiber of the flax plant, used to make cloth.

Hemp: A tough fiber from the hemp plant, used to make rope and rough cloth.

Cultivated: Used to grow crops.

Deposit: Place for safekeeping.

Phenomenon: Fact or event that can be observed.

Subsistence: Means to support life.

Casualties: Losses that occur by chance.

Caprice: Unpredictable or irrational ideas or actions.

Subservience: Servitude.

Venality: Openness to being bribed or bought.

Retarded: Slowed.

Aggregate: Total.

Barometer: Instrument that detects changes.

Twirling a distaff: Spinning a staff holding fibers such as wool or cotton.

Loss by the transportation of commodities: Expenses of shipping goods to and from Europe.

Vigour: Active in body or mind.

Degeneracy: Corruption.

Canker: Spreading sore.

or that one half should be called off from that to exercise manufactures and handicraft arts for the other? Those who labor in the earth are the chosen people of God, if ever he had a chosen people, whose breasts he has made his peculiar **deposit** for substantial and genuine virtue. It is the focus in which he keeps alive that sacred fire, which otherwise might escape from the face of the earth. Corruption of morals in the mass of cultivators is a **phenomenon** of which no age nor nation has furnished an example. It is the mark set on those, who not looking up to heaven, to their own soil and industry, as does the husbandman, for their **subsistence**, depend for it on the **casualties** and **caprice** of customers. Dependence begets **subservience** and **venality**, suffocates the germ of virtue, and prepares fit tools for the designs of ambition. This, the natural progress and consequence of the arts, has sometimes perhaps been **retarded** by accidental circumstances: but, generally speaking, the proportion which the **aggregate** of the other classes of citizens bears in any state to that of its husbandmen, is the proportion of its unsound to its healthy parts, and is a good enough **barometer** whereby to measure its degree of corruption. While we have land to labor then, let us never wish to see our citizens occupied at a workbench, or **twirling a distaff**. Carpenters, masons, smiths, are wanting in husbandry: but, for the general operations of manufacture, let our workshops remain in Europe. It is better to carry provisions and materials to workmen there, than bring them to the provisions and materials, and with them their manners and principles. The **loss by the transportation of commodities** across the Atlantic will be made up in happiness and permanence of government. The mobs of great cities add just so much to the support of pure government, as sores do to the strength of the human body. It is the manners and spirit of a people which preserve a republic in **vigour**. A **degeneracy** in these is a **canker** which soon eats to the heart of its laws and constitution.

What happened next . . .

In 1789 President George Washington (1732–1799; served 1789–97) chose Jefferson as his secretary of state. While holding this position, Jefferson came into direct confrontation with the nation's secretary of the treasury, Alexander Hamilton (1755–1804; see Chapter 2), a strong supporter of industrialization. Hamilton sought a stronger federal government with less power held only by the states. He was a champion of the "infant industries," or the newly established manufacturing businesses in the United States, and believed the government should help them. In Jefferson's opinion, Hamilton's financial measures helped the few at the expense of the many, encouraged corruption in the economy, and gave too much power to the government. The public argument between Jefferson and Hamilton represented the national debate over the direction the country should take.

Jefferson became president on March 4, 1801. During his two terms in office, he attempted to create his republican vision of a land of independent farmers. By reducing the means and powers of the government, Jefferson sought to promote peace, equality, and individual freedom. The scientist within Jefferson, however, was greatly interested in the new technologies being invented and used in the United States, and his opposition to them gradually decreased as he grew older.

During the years of Jefferson's presidency (1801–9), the United States was a largely agricultural nation, with more than 90 percent of its population living in rural areas, and fully 80 percent working on farms. Industry began to develop very slowly in the early part of the nineteenth century, and then very rapidly in the second half of the century. By 1920 more than half of the nation's population lived in cities. At the beginning of the twenty-first century, more than 80 percent of Americans lived in urban areas.

Did you know . . .

- During the presidency of George Washington there was only one political party—the Federalists. No political party system existed. The two-party system came about when people like Jefferson organized in opposition to the Federalist policies of Alexander Hamilton. The Federalists believed in a strong federal government, national banks, and government aid of industrialization. Jefferson became the leader of the new party, the Republicans (also known as the

Thomas Jefferson. *(© Bettmann/Corbis.)*

Democratic-Republicans), who believed in stronger states' rights, less federal interference in people's lives, and a republic of land-owning farmers.

- Though Jefferson believed that "those who labor in the earth are the chosen people of God," he did keep his own slaves and held conflicting views about slave labor in the United States. Jefferson did not believe blacks were equal to white Americans, but by the end of his life he was convinced that slavery was morally wrong. Agonizing over the issue, he wrote a plan for the gradual emancipation (freeing) of slaves. His plan stated that the freed slaves would not live in communities with their former owners. Rather they would be sent to live in colonies in some remote land. Jefferson never submitted his plan to the government of Virginia.

Consider the following . . .

- Explain why Thomas Jefferson believed that the growth of manufacturing in the United States was a threat to the values of the new nation. What was it about working as a farmer that Jefferson believed was morally superior to industry? Discuss some of the ideas expressed in the passage above to summarize his opposition to manufacturing in the new nation.

- Can you envision the United States today if Thomas Jefferson and his supporters had been successful in preventing industry from developing in the United States? Do you think any good might have resulted had the country remained largely agricultural? What negative results might have occurred?

For More Information

Books

Davis, David Brion and Steven Mintz, eds. *The Boisterous Sea of Liberty: A Documentary History of America from Discovery through the Civil War.* New York: Oxford University Press, 1998.

Ellis, Joseph J. *The Founding Brothers: The Revolutionary Generation.* New York: Alfred A. Knopf, 2001.

Hindle, Brooke, and Steven Lubar. *Engines of Change: The American Industrial Revolution, 1790–1860.* Washington, DC and London: Smithsonian Institution Press, 1986.

Kasson, John F. "Republican Values as a Dynamic Factor." In *The Industrial Revolution in America.* Edited by Gary J. Kornblith. Boston, MA: Houghton Mifflin, 1998.

Koch, Adrienne, and William Penn, eds. *The Life and Writings of Thomas Jefferson.* New York: Modern Library, 1944.

Randall, Willard Sterne. *Thomas Jefferson: A Life.* New York: Henry Holt and Company, 1993.

Web Sites

"Biography of Thomas Jefferson." *The White House.* http://www.whitehouse.gov/history/presidents/tj3.html (accessed on July 6, 2005).

Congressional Report on Manufactures

Excerpt from **Report to Congress on the Subject of Manufactures**
**Presented to the Speaker of the House of Representatives,
December 5, 1791**
Published in the *Annals of the Second Congress*, Appendix, 1791–1793

> "In general, women and children are rendered more useful . . . by manufacturing establishments, than they would otherwise be."

Alexander Hamilton (1755–1804) was the first secretary of the treasury of the United States and one of its founding fathers. The founding fathers are the members of the Constitutional Convention who drafted the U.S. Constitution in 1787. Like his opponent in government, Thomas Jefferson (1743–1826), Hamilton greatly affected the shape of the new nation.

Hamilton was raised in the West Indies. He was the illegitimate (born of parents not married to each other) child of an aristocratic but unsuccessful Scottish trader who abandoned the family when Hamilton was about ten years old. When Hamilton's mother died in 1768, her relatives recognized his intelligence and arranged for him to attend preparatory school in New Jersey. After finishing his undergraduate studies, Hamilton then enrolled at King's College (now Columbia University) in 1773. As a student Hamilton wrote and published three highly praised pamphlets that brought him to the attention of General George Washington (1732–1799) just as the American Revolution (1775–83; the American colonists' fight

Alexander Hamilton believed that the employment of women and children was one of the benefits of industry. *(© Stapleton Collection/Corbis.)*

for independence from England) was beginning. At the age of twenty-two, Hamilton joined Washington's military staff as an aide-de-camp, or military assistant, with the rank of lieutenant colonel. He remained on the staff for four years and became one of Washington's most valued aides.

During the war the Articles of Confederation, a governing document for the nation seeking its freedom, had been written. The Articles provided the original thirteen states (Connecticut, Delaware, Georgia, Maryland, Massachusetts, New Hampshire, New Jersey, New York, North Carolina, Pennsylvania, Rhode Island, South Carolina, and Virginia) with more power than the central government. Hamilton believed the Articles of Confederation were weak and impossible to enforce. As a delegate to the 1787 Philadelphia meeting of the Constitutional Convention, he argued for a strong national government with almost unlimited power over the states. He proposed a government structure that featured a president who would be chosen for life and a senate whose members would be named by electors chosen by the people and who would also serve for life. He wanted to eliminate elected state governments by giving the president the authority to appoint the state governors and to veto (reject) all local and state laws. His views were in the minority and largely ignored.

With James Madison (1751–1836), a delegate from Virginia, and John Jay (1745–1829), the secretary for foreign affairs, Hamilton wrote a series of essays that were published in a New York newspaper between October 1787 and May 1788. These essays, published as a collection known as *The Federalist Papers,* argued his case for a strong national government. His essays influenced the men who drafted the U.S. Constitution.

Upon taking office, President George Washington (served 1789–97) appointed Hamilton as the first secretary of the treasury. Hamilton went to work with remarkable energy, and the country's foreign debt was repaid by the end of 1795. The Bank of the United States was established and funded. The U.S. currency (money system) grew strong. Hamilton believed that the federal government should take an active part in the national economy. He urged federal agencies to encourage new industry by protecting "infant," or newly formed, U.S. industries until they had established relationships with customers who were used to buying imported goods, and were thus able to compete on an equal basis with imports. Hamilton was convinced that the United States needed to balance its agricultural economy with industry to decrease dependence on European manufacturers and to stabilize the economy.

Hamilton was by no means the first champion of industrialization. An early supporter of U.S. manufacturing was Tench Coxe (1755–1824), a merchant from Philadelphia who became a noted political economist. His pamphlet, *An Enquiry into the Principles on Which a Commercial System for the United States of America Should be Founded* (1787), excited the supporters of U.S. industrialization. Coxe believed that the United States would be able to make industry a foundation of its democratic goals of independence and equality among citizens. He believed in a balance between agriculture and industry, and envisioned a time when machines could free humans from work and produce the goods Americans needed, leading to higher standards of life for all. With labor-saving machinery doing the work, Americans could continue to live independently, and with more money, on their farms. Coxe became a member of the United Company of Philadelphia for Promoting American Manufactures in 1775 and became president of the Pennsylvania Society for the Encouragement of Manufactures and the Useful Arts (founded in 1787). In 1790 Hamilton appointed him to be assistant secretary in the Treasury Department. Coxe produced the first draft of Hamilton's famous report to Congress about the benefits of industrialization.

Tench Coxe was an early supporter of U.S. industrialization. *(Archive Photos Inc. Reproduced by permission.)*

On December 5, 1791, Hamilton presented the *Report to Congress on the Subject of Manufactures.* After completing his own thorough study of the existing factories in the United States, he had expanded greatly on Coxe's initial draft. His *Report* is now famous for its accurate prediction of the future of the industrial United States as it would appear in the years after the American Civil War (1861–65; a war between the Union [the North], who were opposed to slavery, and the Confederacy [the South], who were in favor of slavery). In this report Hamilton argued that by increasing the nation's industries the United States would achieve true independence by decreasing its reliance on other nations for military and essential supplies. Further, he foresaw the vast growth in population that would occur in the nineteenth century as more and more European immigrants arrived in America to make their homes in the new nation. He knew they would require jobs on a massive scale.

Alexander Hamilton. *(AP/Wide World Photos. Reproduced by permission.)*

Believing the only way to support a growing population was to diversify the economy with a variety of industries, Hamilton asserted that the government should promote manufacturing by charging duties (taxes) on or stopping the import of rival products from other nations. Domestic manufactured goods, however, would be free from export duties and new inventions would be encouraged, especially inventions related to machinery. Hamilton understood that it would be necessary for the federal government to regulate industries in order to guarantee quality and safety and to avoid monopolies (exclusive possession or right to produce a particular good or service). He was ahead of his time in this area—it was not until the early twentieth century that the nation's government began to regulate business.

Things to remember while reading *Report to Congress on the Subject of Manufactures*:

- In 1791, when Hamilton presented his report to Congress, the United States had very little industry. English immigrant Samuel Slater (1768–1835), a textile worker who constructed the first mechanized textile mills in the country, had arrived only two years before. His first mill—and the nation's first factory—had not yet been built. Transportation was mainly by foot or horse, and there were few roads for travel or freight. It would be two years before Eli Whitney (1765–1825) invented the cotton gin and several more years before the machine makers, a group of inventors working mainly in the workshops of the Northeast, began the remarkable development of industrial technology that paved the way for mass production—the manufacturing of goods on a large scale through the use of machines and managed labor. Yet

Hamilton understood the nature of industrialization, and was able to accurately foresee many of the changes that were about the take place in the United States.

- In the first textile mills in the Northeast, children were often preferred as the workers who operated the machines. They were easier to control, their hands were small and fast, and most importantly, they worked for very low wages. When Samuel Slater opened his first mills in the 1790s, he paid boys and girls aged between seven and twelve to operate the spinning machines. Most Americans were used to children working, particularly on the farms, and there was not yet a widespread movement to end child labor. In listing the employment of children as one of the benefits of industry, Hamilton expressed what was generally an acceptable viewpoint during the period.

Excerpt from Report to Congress on the Subject of Manufactures

The **expediency** of encouraging manufactures in the United States, which was not long since deemed very questionable, appears at this time to be pretty generally admitted. The **embarrassments** which have obstructed the progress of our **external trade,** have led to serious reflections on the necessity of enlarging the **sphere** of our domestic commerce. . . .

It ought to be readily **conceded,** that the **cultivation of the earth**—as the primary and most certain source of national supply—as the immediate and chief source of **subsistence** to man—as the principal source of those materials which constitute the **nutriment** of other kinds of labor—as including a state most favourable to the freedom and independence of the human mind—one, perhaps, most **conducive** to the multiplication of the human species—has **intrinsically** a strong claim to **pre-eminence** over every other kind of industry.

But, that it has a title to any thing like an **exclusive predilection,** in any country, ought to be admitted with great caution. That it is even more productive than every other branch of Industry requires more evidence, than has yet been given in support of the position. That its

Expediency: Appropriateness.

Embarassments: Things that stand in the way.

External trade: Trade with other nations.

Sphere: Range.

Conceded: Accepted as true.

Cultivation of the earth: Preparation of the earth for farming.

Subsistence: Means to support life.

Nutriment: Substances (foods) that promote growth or nourishment.

Conducive: Assisting.

Intrinsically: Essentially.

Pre-eminence: Superiority.

Exclusive predilection: A preference that rules out all other choices.

real interests, precious and important as without the help of exaggeration they truly are, will be advanced, rather than injured by the due encouragement of manufacture, may, it is believed, be satisfactorily demonstrated.

It is now proper to . . . **enumerate** the principal circumstances, from which it may be **inferred,** that manufacturing establishments not only **occasion** a positive **augmentation** of the produce and revenue of the society, but that they contribute essentially to rendering them greater than they could possibly be, without such establishments. These circumstances are:

1. The division of labor.

2. An extension of the use of machinery.

3. Additional employment to classes of the community not ordinarily engaged in the business.

4. The promoting of emigration from foreign countries.

5. The furnishing greater scope for the diversity of talents and **dispositions** which discriminate men from each other.

6. The **affording** a more ample and various field for **enterprise.**

7. The creating in some instances a new, and securing in all, a more certain and steady demand for the surplus produce of the soil.

Each of these circumstances has a considerable influence upon the total mass of industrious effort in a community. Together, they add to it a degree of energy and effect, which are not easily conceived. . . .

I. As to the division of labor

It has justly been observed, that there is scarcely anything of greater **moment** in the economy of a nation, than the proper division of labor. The separation of occupations causes each to be carried to a much greater perfection, than it could possibly acquire, if they were blended. This arises principally from three circumstances.

First. The greater skill and **dexterity** naturally resulting from a constant and undivided **application to a single object.** It is evident, that these properties must increase, in proportion to the separation and simplification of objects and the steadiness of the attention devoted to each; and must be less, in proportion to the complication of objects, and the number among which the attention is distracted [divided].

Enumerate: Count.

Inferred: Concluded.

Occasion: Bring about.

Augmentation: Increase.

Dispositions: Moods and attitudes.

Affording: Making available.

Enterprise: A project or undertaking; a business.

Moment: Importance.

Dexterity: Skill in working with one's hands.

Application to a single object: Performance of only one task.

*Second. The economy of time—by avoiding the loss of it, **incident to** a frequent transition from one operation to another of a different nature. . . .*

*Third. An extension of the use of machinery. A man occupied on a single object will have it more in his power, and will be more naturally led to exert his imagination in devising methods to **facilitate** and **abridge** labor, than if he were **perplexed** by a variety of independent and dissimilar operations. Besides this, the **fabrication** of machines, in numerous instances, becoming itself a distinct trade, the artist who follows it, has all the advantages which have been enumerated, for improvement in his particular art; and in both ways the invention and application of machinery are extended.*

*And from these causes united, the mere separation of the occupation of the **cultivator**, from that of the **artificer**, has the effect of augmenting the productive powers of labor, and with them, the total mass of the produce or **revenue** of a country. In this single view of the subject, therefore, the **utility** of artificers or manufacturers, towards promoting an increase of productive industry, is apparent.*

II. As to an extension of the use of machinery

*The employment of machinery forms an item of great importance in the general mass of national industry. 'Tis an artificial force brought in aid of the natural force of man; and, to all the purposes of labor, is an increase of hands; an **accession** of strength, **unencumbered** too by the expense of maintaining the laborer. May it not therefore be fairly inferred, that those occupations, which give greatest scope to the use of this **auxiliary**, contribute most to the general stock of industrial effort, and, in consequence, to the general product of industry?*

*It shall be taken for granted, and the truth of the position referred to observation, that manufacturing pursuits are **susceptible** in a greater degree of the application of machinery, than those of agriculture. . . .*

*The cotton mill invented in England, within the last twenty years, is a **signal illustration** of the general proposition, which has been just advanced. In consequence of it, all the different processes for spinning cotton are performed by means of machines, which are put in motion by water, and attended chiefly by women and children; (and by a smaller) number of (persons, in the whole, than are) **requisite** in the ordinary mode of spinning. And it is an advantage of great moment that the operations of this mill continue with convenience, during the night, as well as through the day. The **prodigious** affect of such a machine is*

Incident to: Due to.

Facilitate: Make easier.

Abridge: Make shorter.

Perplexed: Filled with uncertainty.

Fabrication: Creation.

Cultivator: Farmer.

Artificer: Maker of manufactured goods.

Revenue: Income.

Utility: Fitness.

Accession: Increase.

Unencumbered: Unburdened.

Auxiliary: Extra help.

Susceptible: Open to influence.

Signal illustration: Primary example.

Requisite: Necessary.

Prodigious: Making more numerous or bigger.

Conceived: Understood.

Attributed: Explained by indicating a cause.

Industrious: Active.

Collateral: Secondary.

Husbandman: Farmer.

*easily **conceived.** To this invention is to be **attributed** essentially the immense progress, which has been so suddenly made in Great Britain in the various fabrics of cotton.*

III. As to the additional employment of classes of the community, not ordinarily engaged in the particular business

*. . . .In places where those institutions prevail, besides the persons regularly engaged in them, they afford occasional and extra employment to **industrious** individuals and families, who are willing to devote the leisure resulting from the intermissions of their ordinary pursuits to **collateral** labors, as a resource of multiplying their acquisitions or [their] enjoyments. The **husbandman** himself experiences a new source of profit and support from the increased industry of his wife and daughters; invited and stimulated by the demands of the neighboring manufactories. . . . It is worthy of particular remark, that, in general, women and children are rendered more useful and the latter more early useful by manufacturing establishments, than they would otherwise be. Of the number of persons employed in the cotton manufactories of Great Britain, it is computed that four-sevenths, nearly, are women and children; of whom the greatest proportion are children and many of them of a very tender age.*

What happened next . . .

Hamilton's recommendations for developing and stimulating the economy were not well received in Congress. Many felt he was promoting his own personal interests at the expense of agriculture. Others feared the powerful federal government he proposed. His plan was never put to a vote.

Though Tench Coxe, the writer of the first draft of *Report on Manufactures,* was strongly pro-industry, he was not as firmly attached to Hamilton's Federalist Party. (Federalists believe in a strong federal government, national banks, and government aid of industrialization.) In 1803, after Coxe had publicly argued with the Federalists, Republican president Thomas Jefferson (served 1801–9) appointed him Purveyor of Public Supplies and Coxe joined the Republicans.

Did you know . . .

- Alexander Hamilton was known for his arrogant and forceful personality, which won him many enemies. One of those enemies was Aaron Burr (1756–1836). The rivalry between the two had probably started in 1791, when Burr abandoned Hamilton's Federalist Party to run as a Democratic-Republican candidate for the U.S. Senate seat in New York. (Democratic-Republicans, also known as Republicans, believed in stronger states' rights, less federal interference in people's lives, and a republic of landowning farmers.) Burr incurred Hamilton's wrath when he defeated Hamilton's father-in-law in the elections. In 1792 Burr offered to join the Federalists once again in order to run for governor of New York. Hamilton's strong opposition eliminated him from candidacy. Hamilton also opposed Burr's attempt to be the Federalist vice-presidential candidate in 1792. In the presidential election of 1800, there was a tie between the two Republican candidates, Jefferson and Burr. During this period in U.S. history, the candidate with the most votes became president and the one with the second largest number of votes became vice president. In case of a tie, the outcome was settled by Congress. Despite his longtime rivalry with Jefferson, Hamilton pushed his friends in Congress to elect Jefferson over Burr because he disliked Burr so strongly. With Hamilton's backing, Jefferson unexpectedly won by only one vote. In 1804 Burr was once again defeated in the election for governor of New York. During the campaign, Hamilton had publicly spoken negatively of Burr. The angry Burr challenged Hamilton to a duel, which took place on July 11, 1804. It is said that Hamilton shot into the air rather than firing upon Burr and was fatally wounded by his enemy. He died the next day.

Consider the following . . .

- Compare and contrast the views of Alexander Hamilton and Thomas Jefferson (see Chapter 1) on the benefits and disadvantages of industrialism. Try to find several strong arguments for each side of the issue.

- Briefly research the political parties that existed at the time of Thomas Jefferson's presidency: the Democratic-Republicans and the Federalists. Describe the basic sets of beliefs of each of these parties.

For More Information

Chernow, Ron. *Alexander Hamilton.* New York: Penguin Press, 2004.

Davis, David Brion, and Steven Mintz, eds. *The Boisterous Sea of Liberty: A Documentary History of America from Discovery through the Civil War.* New York: Oxford University Press, 1998.

Ellis, Joseph J. *The Founding Brothers: The Revolutionary Generation.* New York: Alfred A. Knopf, 2001.

Hamilton, Alexander. "Report to Congress on the Subject of Manufactures." *Annals of the Second Congress,* Appendix, 1791–1793.

Hindle, Brooke, and Steven Lubar. *Engines of Change: The American Industrial Revolution, 1790–1860.* Washington, DC and London: Smithsonian Institution Press, 1986.

Kasson, John F. "Republican Values as a Dynamic Factor." In *The Industrial Revolution in America.* Edited by Gary J. Kornblith. Boston, MA: Houghton Mifflin, 1998.

Cotton Gin Petition

Cotton Gin Petition
Written by Eli Whitney on June 20, 1793
Reprinted in *The Papers of Thomas Jefferson, Vol. 26:
11 May to 31 August 1793,* 1995

Eli Whitney (1765–1825) was one of the great inventors of the early Industrial Revolution in the United States. Whitney perfected the cotton gin, a machine that separates the seeds from the fibers of cotton. Although his cotton gin transformed the Southern economy and changed history, Whitney experienced little financial gain due to problems in the patent system of the new nation. A patent is a legal document issued by a government granting exclusive authority to an inventor for making, using, and selling an invention.

Whitney showed a strong interest in mechanical work from his early boyhood in Westboro, Massachusetts. Although he worked on his father's farm, he preferred his father's shop, where by the age of fifteen he labored part-time making nails for sale. As much as he enjoyed working as a mechanic, he decided to obtain an academic education. He attended Yale College, graduating in 1792. Whitney then traveled to Georgia to study for a law degree. He stayed with Catharine Littlefield Greene, the widow of American Revolutionary War (1775–83; the American colonists' fight

"With this Ginn, if turned with horses or by water, two persons will clean as much cotton in one Day, as a Hundred persons could cleane in the same time with the ginns now in common use."

THE COTTON GIN.

Slaves using the cotton gin. *(© Bettmann/Corbis.)*

for independence from England) hero General Nathanael Greene (1742–1786), on her plantation at Mulberry Grove, near Savannah. Whitney formed a lasting relationship there with Phineas Miller, the plantation manager and later the second husband of Mrs. Greene.

While living on the plantation, Whitney became fascinated with the time-consuming process used by slaves to remove seeds from picked cotton. Cotton gins of various designs were then in use in different parts of the world, but none had ever worked well. Cleaning continued to be done by hand and it took a slave a full day to clean one pound of cotton.

At Mrs. Greene's urging, Whitney focused his mechanical abilities on the problem, and within ten days he produced a design for a gin. By April 1793 he had made a working model that cleaned fifty pounds of cotton a day. The machine worked by turning a crank (lever) that caused a cylinder (tube-shaped chamber or tank) covered with wire teeth to revolve. The teeth pulled the cotton fiber, carrying it through slots in the cylinder as it revolved. Since the slots were too small for the seeds to pass through, they were left behind. A roller with brushes then removed the fibers from the wire teeth.

The cotton gin was a very simple machine that would have a tremendous impact on the American textile industry and the Southern economy. There was a dramatic increase in the production of processed cotton. One large gin could process fifty times the cotton that a laborer could process in a day. Soon plantations and farms were supplying huge amounts of cotton to textile mills in England and in the northeastern United States. In 1792 the United States exported 138,328 pounds of cotton. In 1794 that figure rose to 1.6 million pounds. The following year, nearly 6.3 million pounds were exported, and by 1800 the production of cotton in the United States had risen to 35 million pounds, of which almost 18 million were exported. Whitney had hoped that by making the task of cleaning cotton so inexpensive he might help eliminate slavery. Instead the resulting boom in the cotton business in the South gave new life to the institution, and southern planters became even more dependent on slavery.

Whitney did not profit financially from the cotton gin mainly because the new U.S. patent system failed him. Congress passed the first patent act in 1790. Patents were viewed as a way to financially reward inventors for their work. They were also a means to convince an inventor to provide the public with an in-depth description of how his invention worked and how it was made so that the invention would last beyond the life of its inventor. In exchange for making the workings of his or her invention known, the inventor received the exclusive right to make the invention and profit from it for a set amount of time. When that period was over, anyone could produce the invention. Whitney applied for a patent for the cotton gin in 1793, sending a petition and a drawing of his invention to Secretary of State Thomas Jefferson (1743–1826). He received his patent in March 1794.

Eli Whitney, inventor of the cotton gin. *(Courtesy of The Library of Congress.)*

After receiving his patent, Whitney entered into a business partnership with Phineas Miller. They planned to build cotton gins and install them on farms throughout the South. The partners intended to do the cotton ginning themselves and charge the plantation owners a high fee for it. With their monopoly (the exclusive possession or right to produce a particular good or service) on the cotton gin, it was likely they would become extremely wealthy. The cotton farmers were not happy with this arrangement, which cut deeply into their profits. Since they could plainly see how the gin worked, many simply built their own. Furthermore, Whitney and Miller could not produce enough machines to gin the rapidly increasing cotton crops of the South. Infringing machines—machines that violated Whitney's patent—were built in large numbers to do the work. Whitney sued the people who infringed on his patent in 1797, but he lost the case because the judges in the South were prone to upholding the interests of the plantation owners. It was to be ten years before the court decided in favor of his patent. In the meantime, Miller had died in 1803, poor and bitter after the long struggle. In 1812 Whitney made an application to Congress for the renewal of his expired patent, but his request was refused.

Things to remember while reading the Cotton Gin Petition:

- There were no patent laws in place when the United States won its independence from England. If an invention was made and other people saw it, they were free to copy the invention. But the U.S. Constitution did contain a provision, or clause, in Article I, Section 8 about patents, giving Congress the power "to promote the progress of Science and useful Arts by securing for limited Time to Authors and Inventors the exclusive right to their respective Writings and Discoveries."

- After Congress passed the Patent Act of 1790 Thomas Jefferson, as secretary of state, served as the first administrator of the patent system. In the system's early years, the number of patent applications was small and Jefferson, who was a scientist, was able to examine each of them carefully.

- The Patent Act defined as patentable "any useful art, manufacture, engine, machine, or device, or any improvement therein not before known or used." The inventor was to supply government officials with detailed descriptions and drawings or a model of his or her invention. Part of the requirement was that the invention was original in some way, and that even if the basic idea for it had already existed, the invention had never before been made in exactly the way the applicant was making it.

- The Patent Act limited patents to fourteen-year periods with no possibility of extension. Inventors complained about this limitation since it often took several years to get their inventions on the market.

- As more and more inventors filed patent applications, the process of examining them became too big a burden for the secretary of state. In 1836 the Patent Office of the United States was created, providing a panel of experts to examine patent claims.

- The spelling and punctuation in the document are Whitney's and reflect earlier standards of the English language.

Cotton Gin Petition

*To the Honourable Thomas Jefferson Esquire Secretary, of State for the United States of America: The Petition of Eli Whitney, of the County of Worcester and Commonwealth of Massachusetts, humbly **sheweth**: That having invented a Machine for the Purpose of ginning Cotton, he is desirous of obtaining an **exclusive Property** in the same.*

Sheweth: Showeth; shows.

Exclusive property: The sole right to produce or sell.

Alledges: Alleges.

*Concerning which invention, your Petitioner **alledges** as follows (viz) first.*

That it is entirely new and constructed in a different manner and upon different principles from any, other Cotton Gin or Machine heretofore known or used for that purpose.

2d. That with this Ginn, if turned with horses or by water, two persons will clean as much cotton in one Day, as a Hundred persons could cleane in the same time with the ginns now in common use.

3d. That the Cotton which is cleansed in his Ginn contains fewer broken seeds and impurities, and is said to be more valuable than Cotton, which is cleaned in the usual way.

Your Petitioner, therefore, Prays your Honour to Grant him the said Whitney, a Patent for the said Invention or Improvement: and that your Honour cause Letters Patent to be made out, in the Name of the United States, granting to him, our said petitioner, his heirs Administrators and Assigns, for the term of fourteen Years, the full and exclusive right and liberty of making, constructing using and vending to others to be used, the said Invention or improvement.

ELI WHITNEY

Philadelphia

20th June 1793

What happened next . . .

The cotton gin was not Whitney's only contribution to the Industrial Revolution. While struggling in court over his patent, Eli Whitney turned to the manufacture of guns for the military. When he began this effort, he had no workers, no capital (accumulated wealth or goods devoted to the production of other goods), and knew nothing about making muskets, which were large firearms carried on the shoulder and loaded through their muzzles. Still, he was able to earn a contract from the United States government in 1798 hiring him to deliver four thousand muskets in just over a year and another six thousand firearms in 1800. In the late eighteenth century, a contract for ten thousand muskets in two years had never existed before. The reason this had never happened was that neither the technology nor the processes of mass production were in place. Mass production is the manufacture of goods in quantity by using machines and standardized designs and parts. It took Whitney three years to deliver just five hundred firearms and the rest were delivered almost nine years behind schedule. One of the first things Whitney undertook was the creation of the machines that would make his gun parts. Whitney set out to make interchangeable parts (standardized units of a machine that could be used in any machine of that model) for his guns, greatly reducing assembly time. At one point Whitney reportedly took all the parts for ten muskets to government officials, dumped the parts in front of them, and challenged them to assemble the firearms. The officials successfully built the guns, and a new system of production was born. While his muskets were neither timely nor particularly successful, Whitney's manufacturing methods were revolutionary. He had pioneered the use of interchangeable parts assembled on a production line, leading to mass production techniques still used by industries in the early twenty-first century.

Did you know . . .

- Some of the founding fathers (members of the convention that drafted the U.S. Constitution in 1787) were not sure that federal protection of inventions was a good idea. American statesman and philosopher Benjamin Franklin (1706–1790), for one, believed that the inventor should freely give his ideas to society. True to his word, he never patented his famous Franklin stove. Thomas Jefferson was another inventor who never sought a patent; as a politician he was reluctant to see the government grant monopolies. On the other hand, President James Madison (1751–1836; served 1809–17) and statesman Alexander Hamilton (1755–1804) were in favor of supporting the work of inventors by protecting their property rights.

- Eli Whitney was not the only inventor who found that the early patent system did not provide enough protection for an invention. Steamboat innovators John Fitch (1743–1798) and James Rumsey (1743–1792) both received patents on their steamboats in the same year (1791),

Steamboat inventor John Fitch. *(Courtesy of The Library of Congress.)*

leaving them to argue in public against each other's claim to be the first steamboat builder. They both failed to get financing for their projects at least partly due to their competing patents for their steamboat design. Oliver Evans (1755–1819), who held several patents for factory mechanization and steam-engine improvements, was so discouraged by his long fight for property rights for his inventions that he burned all the records of them. It took many years for the U.S. Patent Office to improve the system.

Consider the following . . .

- In what ways do you think the U.S. patent system affected the Industrial Revolution in the United States? If inventors and innovators had not been able to patent their inventions, do you think they would have accomplished the same results? Explain the motivations and rewards for inventors with and without a patent system.

- Eli Whitney is considered one of the most significant inventors in American history, yet his cotton gin was a very simple tool and his manufacturing method was not very effective. What are some of the reasons he is viewed as an important figure in U.S. industrialization?

For More Information

Books

Catanzariti, John, ed. *The Papers of Thomas Jefferson, Vol. 26: 11 May to 31 August 1793*. Princeton, NJ: Princeton University Press, 1995.

Hindle, Brooke, and Steven Lubar. *Engines of Change: The American Industrial Revolution, 1790–1860*. Washington, DC and London: Smithsonian Institution Press, 1986.

McCormick, Anita Louise. *The Industrial Revolution in American History.* Berkeley Heights, NJ: Enslow Publishers, 1998.

Vaughan, Floyd Lamar. *The United States Patent System: Legal and Economic Conflicts in American Patent History.* Westport, CT: Greenwood, 1973.

Web Sites

Eli Whitney Museum. http://www.eliwhitney.org/cotton.htm (accessed on July 6, 2005).

Patent Act of 1790, Ch. 7, 1 Stat. 109–112 (April 10, 1790). http://ipmall. info/hosted_resources/lipa/lipa_patent_index.asp (accessed on July 6, 2005).

Loom and Spindle

Excerpts from Loom and Spindle: or, Life among the Early Mill Girls
By Harriet Hanson Robinson
Originally published by T. Y. Cromwell in 1898
Revised edition published by Hawaii Press Pacific, 1976

> "One of the girls stood on a pump, . . . declaring that it was their duty to resist all attempts at cutting down the wages. This was the first time a woman had spoken in public in Lowell. . . ."

During the early nineteenth century, the country's first factories were being established in New England. In 1814 Francis Cabot Lowell (1775–1817) built the first complete cotton factory—with both spinning and weaving processes in one building—in Waltham, Massachusetts. By 1823, after Lowell's death, his business associates had built larger mills in Lowell, along the Merrimack River. The mills used power looms that required workers with quick hands for smooth operation. The mill workforces were made up mainly of young women, many from the farms of New England. Bright, eager, and willing to work for less money than men, the "Lowell girls," as they came to be called, filled the mill owners' needs and became the first industrial workforce in the United States.

Mill work was appealing to many young women. The biggest attraction was that it paid more than women could make elsewhere. In the Lowell mills in the 1830s women earned $2.40 to $3.20 a week plus room and board. This amount was one-half to one-third the wages paid to men for similar work, but it was still more than double the money a woman would receive working as a domestic servant or seamstress. Some

Like this girl, Harriet Hanson Robinson worked in a textile mill in her youth.
(© Corbis.)

women were excited by the promise of a few years of independence before marriage, as it was considered unacceptable for a married woman to work outside the home. Others were in desperate need of income for their families.

Since most Americans in the early 1900s believed that women should be at home caring for their families, mill owners sought to make the practice of hiring women acceptable to the laborers' families and to the general public. To achieve this they attempted to create a respectable environment for the young women. They were housed in company-owned boardinghouses, where their safety and daily behavior could be

Harriet Hanson Robinson. *(Courtesy of The Library of Congress.)*

supervised by mature women who were paid by the mill owners. The workers' characters were checked before they were hired, so no unsuitable women would be introduced to the group. The young women had curfews (rules about when they had to be in their rooms in the evening) and chaperones (adults who accompanied them when they visited with a male) and they were required to attend church regularly. Nevertheless, many found time to pursue an education and to share their experiences through writing, and because of their writings we know more about this early industrial workforce than we know of many more recent groups of laborers.

One of the Lowell girls who recorded the experience in her memoirs was author and activist Harriet Hanson Robinson (1825–1911). She was born Harriet Hanson on August 2, 1825, in Boston, Massachusetts. In 1831, when she was only six years old, her father died, and her mother was faced with the difficult task of feeding and caring for four young children alone. Harriet's mother set up a small shop to sell food, candy, and firewood, but supporting her family was difficult and they lived in poverty. In 1832 Hanson and her children moved twenty miles north of Boston to the booming mill town of Lowell, Massachusetts, where she began managing a boardinghouse for female mill workers.

In Lowell, Robinson helped her mother manage the boardinghouse, which was home to forty workers. When she was ten years old, she went to work in the mills to help pay the family's expenses. She worked from 1834 to 1848, during the early days of the cotton factories when mill owners were still experimenting with management methods. Francis Lowell had hoped to design a factory system that treated its workers well, and he regarded the laborers in his mills as his responsibility, both during and after work hours.

Robinson's experiences as a mill worker are vividly depicted in a book called *Loom and Spindle: or, Life among the Early Mill Girls,* published in 1898. She presented a positive view of the opportunities for women offered by the mills. According to Robinson, many women took advantage of their independence to educate themselves and came away from the experience more confident and self-assured than when they had started. To many historians, Robinson's picture of life in the mills during this time is unusually optimistic. Indeed, Robinson's situation was more favorable than most. She lived with her own family—many girls had to leave home and travel far away to work in the mills—and she held a skilled but relatively easy job that allowed time for reading. By the late 1830s, however, things were already changing, as Robinson confirms in her memoirs.

Things to remember while reading the excerpts from *Loom and Spindle: or, Life among the Early Mill Girls*:

- By 1831 women made up almost forty thousand of the fifty-eight thousand factory workers in the textile industry. This figure includes a high percentage of young girls, but the exact numbers and ages of the girls were not recorded.

- Working conditions were tough at the Lowell mill. Work routines were strict, with twelve- to fourteen-hour days that started very early in the morning. Factory bells announced times for leaving and entering the plant, and the employees were fined if they were late. Because cotton thread breaks more easily in dry air, overseers sealed windows shut and sprayed water in the air to keep the moisture in the air high. Along with being hot and humid, the moisture often caused lung ailments.

- Many women mill workers spent a great deal of their free time educating themselves. After a long day of work, they often read or met in study groups, and they attended lectures and church meetings over the weekends. Like Robinson, many of the young women wrote memoirs, letters, and stories about their experiences, documenting their years of independence.

- By the mid-1830s increased competition was driving textile prices down. In 1834, in order to lower their expenses, the Lowell mill owners cut their workers' wages by 25 percent. The workers responded by staging a strike and organizing a labor union called the Factory Girls Association. Two years later mill owners increased boardinghouse rates and again cut wages. The Lowell workers organized another strike in 1836. Neither of these efforts succeeded in changing the mill owners' policies.

Excerpt from Loom and Spindle: or, Life among the Early Mill Girls

Child-life in the Cotton Mills

*I had been to school constantly until I was about ten years of age, when my mother, feeling obliged to have help in her work besides what I could give, and also needing the money which I could earn, allowed me, at my urgent request (for I wanted to earn money like the other little girls), to go to work in the mill. I worked first in the spinning-room as a "doffer." The doffers were the very youngest girls, whose work it was to doff, or take off, the full **bobbins**, and replace them with the empty ones.*

*I can see myself now, racing down the alley, between the **spinning-frames**, carrying in front of me a bobbin-box bigger than I was. These **mites** had to be very swift in their movements, so as not to keep the spinning-frames stopped long, and they worked only about fifteen minutes in every hour. The rest of the time was their own, and when the overseer was kind they were allowed to read, knit, or even to go outside the mill-yard to play. . . .*

*When not doffing, we were often allowed to go home, for a time, and thus we were able to help our mothers in their housework. We were paid two dollars a week; and how proud I was when my turn came to stand up on the bobbin-box, and write my name in the paymaster's book, and how **indignant** I was when he asked me if I could "write." "Of course I can," said I, and he smiled as he looked down on me.*

The working-hours of all the girls extended from five o'clock in the morning until seven in the evening, with one-half hour for breakfast and

Bobbins: Spools or reels that hold thread or yarn for spinning or weaving.

Spinning frames: Machines that draw, twist, and wind yarn.

Mites: Small ones; the children working in the mill.

Indignant: Angry because of something unjust.

for dinner. Even the doffers were forced to be on duty nearly fourteen hours a day, and this was the greatest hardship in the lives of these children. For it was not until 1842 that the hours of labor for children under twelve years of age were limited to ten per day; but the "ten-hour law" itself was not passed until long after some of these little doffers were old enough to appear before the legislative committee on the subject, and plead, by their presence, for a reduction of the hours of labor. . . .

The Lowell Mill Girls Go on Strike, 1836

*One of the first strikes of cotton-factory **operatives** that ever took place in this country was that in Lowell, in October, 1836. When it was announced that the wages were to be cut down, great indignation was felt, and it was decided to strike, **en masse**. This was done. The mills were shut down, and the girls went in procession from their several corporations to the "grove" on Chapel Hill, and listened to "**incendiary**" **speeches** from early labor reformers.*

*One of the girls stood on a pump, and **gave vent to** the feelings of her companions in a neat speech, declaring that it was their duty to resist all attempts at cutting down the wages. This was the first time a woman had spoken in public in Lowell, and the event caused surprise and **consternation** among her audience.*

*Cutting down the wages was not their only **grievance**, nor the only cause of this strike. Hitherto the corporations had paid twenty-five cents a week towards the board of each operative, and now it was their purpose to have the girls pay the sum; and this, in addition to the cut in the wages, would make a difference of at least one dollar a week. It was estimated that as many as twelve or fifteen hundred girls turned out, and walked in procession through the streets. They had neither flags nor music, but sang songs, a favorite (but rather inappropriate) one being a parody on "I won't be a nun."*

> *Oh! isn't it a pity, such a pretty girl as I*
> *Should be sent to the factory to pine away and die?*
> *Oh! I cannot be a slave,*
> *I will not be a slave,*
> *For I'm so fond of liberty*
> *That I cannot be a slave.*

*My own recollection of this first strike (or "turn out" as it was called) is very vivid. I worked in a lower room, where I had heard the proposed strike fully, if not **vehemently**, discussed; I had been an **ardent** listener to what was said against this attempt at "oppression" on the part of the corporation, and naturally I took sides with the strikers. When the day came on which the girls were to turn out, those in the upper rooms*

Operatives: Workers who ran the machines in the mills.

En masse: As a whole group.

Incendiary speeches: Speeches causing excitement or rebellion.

Gave vent to: Expressed.

Consternation: Dismay.

Grievance: Cause of distress regarded as a reason for complaint.

Vehemently: With intense emotion.

Ardent: Enthusiastic.

Irresolute: Unsure or wavering.

Bravado: False courage.

Suffrage: Voting.

Functionary: Official.

Accede: Agree to.

Old guard: Those who had been there for a long time.

started first, and so many of them left that our mill was at once shut down. Then, when the girls in my room stood **irresolute,** uncertain what to do, asking each other, "Would you?" or "Shall we turn out?" and not one of them having the courage to lead off, I, who began to think they would not go out, after all their talk, became impatient, and started on ahead, saying, with childish **bravado,** "I don't care what you do, I am going to turn out, whether any one else does or not"; and I marched out, and was followed by the others.

As I looked back at the long line that followed me, I was more proud than I have ever been since at any success I may have achieved, and more proud than I shall ever be again until my own beloved State gives to its women citizens the right of **suffrage.**

The agent of the corporation where I then worked took some small revenges on the supposed ringleaders; on the principle of sending the weaker to the wall, my mother was turned away from her boarding-house, that **functionary** saying, "Mrs. Hanson, you could not prevent the older girls from turning out, but your daughter is a child, and her you could control."

It is hardly necessary to say that so far as results were concerned this strike did no good. The dissatisfaction of the operatives subsided, or burned itself out, and though the authorities did not **accede** to their demands, the majority returned to their work, and the corporation went on cutting down the wages.

And after a time, as the wages became more and more reduced, the best portion of the girls left and went to their homes, or to the other employments that were fast opening to women, until there were very few of the **old guard** left; and thus the status of the factory population of New England gradually became what we know it to be today.

What happened next . . .

In 1848 Robinson married journalist William Stevens Robinson (1818–1876), a strong supporter of the antislavery movement. They had several children and Robinson worked in the home as a housewife. After her husband's death, Robinson became active in the women's suffrage movement. She was the first woman to appear before the Select Committee on Woman

Suffrage in Congress, and she argued the case for suffrage before the legislature of Massachusetts. In 1881 Robinson published the book *Massachusetts in the Woman Suffrage Movement*. She died in 1911, nine years before American women received the right to vote through the Nineteenth Amendment to the U.S. Constitution.

By the 1850s the number of native-born American women working in the textile mills had greatly decreased. Working conditions had grown worse and wages had been reduced. The mill managers no longer wanted to hire young women from the farms of New England since they had proved themselves likely to protest unfair work conditions. As a result, the supervised boardinghouse system was dropped.

By the mid- to late 1800s, mill girls were almost entirely replaced by Irish, Italian, and Portuguese immigrants who were willing to work for lower wages. Housing in mill towns like Lowell, Lawrence, and Holyoke, Massachusetts, became hard to find, and terrible overcrowding occurred as more immigrants arrived in search of jobs. Cramped conditions, improper air circulation, and unclean surroundings caused outbreaks of contagious diseases. One out of every three spinners (those who operated spinning machines), many under the age of twenty-five, died before completing ten years in the factory. Mill work had changed a great deal since the days when Robinson was employed at Lowell.

Did you know . . .

- Women have been responsible for making cloth and clothing in many cultures throughout the ages. In England the word "spinster" came into use sometime in the thirteenth century and referred to any woman who spun wool for a living. Since unmarried women were more likely to have to work for a living, and the most common work for women was spinning, over the centuries the term "spinster" also became a word meaning any unmarried woman. It is not surprising that in the United States textile manufacturing was the first industry to have a large female workforce, since for so long women had been associated with the art of making cloth.

- Other industries with large numbers of women in their workforces in the early nineteenth century included ready-made clothing, fur, hat, shoe, umbrella, button, glove, and furniture manufacturing.

Consider the following . . .

- Some writers describing the Lowell mill girls focused on the opportunities that were granted them by the textile mills: independence, education, deep bonds of friendship among the workers, a safe place to live, and supervision over their daily lives. The young women in the early days of the Lowell mills distinguished themselves as writers and artists, and many left the mills with far greater knowledge of the world than when they arrived. On the other hand, critics also stressed the overly strict attitude of the mill owners and their exploitation (taking unfair advantage of for their own gain) of the factory workers. What do you think—did the mills present young women with good opportunities, abuse them, or a little of both?

- When she wrote about her days as a Lowell girl, do you think Harriet Hanson Robinson looked back on it as a good experience? What clues are there in the excerpt about how she felt about those days?

For More Information

Books

Dublin, Thomas. *Women at Work: The Transformation of Work and Community in Lowell, Massachusetts, 1826–1860.* New York: Columbia University Press, 1979.

Foner, Philip S., ed. *The Factory Girls.* Urbana: University of Illinois Press, 1977.

Robinson, Harriet Hanson. *Loom and Spindle: or, Life among the Early Mill Girls.* Rev. ed. Kailua: Hawaii Press Pacific, 1976.

Selden, Bernice. *The Mill Girls: Lucy Larcom, Harriet Hanson Robinson, Sarah G. Bagley.* New York: Atheneum, 1983.

Web Sites

Cummings, Patricia L. "The Mill Girls of Spindle City." *Quilter's Muse.* http://www.quiltersmuse.com/mill_girls_of%20spindle%20city.htm (accessed on July 6, 2005).

"The Mill Girls." *The National Park Service.* http://www.nps.gov/lowe/loweweb/Lowell_History/Millgirls.htm (accessed on July 6, 2005).

The Lowell Offering

"A Second Peep at Factory Life"
By Josephine L. Baker
Article from the *Lowell Offering*
Published in Vol. V: 97–100, 1845

In the 1820s the textile mills in Lowell, Massachusetts, began operating successfully using a workforce made up largely of young, unmarried women. For these daughters of northern farmers and laborers, the factory life was temporary and they would only labor for a few years before returning to their homes to marry and raise families. It was not an accepted practice for young women to work for wages in factories at that time, but the growth of industrialization was changing social standards. From their writings, it is apparent that the Lowell "mill girls," as they called themselves, were taking full advantage of the opportunities offered them through their employment in the factories. During their free time they sought to educate and improve themselves, and they often wrote about their lives, including their experiences in the mills. In later years, when the mill girls began to protest against poor working conditions, they learned to organize, speak in public, and challenge bosses.

Many of the Lowell workers were eager to experience independence for the first, and perhaps the only, time in their lives. They worked up to fourteen hours a day, and yet it was

"The time has come when something, besides the clothing and feeding of the body is to be thought of; when the mind is to be clothed and fed; and this cannot be as it should be, with the present system of labor."

THE LOWELL OFFERING:

A REPOSITORY

OF

ORIGINAL ARTICLES ON VARIOUS SUBJECTS,

WRITTEN

BY FACTORY OPERATIVES.

"Full many a gem of purest ray serene,
The dark, unfathomed caves of ocean bear;
Full many a flower is born to blush unseen,
And waste its sweetness on the desert air."

No. 1. Price 6¼cts.

THIS NUMBER WHOLLY WRITTEN

BY FEMALES EMPLOYED IN THE MILLS.

CONTENTS:

LOWELL, MASS.
PRINTED BY A. WATSON, 15 CENTRAL STREET.
For Sale at all the Bookstores; and by Tower, in the angle of Central and Gorham sts.;
and at Billings' Variety Store, Merrimack st. opposite Tremont Corporation.

Title page of an 1840 issue of the *Lowell Offering*. *(Courtesy of Rotch Visual Collections, M.I.T.)*

common for the young mill operators to spend their evening hours participating in reading groups, attending night school, going to lectures, or just reading on their own. One popular reading group was sponsored by the First Universalist Church in Lowell, where the young women met and read to each other from their own writings. Impressed with the large quantity of literary material the women produced, the pastor of the church, Abel C. Thomas (1807–1880), organized the *Lowell Offering* in 1840. The first publication was simply a pamphlet, which included a collection of essays, letters, and poetry written by the mill girls. As more volumes were published, the *Offering* quickly grew into a monthly magazine, written and edited by the mill girls.

In 1841 Reverend Thomas moved to another congregation. At the time, the *Offering* was sold for around 6 cents per issue, but the price was not enough to cover the publishing costs, and the mill owners began to subsidize it (assist by providing money for operation), although it was still edited and written by the women mill workers. In October 1842 Harriet Farley (1817–1907) became the editor. She was joined in 1843 by coeditor Harriet F. Curtis (1813–1889).

The articles in the magazine covered a variety of subjects from astronomy to religion to housekeeping. Most, though, were about factory work and life in the industrial town. The young women were well aware that a lot of attention was focused on them, since as working women in the United States they represented an extreme departure from the normal female role in society. They frequently wrote articles attempting to argue or prove that they were thoughtful, capable, and intelligent. Since factory work was considered lowly, the mill girls also wanted to show that their work was not without honor, and they struggled to present the self-sacrifice and discipline necessary to work in the factories.

During the five years the *Offering* was published, conditions at the Lowell mills became worse. The managers cut wages and increased workloads, and the women became unhappy. Sarah Bagley wrote in a July 3, 1845, article in the weekly workers' newspaper *Voice of Industry:*

> One would suppose [based on the low wages of workers] that the Lowell mills were filled with farmers' daughters who could live without labor and who go there merely as a resort for health and recreation, instead of a large portion of

poverty's daughters whose fathers do not possess one foot of land, but work day by day for the bread that feeds their families. Indeed, many of the operatives are foreigners free to work there according to the mandates of heartless power, or to go to the poor house, beg, or do worse.

However, while some of the articles in the *Offering* reflected the growing dissatisfaction with working conditions, the magazine did not publish articles that were directly critical of the management. Some believed this was due to Farley, the editor. Bagley, who also wrote for the *Offering,* called Farley "the mouthpiece of the corporations" (as quoted by Philip S. Foner in *The Factory Girls*). In a very public dispute, Bagley claimed that Farley had refused to publish articles about the declining working conditions of the laborers. Farley claimed this was not true. Others clearly felt dissatisfaction with the *Offering,* as it quickly lost its readership and ceased publication by December 1845.

Things to remember while reading "A Second Peep at Factory Life":

- The author of the article below, Josephine L. Baker, wrote as if she were speaking to a visitor to whom she was giving a tour of the textile factory. In the piece, she describes factory life and some of the machinery used by the laborers, and then openly and honestly discusses working conditions at the factory. The article was written in the last year of publication of the *Lowell Offering,* when frustration among workers was running high.

- During its five years of publication, seventy young women wrote articles for the *Lowell Offering.* Although this is a large number, there is no way to know if these contributors were representative of the Lowell mill girls as a whole. Whether there was censorship by the mill owners and the editor is also unknown.

- English novelist Charles Dickens (1812–1870) paid a visit to the Lowell mills while traveling in the United States. He describes the mills and the workers in his *American Notes and Pictures from Italy* (1874). Dickens read all four hundred pages of the published volumes of the *Lowell Offering,* and commented: "Of the merits of the *Lowell Offering* as a literary production, I will only observe, putting entirely out of sight the fact of the articles having been written by these girls after the arduous [difficult to accomplish] labours of the day, that it will compare advantageously [favorably] with a great many English Annuals." Dickens continued, "It is pleasant to find that many of its Tales are of the Mills and of those who work in them; that they inculcate [show] habits of self-denial and contentment, and teach good doctrines of enlarged benevolence. A strong feeling for the beauties of nature, as displayed in the solitudes the writers have left at home, breathes through its pages like wholesome village air."

English novelist Charles Dickens was impressed by the writings of the Lowell mill girls. *(AP/Wide World Photos. Reproduced by permission.)*

"A Second Peep at Factory Life"

*There is an old saying, that "When we are with the Romans, we must do as the Romans do." And now, kind friend, as we are about to renew our walk, I beg that you will give heed to it, and do as factory girls do. After this **preliminary**, we will proceed to the factory.*

*There is the **"counting-room,"** a long, low, brick building, and opposite is the "store-house," built of the same material, after the same model. Between them, swings the **ponderous** gate that shuts the mills in from the world without. But, stop; we must get "a pass," ere we go through, or "the watchman will be after us." Having obtained this, we will stop on the slight elevation by the gate, and view the mills. The one to the left rears high its huge sides of brick and **mortar,** and the **belfry,** towering far above the rest, stands out in bold relief against the rosy sky. The almost innumerable windows glitter, like gems, in the morning sunlight. It is six and a half stories high, and, like the fabled monster of old, who guarded the*

Preliminary: Introductory part.

Counting-room: Room in which a merchant, trader, or manufacturer keeps his financial records and does business.

Ponderous: Heavy.

Mortar: The substance that is applied between bricks in building.

Belfry: Bell tower.

Sacred waters of Mars: In the sacred grove of Mars, the Roman god of war, there was a fountain of pure water. This fountain was guarded by a large serpent.

Gigging: Raising the nap, or the furry surface, of the cloth.

Fulling: Shrinking and thickening cloth by moistening and heating it.

Burling: Knotting.

Shearing: Cutting or trimming.

Fine-drawing: Sewing so a seam is not visible.

Exquisite fancy: Beautiful and ornamental.

Looms: Weaving machines.

Dressing: Finishing.

Lathe: Machine tool that rotates for shaping things.

Shuttle: Device that carries threads across a loom in the weaving process.

Jennies: Early spinning machines used to make thread or yarn.

Etiquette: Social conduct displayed by one with good manners.

Unceremoniously: Abruptly.

Carding-room: A place where fibers are combed and gathered into a loose rope.

Terra firma: Latin phrase meaning "solid ground."

Clouded brows: Troubled expressions.

sacred waters of Mars, it seems to guard its less aspiring sister to the right; that is five and a half stories high, and to it is attached the repair-shop. If you please, we will pass to the larger factory,—but be careful, or you will get lost in the mud, for this yard is not laid out in such beautiful order, as some of the factory yards are, nor can it be.

*We will just look into the first room. It is used for cleaning cloth. You see the scrubbing and scouring machines are in full operation, and **gigging** and **fulling** are going on in full perfection.... In the second room the cloth is "finished," going through the various operations of **burling, shearing,** brushing, inking, **fine-drawing,** pressing, and packing for market. This is the pleasantest room on the corporation, and consequently they are never in want of help. The shearing, brushing, pressing and packing is done by males, while the burling, inking, marking and fine-drawing is performed by females. We will pass to the third room, called the "cassimere weaving-room," where all kinds of cloths are woven, from plain to the most **exquisite fancy.** There are between eighty and ninety **looms,** and part of the **dressing** is also done here. The fourth is the "broad weaving-room," and contains between thirty and forty looms; and broad sure enough they are. Just see how lazily the **lathe** drags backward and forward, and the **shuttle**—how spitefully it hops from one end of it to the other.... Now if you please we will go up to the next room, where the spinning is done. Here we have spinning jacks or **jennies** that dance merrily along whizzing and singing, as they spin out their "long yarns," and it seems but pleasure to watch their movements; but it is hard work, and requires good health and much strength. Do not go too near, as we shall find that they do not understand the established rules of **etiquette,** and might **unceremoniously** knock us over. We must not stop here longer, for it is twelve o'clock, and we have the "**carding-room**" to visit before dinner. There are between twenty and thirty sets of cards located closely together, and I beg of you to be careful as we go amongst them, or you will get caught in the machinery.... And—but the bell rings.*

*Now look out—not for the engine—but for the rush to the stairway. O mercy! what a crowd. I do not wonder you gasp for breath; but, keep up courage; we shall soon be on **terra firma** again. Now, safely landed, I hope to be excused for taking you into such a crowd. Really, it would not be fair to let you see the factory girls and machinery for nothing. I shall be obliged to hurry you, as it is some way to the boarding-house, and we have but thirty minutes from the time the bell begins to ring till it is done ringing again; and then all are required to be at their work. There is a group of girls yonder, going our way; let us overtake them, and hear what they are talking about. Something unpleasant I dare say, from their earnest gestures and **clouded brows.***

"Well, I do think it is too bad," exclaims one.

"So do I," says another. "This cutting down wages is not what they cry it up to be. I wonder how they'd like to work as hard as we do, digging and drudging day after day, from morning till night, and then, every two or three years, have their wages reduced. I rather guess it wouldn't set very well."

"And, besides this, who ever heard, of such a thing as their being raised again," says the first speaker. "I confess that I never did, so long as I've worked in the mill, and that's been these ten years."

"Well, it is real provoking any how," returned the other, "for my part I should think they had made a clean sweep this time. I wonder what they'll do next."

"Listeners never hear any good of themselves" is a **trite** saying, and, for fear it may prove true in our case, we will leave this busy group, and get some dinner. There is an open door inviting us to enter. We will do so. You can hang your bonnet and shawl on one of those hooks, that extend the length of the entry for that purpose, or you can lay them on the banisters, as some do. Please walk into the dining room. Here are two large square tables, covered with checked clothes and loaded down with smoking **viands**, the odor of which is very inviting. But we will not stop here; there is the long table in the front room, at which ten or fifteen can be comfortably seated. You may place yourself at the head. Now do not be bashful or wait to be helped, but comply with the oft-made request, "help yourself" to whatever you like best; for you have but a few minutes allotted you to spend at the table. The reason why, is because you are a rational, intelligent, thinking being, and ought to know enough to swallow your food whole; whereas a horse or an ox, or any other dumb beast knows no better than to spend an hour in the useless process of **mastication**. The bell rings again, and the girls are hurrying to the mills; you, I suppose, have seen enough of them for one day, so we will walk up stairs and have a **tete-a-tete**.

You ask, if there are so many things objectionable, why we work in the mill. Well, simply for this reason,—every situation in life, has its trials which must be **borne,** and factory life has no more than any other. There are many things we do not like; many occurrences that send the warm blood **mantling** to the cheek when they must be borne in silence, and many harsh words and acts that are not called for. There are objections also to the number of hours we work, to the length of time **allotted** to our meals, and to the low wages allowed for labor; objections that must and will be answered; for the time has come when something, besides the clothing and feeding of the body is to be thought of; when the mind is to be clothed and fed; and this cannot be as it should be, with the present

Trite: Unoriginal.

Viands: Foods.

Mastication: Chewing.

Tete-a-tete: Literally head-to-head in French; a private chat.

Borne: Endured.

Mantling: Spreading over a surface.

Allotted: Allowed.

system of labor. Who, let me ask, can find that pleasure in life which they should, when it is spent in this way. Without time for the laborer's own work, and the improvement of the mind, save the few evening hours; and even then if the mind is enriched and stored with useful knowledge, it must be at the expense of health. And the feeling too, that comes over us (there is no use in denying it) when we hear the bell calling us away from repose that tired nature loudly claims—the feeling, that we are obliged to go. And these few hours, of which we have spoken, are far too short, three at the most at the close of day. Surely, methinks, every heart that lays claim to humanity will feel 'tis not enough. But this, we hope will, ere long, be done away with, and labor made what it should be; pleasant and inviting to every son and daughter of the human family.

There is a brighter side to this picture, over which we would not willingly pass without notice, and an answer to the question, why we work here? The time we do have is our own. The money we earn comes promptly; more so than in any other situation; and our work, though **laborious,** *is the same from day to day; we know what it is, and when finished we feel perfectly free, till it is time to* **commence** *it again.*

Besides this, there are many pleasant associations connected with factory life, that are not to be found elsewhere.

There are lectures, evening schools and libraries, to which all may have access. The one thing needful here, is the time to improve them as we ought.

There is a class, of whom I would speak, that work in the mills, and will while they continue in operation. Namely, the many who have no home, and who come here to seek, in this busy, bustling "City of Spindles," a competency that shall enable them in after life, to live without being a burden to society,—the many who toil on, without a murmur, for the support of an aged mother or orphaned brother and sister. For the sake of them, we earnestly hope labor may be reformed; that the miserable, selfish spirit of competition, now in our midst, may be thrust from us and **consigned to eternal oblivion.**

J. L. B.

What happened next . . .

In 1846 Irish immigrants who had fled their native country due to a terrible famine (extreme shortage of food) arrived in large numbers in Lowell and the surrounding cities. They were very poor and willing to work for low wages. By 1860 they made up about one-half of Lowell's mill workers. Immigrants from other countries made up most of the rest of the workforce.

In 1844 Sarah Bagley, hoping to improve the mill environment, helped found the Lowell Female Reform Association (LFRA). She spoke before the Massachusetts legislature and claimed that new requirements forcing mill workers to oversee more machines were endangering their physical health because of the tremendous and continuous stress it placed upon the worker and the increased likelihood of accidents. As a result the legislature conducted an investigation into worker health and safety, but no action was taken to improve conditions. The LFRA then formed a partnership with a labor organization known as the New England Workingmen's Association. In 1845 Bagley became the editor of the organization's weekly newspaper, *The Voice of Industry*, and began her major campaign, the Ten Hours Movement, which was an attempt to limit the workday to ten hours. For the next couple of years, she was known as one of the most forceful writers and speakers for this cause. In 1848 she disappeared from historical records, but she is remembered as the first woman trade union leader.

Amelia Bloomer, publisher of *The Lily*, wearing "bloomers." *(© Bettmann/Corbis.)*

Did you know ...

- The *Lowell Offering* was the first of several periodicals produced and written by women for women readers in the United States during the nineteenth century. Amelia Bloomer (1818–1894) published the successful magazine *The Lily* from 1849 to 1856 to promote temperance (abstinence from drinking alcohol) and women's dress reform. From 1853 to 1855, Paulina Wright Davis (1813–1876) published *Una*, the first U.S. women's rights newspaper. In 1868 women's rights advocates Elizabeth Cady Stanton

(1815–1902) and Susan B. Anthony (1820–1906) founded *The Revolution*, a feminist weekly newspaper that also covered many other political topics. The *Woman's Era*, published from 1894 to 1903, was the first newspaper created by and for African American women.

Consider the following . . .

- The author of the article "A Second Peep at Factory Life" presents her description of the cotton mill in a very unusual way. What effect does she achieve by writing as if talking directly to an interested visitor to the factory? Why do you think she chose to write in that way?

- Do you think the narrator of the article is happy with her work at the mill? Do you think she is proud of her work? Finally, do you think she intends to continue working there? Explain.

For More Information

Books

Dickens, Charles. *American Notes and Pictures from Italy.* London: Chapman and Hall, 1874.

Eisler, Barbara, ed. *The Lowell Offering: Writings by New England Mill Women, 1840–1845.* Philadelphia: J.B. Lippincott, 1977.

Foner, Philip S., ed. *The Factory Girls.* Urbana: University of Illinois Press, 1977.

Selden, Bernice. *The Mill Girls: Lucy Larcom, Harriet Hanson Robinson, Sarah G. Bagley.* New York: Atheneum, 1983.

Periodicals

Baker, Josephine L. "A Second Peep at Factory Life." From *Lowell Offering,* vol. V (1845): 97–100. This article can also be found online at http://www.albany.edu/history/history316/SecondPeepatFactoryLife.html (accessed on July 6, 2005).

"Mind Among the Spindles: The Lowell Offering." *Cobblestone,* March 2001.

Web Sites

"The Mill Girls." *The National Park Service.* http://www.nps.gov/lowe/loweweb/Lowell_History/Millgirls.htm (accessed on July 6, 2005).

The Canal Boat

Excerpt from "The Canal Boat"
By Nathaniel Hawthorne
Originally published in the *New England Magazine,* 1835
Amended version available online from the University of Rochester,
Department of History, Erie Canal Library
http://www.history.rochester.edu/canal/bib/hawthorne/
canalboat.htm

When the Industrial Revolution began in the United States in the late eighteenth and early nineteenth centuries, it was extremely difficult and expensive to transport goods across the country. In the early 1800s the Allegheny Mountains (a range in the Appalachian system extending through Pennsylvania, Maryland, Virginia, and West Virginia) formed the western frontier of the nation. Beyond the Alleghenies lay the Old Northwest (the modern states of Ohio, Indiana, Illinois, Michigan, and Wisconsin), a land rich in natural resources such as timber, minerals, and fertile soil. However, there were few roads, and those that did exist were muddy and filled with boulders and tree stumps. For the country to continue to grow and prosper under the development of industry, more efficient transportation systems were needed. This problem eased slightly in 1807 when steamboats were first used on some of the country's major rivers, but it still remained difficult to transport materials across the land to the waterways.

In the early nineteenth century, scientists, politicians, and businessmen began to study the possibility of building

"Surely, the water of this canal must be the most fertilizing of all fluids; for it causes towns . . . to spring up."

The entrance of the Erie Canal. *(© Corbis.)*

canals—shallow, human-made waterways that could connect larger, natural waterways. Foremost among the supporters of canal-building was the mayor of New York City (and future governor of the state), DeWitt Clinton (1769–1828). Clinton worked hard to raise interest, as well as $7 million from the state of New York, to build the Erie Canal, a 363-mile-long waterway that would connect the Hudson River in New York to Lake Erie in the Midwest. Nothing like it had ever been built, and skeptics, predicting a grand failure, referred to the canal as "Clinton's Ditch."

Construction began at Rome, New York, in 1817. Four men with little building experience were appointed as the giant project's principal engineers. They completed the work in eight years and almost managed to stay within the budget that had been set. The engineers designed fresh methods of digging the canal using plows and root cutters powered by horses and other livestock. Several new inventions were used in the construction, including a machine that could be used to pull down a tree of any height without an ax and a wheeled machine that could pull thirty to forty tree stumps a day using only seven laborers. The laborers who built the canal were mainly local farmers and mechanics mixed with a small number of Irish immigrants. Locals along the course of the canal were happy to help, and many farmers donated the land from which it was cut.

The Erie Canal was about four feet deep and forty feet wide. Along one bank was a ten-foot-wide towpath for the horses, mules, and oxen that pulled the boats through the canal waters. There was a 568-foot rise in elevation between the Hudson River and Lake Erie, so a system of eighty-three locks was built to raise or lower the boats in the canal to adjust to the different water levels. A lock consists of two gates and room for the boat within them. On one side of the lock, the water is either higher or lower than it is on the other side. As the boat approaches, one gate opens to let the boat enter and then closes behind it. Water then fills the chamber between the gates (or is let out of it) and the boat rises (or sinks) to the water level on the other side of the second gate. Then the second gate is opened and the boat continues on. The original locks in the Erie Canal were ninety feet long and fifteen feet wide.

The Erie Canal was an engineering wonder and quickly became the American superhighway of its day. Upon its completion in October 1825, New Yorkers held a ten-day celebration. As part of the grand ceremony, Governor Clinton set out from Buffalo, New York, in a packet boat called the *Seneca Chief* headed for the harbor at New York City, which lies at the mouth of the Hudson River where it runs into the Atlantic Ocean. Cannons spaced along the entire five hundred miles of the route fired in succession to announce his departure. The last cannon boomed one hundred minutes after the first, and then the process began again in reverse order. When he arrived in New York Harbor on November 4, Clinton dumped two kegs

Hawthorne traveled the Erie Canal in a horse-drawn packet boat, like those shown here. *(© Corbis.)*

of Lake Erie water into the harbor to symbolize what he called "the Marriage of the Waters": the connection between the Atlantic Ocean and the Great Lakes.

The canal had a large impact on the economy of New York and the nation as a whole. It opened an inexpensive route for western goods, especially lumber, grain, and flour, to flow into the Hudson and then out into world markets from the piers of Manhattan and Brooklyn. Imported and U.S.-manufactured products also moved west along the new channel, quickly making the port of New York the busiest and most important in the country. Between 1830 and 1847 well over half of all American imports traveled through New York's harbor. This enormous volume resulted from the fact that the Erie Canal cut the cost of sending goods from Buffalo to New York City to less than $8 per ton from the previous cost of $100 per ton before the canal was built.

The completion of the Erie Canal created a thriving economy not just in New York City but all along its line. In the western part of the state, where there had been little settlement, new farms sprang up to the north and south of the canal route. More impressive still was the growth of canal towns in New York such as Lockport, Rochester, and Buffalo. Rochester's population increased from 1,502 to 36,403 between 1820 and 1850, and the city became a major grain processor, shipping out 369,000 barrels of flour in 1836 alone. Areas outside of New York also profited from the canal. Most significantly, the Erie Canal provided a waterway and transportation option directly from the Atlantic Ocean and the East Coast to the hard-to-reach Great Lakes. The Great Lakes soon became crowded with hundreds of steamships, and giant industries arose along their shores. Small towns on the banks of the lakes, including Chicago, Illinois, Detroit, Michigan, and Cleveland, Ohio, grew into massive cities.

Things to remember while reading the excerpt from "The Canal Boat":

- The Erie Canal made it possible for sightseers to travel to many locations that had not been accessible in the past. One of these destinations was Niagara Falls in New York. In September 1832 Nathaniel Hawthorne (1804–1864), a young and largely unknown writer, took a packet boat up the Erie Canal and visited Niagara Falls. At the time of Hawthorne's travels, the area around the new canal was in the process of changing. Commercial centers had arisen along the route but most were still in their early stages.

- Canal passengers could choose from two types of vessels to travel on: the cheaper regular or line boats, which carried freight as well, and the more elegant luxury or packet boats, such as the one Hawthorne chose. Packet boats were generally from fifty to seventy feet long, with large cabins that extended most of their length. They were pulled along by a team of horses, mules, or oxen managed by a handler called a hoggee, and the animals were changed every few miles at stops along the way. The boats were divided into four or five cabins: a small forward (near the front) space for the six crew members, a ladies' cabin and room also forward, the cook's quarters, and a larger middle or rear cabin that served as a sleeping parlor for the men and a dining room for all. Passengers slept on bunks or narrow shelves fitted to the walls. When the boats were overcrowded, which was often, passengers slept on the floors, tables, and anywhere else they could find room. During daytime travel passengers used the roof of the long cabin as a deck from which to sit and watch the passing scenery.

- In 1832 a trip on a packet boat on the Erie Canal from New York City to Buffalo took around four days, as the boat traveled at a rate of about 3.5 miles per hour. Passengers paid approximately 5 cents per mile to travel on a packet, and the price included a berth (place to sit or sleep) and three meals a day.

Nathaniel Hawthorne. *(© Hulton-Deutsch Collection/Corbis.)*

Excerpt from "The Canal Boat"

I was inclined to be poetical about the Grand Canal. In my imagination, De Witt Clinton was an enchanter, who had waved his magic wand from the Hudson to Lake Erie, and united them by a watery highway, crowded with the commerce of two worlds, till then inaccessible to each other. This simple and mighty conception had **conferred inestimable** *value on spots which Nature seemed to have thrown carelessly into the great body of the earth, without foreseeing that they could ever attain importance. I pictured the surprise of the sleepy Dutchmen when the new river first glittered by their doors, bringing them hard cash or foreign* **commodities,** *in exchange for their* **hitherto** *unmarketable produce. Surely, the water of this canal must be the most fertilizing of all fluids; for it causes towns—with their masses of brick and stone, their churches and theatres, their business and hubbub, their luxury and refinement, their gay dames and polished citizens—to spring up, till, in time, the wondrous stream may flow between two continuous lines of buildings, through one* **thronged** *street, from Buffalo to Albany. I*

Conferred: Gave.

Inestimable: Unknown.

Commodities: Goods.

Hitherto: Until this time.

Thronged: Crowded.

embarked about thirty miles below Utica, determining to voyage along the whole extent of the canal, at least twice in the course of the summer.

Behold us, then, fairly afloat, with three horses harnessed to our vessel, like the steeds of **Neptune** to a huge scallop-shell, in mythological pictures. Bound to a distant port, we had neither chart nor compass, nor cared about the wind, nor felt the heaving of a **billow**, nor dreaded shipwreck, however fierce the **tempest**, in our adventurous navigation of an **interminable** mud-puddle—for a mud-puddle it seemed, and as dark and **turbid** as if every kennel in the land paid contribution to it. With an **imperceptible** current, it holds its drowsy way through all the dismal swamps and unimpressive scenery, that could be found between the great lakes and the sea-coast. Yet there is variety enough, both on the surface of the canal and along its banks, to amuse the traveller, if an overpowering **tedium** did not deaden his perceptions.

Sometimes we met a black and rusty-looking vessel, laden with lumber, salt from Syracuse, or Genesee flour, and shaped at both ends like a square-toed boot; as if it had two **sterns**, and were fated always to advance backward. On its deck would be a square hut, and a woman seen through the window at her household work, with a little tribe of children, who perhaps had been born in this strange dwelling and knew no other home. Thus, while the husband smoked his pipe at the helm, and the eldest son rode one of the horses, on went the family, travelling hundreds of miles in their own house, and carrying their fireside with them. The most frequent species of craft were the "line boats," which had a cabin at each end, and a great bulk of barrels, bales, and boxes in the midst; or light packets, like our own, decked all over, with a row of curtained windows from stem to stern, and a drowsy face at every one. . . .

Had I been on my feet at the time, instead of sailing slowly along in a dirty canal-boat, I should often have paused to contemplate the **diversified panorama** along the banks of the canal. Sometimes the scene was a forest, dark, dense, and **impervious**, breaking away occasionally and receding from a lonely tract, covered with dismal black stumps, where, on the verge of the canal, might be seen a log-cottage, and a sallow-faced woman at the window. Lean and **aguish**, she looked like Poverty personified, half clothed, half fed, and dwelling in a desert, while a tide of wealth was sweeping by her door. Two or three miles further would bring us to a **lock**, where the **slight impediment to navigation** had created a little mart of trade. Here would be found commodities of all sorts, enumerated in yellow letters on the window-shutters of a small grocery-store, the owner of which had set his soul to the gathering of coppers and small change, buying and selling through the week, and counting his gains on the blessed **Sabbath**. The next

Embarked: Came on board.

Neptune: The Roman god of the sea, horses, and earthquakes.

Billow: Great wave.

Tempest: Storm.

Interminable: Seemingly endless.

Turbid: Muddy.

Imperceptible: Extremely slight.

Tedium: Boredom.

Sterns: Rear part of boats.

Diversified panorama: Varied view of an area.

Impervious: Not allowing entrance.

Aguish: Feverish.

Lock: An enclosure in a canal that has gates at each end that are used to raise and lower boats as they pass from one level of water to the next.

Slight impediment to navigation: Minor slowing of boat traffic.

Sabbath: Day of rest and worship for Jews and some Christians.

scene might be the dwelling-houses and stores of a thriving village, built of wood or small gray stones, a church-spire rising in the midst, and generally two taverns, bearing over their **piazzas** the **pompous** titles of "hotel," "exchange," "**tontine**," or "coffee-house." Passing on, we glide now into the unquiet heart of an inland city—of Utica, for instance— and find ourselves amid piles of brick, crowded docks and **quays**, rich warehouses and a busy population. We feel the eager and hurrying spirit of the place, like a stream and **eddy** whirling us along with it. Through the thickest of the **tumult** goes the canal, flowing between lofty rows of buildings and arched bridges of **hewn** stone. Onward, also, go we, till the hum and bustle of struggling enterprise die away behind us, and we are threading an avenue of the ancient woods again. . . .

[*Hawthorne describes the scene on the canal boat as night falls.*] The crimson curtain being let down between the ladies and gentlemen, the cabin became a bed-chamber for twenty persons, who were laid on shelves, one above another. For a long time, our various **incommodities** kept us all awake, except five or six, who were accustomed to sleep nightly amid the uproar of their own snoring, and had little to dread from any other species of disturbance. It is a curious fact, that these snorers had been the most quiet people in the boat, while awake, and became peace-breakers only when others ceased to be so, breathing tumult out of their repose.

Finally, all was hushed in that quarter. Still, I was more broad awake than through the whole preceding day, and felt a feverish impulse to toss my limbs miles apart, and appease the unquietness of mind by that of matter. Forgetting that my berth was hardly so wide as a coffin, I turned suddenly over, and fell like an avalanche on the floor, to the disturbance of the whole community of sleepers. As there were no bones broken, I blessed the accident, and went on deck. A lantern was burning at each end of the boat, and one of the crew was stationed at the bows, keeping watch, as **mariners** do on the ocean. Though the rain had ceased, the sky was all one cloud, and the darkness so intense, that there seemed to be no world, except the little space on which our lanterns glimmered. Yet, it was an impressive scene.

We were traversing the "long level," a dead flat between Utica and Syracuse, where the canal has not rise or fall enough to require a lock for nearly seventy miles. There can hardly be a more dismal tract of country. The forest which covers it, consisting chiefly of white cedar, black ash, and other trees that live in excessive moisture, is now decayed and death-struck, by the partial draining of the swamp into the great ditch of the canal. Sometimes, indeed, our lights were reflected from pools of **stagnant** water, which stretched far in among the trunks of the trees, beneath dense masses of dark **foliage**. But generally, the tall stems and

Piazzas: Open squares.

Pompous: Self-important.

Tontine: Financial establishment.

Quays: Structures built along the banks of the canal for landing boats.

Eddy: Whirlpool.

Tumult: Disorderly movement.

Hewn: Cut.

Incommodities: Discomforts.

Mariners: Sailors.

Stagnant: Unmoving.

Foliage: Leaves.

*intermingled branches were naked, and brought into strong relief, amid the surrounding gloom, by the whiteness of their decay. Often, we beheld the **prostrate** form of some old **sylvan** giant, which had fallen, and crushed down smaller trees under its immense ruin. In spots, where destruction had been riotous, the lanterns showed perhaps a hundred trunks, erect, half overthrown, extended along the ground, resting on their shattered limbs, or tossing them desperately into the darkness, but all of one ashy-white, all naked together, in **desolate** confusion. Thus growing out of the night as we drew nigh, and vanishing as we glided on, based on **obscurity,** and overhung and bounded by it, the scene was ghost-like—the very land of unsubstantial things, **whither** dreams might betake themselves, when they quit the slumberer's brain.*

*My fancy found another **emblem**. The wild Nature of America had been driven to this desert-place by the **encroachments** of civilized man. And even here, where the savage queen was throned on the ruins of her empire, did we penetrate, a vulgar and worldly throng, intruding on her latest solitude. In other lands, Decay sits among fallen palaces; but here, her home is in the forests.*

*Shortly after, our boatman blew a horn, sending a long and **melancholy** note through the forest avenue, as a signal for some watcher in the wilderness to be ready with a change of horses. We had proceeded a mile or two with our fresh team, when the tow-rope got entangled in a fallen branch on the edge of the canal, and caused a momentary delay, during which I went to examine the **phosphoric** light of an odd tree, a little within the forest. It was not the first **delusive** radiance that I had followed. The tree lay along the ground, and was wholly converted into a mass of diseased splendor, which threw a **ghastliness** around. Being full of **conceits** that night, I called it a **frigid** fire; a funeral light, illumining decay and death; an emblem of fame, that gleams around the dead man without warming him; or of genius, when it owes its brilliancy to moral rottenness; and was thinking that such ghost-like torches were just fit to light up this dead forest, or to blaze coldly in tombs. . . .*

Prostrate: Lying flat.

Sylvan: Forest.

Desolate: Dreary.

Obscurity: Absence of light.

Whither: Where; to what place.

Emblem: Symbol.

Encroachments: Advancement.

Melancholy: Sad.

Phosphoric: Containing a substance that radiates light at certain times.

Delusive: Likely to trick or elude.

Ghastliness: Feeling of horror.

Conceits: Fanciful ideas.

Frigid: Extremely cold.

What happened next . . .

At the end of Hawthorne's essay, the canal boat takes off without him, and he happily sets out through the woods on foot to finish his journey.

For two decades after Hawthorne wrote "The Canal Boat," the Erie remained the nation's major highway. No other man-made American water channel ever matched it in size or traffic, although many new canals were hastily built throughout the northeastern and midwestern United States. Other eastern cities, such as Philadelphia, Pennsylvania, and Baltimore, Maryland, could not afford to allow New York to monopolize the western trade. Pennsylvania constructed a system of canals between Philadelphia and Pittsburgh, Pennsylvania, and then built the Pennsylvania Railroad. Baltimore undertook two major transportation improvements, which created the Baltimore and Ohio Railroad and the Chesapeake and Ohio Canal. Farther to the north, Boston constructed a railroad that crossed the state to Albany.

The age of canals was short-lived due to many problems with the waterways. They were expensive to build, cost a great deal to repair, and floods and winter freezes made them less dependable than land transportation. But it was mainly the introduction and spread of the railroads that brought about the decline of canals. Railroads were almost as expensive as canals to construct, but they were cheaper to repair and did not require huge supplies of water. Also, unlike canals, railroads could provide dependable all-weather transport for dry goods and passengers. They were also much faster. Nonetheless, many canals did continue to compete successfully with railroads in the shipment of bulky commodities—crops, lumber, steel, and many others—well into the mid-nineteenth century.

The Erie Canal went through some transformations after Hawthorne wrote his essay. Between 1836 and 1862 the canal was significantly enlarged so that it could accommodate boats carrying up to 250 tons of cargo. Early in the twentieth century, it was equipped with steam and diesel-powered tugboats that moved the boats instead of the old method of using horses and mules. The locks were operated by electricity.

Did you know . . .

- In 1959 the United States and Canada completed a joint waterway project known as the St. Lawrence Seaway. The seaway provided access from the Atlantic Ocean to the Great Lakes along the northern border of the United States.

The Saint Lawrence River flowed out of Lake Ontario in Canada and provided a natural outlet from the Great Lakes to the Atlantic Ocean. However, before the St. Lawrence Seaway was built, small channels and rapids along the river had prevented navigation by vessels much larger than a canoe. In 1954 the American government entered into a cooperative effort with Canada to dig a twenty-seven-foot-deep canal between Montreal, Quebec, and Lake Ontario. This massive project involved fifty-nine thousand workers and $80 million worth of heavy equipment. Tons of heavy rocks, gravel, and slimy marine clay had to be moved to connect the Great Lakes to the sea. In 1958 thirty-eight thousand acres of land along forty miles of the seaway were flooded, providing access for deep-sea ships from the tip of Lake Superior in northern Minnesota to the Atlantic. Once the St. Lawrence Seaway was completed, the Erie Canal was no longer used for commercial shipping. By the early twenty-first century, the Erie, part of New York's Barge Canal System, was used mainly for recreational purposes.

Consider the following . . .

- Hawthorne begins this passage by saying that he began his trip "inclined to be poetical about the Grand Canal." By the end of the excerpt, how does he seem to feel about the canal? Does the canal still inspire the poet in him?
- When he describes the forest from the canal boat at night, Hawthorne creates very strong and eerie images. What are these images and what effect do they have on you, the reader?

For More Information

Books

Bernstein, Peter L. *Wedding of the Waters: The Erie Canal and the Making of a Great Nation.* New York: W. W. Norton & Co., 2005.

Santella, Andrew. *The Erie Canal.* Minneapolis, MN: Compass Point Books, 2005.

Periodicals

Hawthorne, Nathaniel. "The Canal Boat." *New England Magazine,* no. 2 (December 1835): 398–409. Amended version available online from

University of Rochester, Department of History, Erie Canal Library. http://www.history.rochester.edu/canal/bib/hawthorne/canal-boat.htm (accessed on July 6, 2005).

Web Sites

"The Erie Canal." http://www.eriecanal.org/ (accessed on July 6, 2005).

"Traveling the Erie Canal: 1836." *EyeWitness to History.com.* http://www.eyewitnesstohistory.com/eriecanal.htm (accessed on July 6, 2005).

The Education of Henry Adams

Excerpt from The Education of Henry Adams: An Autobiography
Privately printed in 1907; published after Adams's death in 1918
Reprinted by Time Inc. in 1964

American journalist, historian, and novelist Henry Brooks Adams (1838–1918) is best remembered for writings that captured the essence of the changes that occurred during the Gilded Age, the era of industrialization from the early 1860s to the turn of the century in which a few wealthy individuals gained tremendous power and influence. He was born into one of the most well-known political families in the United States. His great-grandfather was John Adams (1735–1826; served 1797–1801), the second president of the United States; his grandfather was John Quincy Adams (1767–1848; served 1825–29), the sixth U.S. president; and his father, Charles Francis Adams (1807–1886), was a diplomat and U.S. senator. As a child, Henry Adams sat at the dinner table with some of the most important statesmen in the nation. His family's experiences and attitudes gave Adams a sense of history and taught him the traditions of the early American leaders.

After graduating from Harvard University in 1858, Henry Adams left the United States to study law in Berlin, Germany. He then went on a lengthy tour of Europe before returning

"On the new scale of power, merely to make the continent habitable for civilized people would require an outlay that would have bankrupted the world. . . . From the moment that railways were introduced, life took on extravagance."

To Adams, the dynamo was a symbol of disunity. *(© Schenectady Museum; Hall of Electrical History Foundation/Corbis.)*

briefly to the United States in 1860 to serve as private secretary to his father, who had been elected to Congress. In March 1861 President Abraham Lincoln (1809–1865; served 1861–65) selected Charles Adams to be minister to Great Britain. Henry accompanied his father as his secretary and remained in England until 1868.

Upon his return to the United States, Adams settled in Washington, D.C., where he reported on the political scene for the *Nation* and other newspapers. Witnessing the dishonesty and greed in the nation's capital during the Gilded Age inspired him to become a critic of and commentator on the questionable conduct of Washington's politicians and businessmen. He focused in particular on scandals that occurred during the administration of President Ulysses S. Grant (1822–1885; served 1869–77). Among the scandals in Grant's administration were: the Credit Mobilier scandal, in which top executives of the Union and Pacific Railroads took huge amounts of federal subsidies (government aid) for their own personal profit; the whiskey ring scandal, in which government officials defrauded the federal government of the taxes collected on whiskey; and the Belknap case, in which Grant's secretary of war, William W. Belknap (1829–1890) resigned after being caught accepting bribes to permit the sale of Native American trading posts in Oklahoma. After a couple of years of writing about governmental corruption, in the autumn of 1870 Adams moved to Boston to become editor of the *North American Review* and an assistant professor of history at Harvard. He left Harvard in 1877 but continued to write well-respected books on American history through the 1890s.

Henry Brooks Adams. (© *Bettmann/Corbis.*)

Adams's two best-known works were written in his later years. In 1904 he completed *Mont-Saint-Michel and Chartres.* The book took the format of a travel guide addressed from an uncle to his nieces, in which he described to them two great achievements in twelfth- and thirteenth-century French architecture: the monastery on the island of Mont-Saint-Michel and the cathedral at Chartres. In his examination of these two monuments, Adams found a powerful symbol of social unity in the Virgin Mary—when everyone in a community passionately worshipped the same symbol, it brought them together. He was fascinated by the difference between the unity of medieval times and the lack of unity of present times, when people did not focus their religious or spiritual worship on a single powerful symbol like the Virgin Mary.

Adams wrote his masterpiece, *The Education of Henry Adams: An Autobiography,* to be a companion volume to *Mont-Saint-Michel and Chartres.* Though *Education* was Adams's autobiography, it was also, like the former volume, his way of documenting the history of an era. To balance his concept of the Virgin Mary as a symbol of unity in the earlier work, in *Education* Adams presented a symbol of the disunity of the nineteenth century in the image of the dynamo, an early form of generator used in power plants that he had observed in the great Paris Exhibition of 1900, in a display of nearly eighty thousand exhibits of modern technology. To Adams, the dynamo was a symbol of all technology, and he felt that technology had replaced religion as the focus of society. Observing the corruption in government and business and the passion exhibited by ordinary people in their attempts to get rich quick in the new industrialized world, Adams judged that money had become the leading force, while the wisdom and moral values of previous times had been forgotten or ignored.

In the excerpt from *Education* Adams describes his return to the United States in 1868 after being in Europe for most of the previous ten years. He had returned to a country so different he did not recognize it. Adams arrived back in the United States with his father and diplomat and historian John Lothrop Motley (1814–1877), who served as the minister to Austria from 1861 to 1867. While away, they had learned the ways of upper-class Europeans, where an old and well-defined aristocracy, made up of people who never actually worked, had refined its leisure pasttimes to an art. Though entertaining, Adams found the traditions of the European aristocracy unsuited to the present age in America, where making money was the primary activity of rich and poor alike. The rising economic and political force in the nation was the new industrialists, and they did not look or act anything like the Europeans with whom he had so recently socialized, or even like the American statesmen who had dined at Adams's table when he was a boy. In the excerpt he describes his impression of the changed nation.

Things to remember while reading the excerpt from *The Education of Henry Adams: An Autobiography*:

- In the excerpt Adams focuses on the railroads and the country's mania to build more railway lines as its first step to industrialization. In 1850 there had been about 9,000 miles of railroad tracks in the country. By the end of the decade there were about 31,000 miles of tracks, and this number continued to grow at a fast rate. Railroads had become the country's biggest business. They linked industrial and agricultural areas and provided a reliable means of transportation between the two for both goods and people. They made it possible to build cities without nearby waterways. They brought the plentiful resources of the United States to American manufacturers. They hastened the settling of the West. Many historians have stated that the United States would not have become the world's top industrial nation without the significant amount of railroad construction that took place in the late nineteenth century, but to Adams the effects of this transformation were not always positive.

Railroad executive Jay Gould. (© *Bettmann/Corbis.*)

- Adams refers in this excerpt to two of the top railroad industrialists at the time of his return to the United States: Cornelius "Commodore" Vanderbilt (1794–1877) and Jay Gould (1836–1892). Vanderbilt made a fortune in steamboats before the Civil War and then in 1865 began to build an enormous New York railroad empire, which made him one of the richest men in the country by the time of his death. Vanderbilt had little education and was known for his rude manners and loud voice. In Adams's times, most readers would have instantly associated these names with the scandals and ruthless business deals they had been involved in.

- Gould was a railroad financier (one who raises and invests money), known for his sharp but unprincipled business practices. Not long after Adams returned to the United States, Gould and his partner James Fisk (1834–1872) developed a scheme to corner the market on gold by buying up most of the gold that was available on the U.S. market. This drove up the price of gold by creating the appearance of increased demand in the market. After the price of gold soared due to their actions, Fisk and Gould sold their gold to other speculators (people who buy and sell in hopes of profiting from changes in the market) before prices had time to collapse. They made large amounts of money, but the rapid fall in gold's value financially ruined the speculators who bought it from them and caused many banks and businesses to fail. The nation's economy went into a steep decline that hit bottom, or crashed, on Friday, September 24, 1869, a day that was later referred to as "Black Friday."

- In the 1860s Gould, Fisk, and a partner, Daniel Drew (1797–1879), started buying great quantities of Erie Railroad stock and thus became controlling directors of the New York railway. At this time Vanderbilt owned a railroad system that extended from New York City to Buffalo, New York. The Erie Railroad was his only competitor and he attempted to gain control of it from Gould. In the conflict that followed, both Vanderbilt and Gould used dishonest means to undercut each other. Vanderbilt started by lowering the rates on his railroad services drastically to take away the Erie's business. Fisk bought a herd of cattle and shipped it at the reduced rate on Vanderbilt's railroad, costing Vanderbilt dearly. Vanderbilt then tried to purchase all available shares of the Erie. Drew, Gould, and Fisk promptly issued one hundred thousand worthless stock certificates for the Erie. Vanderbilt eventually lost the battle, and Jay Gould became very wealthy from the Erie Railroad before driving it into financial ruin.

- Vanderbilt and Gould were among the first of the "robber barons," a relatively small number of U.S. businessmen who, in the years after the Civil War, created gigantic industries and became extremely rich and powerful. In the excerpt Adams compares them to his father and other statesmen of earlier times, whom he calls "ornaments," implying that they looked good but did not achieve many practical ends. Adams acknowledges that the country needs the energy and money of Vanderbilt and Gould and other robber barons in order to become a rich industrial nation. But Adams does not believe that getting rich or even industrialization are worthy goals. He uses satire to hold up the follies of the Gilded Age for his reader's ridicule and scorn.

Excerpt from The Education of Henry Adams: An Autobiography

*At ten o'clock of a July night, in heat that made the tropical rain-shower simmer, the Adams family and the Motley family **clambered** down the side of their **Cunard steamer** into the government tugboat, which set them ashore in black darkness at the end of some North River pier. Had they been **Tyrian** traders of the year BC 10,000, landing from a **galley** fresh from **Gibraltar**, they could hardly have been stranger on the shore of a world, so changed from what it had been ten years before. . . .*

*How much its character had changed or was changing, they could not wholly know, and they could but partly feel. For that matter, the land itself knew no more than they. Society in America was always trying, almost as blindly as an earthworm, to realize and understand itself; to catch up with its own head, and to twist about in search of its tail. Society offered the profile of a long, **straggling caravan**, stretching loosely toward the prairies, its few **score** of leaders far in advance and its millions of immigrants, Negroes, and Indians far in the rear, somewhere in **archaic time**. . . .*

*One could **divine** pretty nearly where the force lay, since the last ten years had given to the great mechanical **energies**—coal, iron, steam—a distinct superiority in power over the old industrial elements—agriculture, handwork, and learning; but the result of this revolution on a survivor from the fifties resembled the action of the earthworm; he twisted about, **in vain**, to recover his starting-point; he could no longer see his own trail; he had become an **estray**; a **flotsam** or **jetsam** of wreckage. . . . His world was dead.*

Clambered: Climbed awkwardly.

Cunard steamer: Transatlantic steamship.

Tyrian: From a city in an ancient country in southwestern Asia called Phoenicia (modern-day Syria and Lebanon).

Galley: Ship of ancient times powered mainly by oars.

Gibraltar: British colony on the southern tip of Spain.

Straggling caravan: Group of travelers wandering off the direct course.

Score: Group of twenty.

Archaic time: Very early ages.

Divine: Discover.

Energies: Resources for producing heat or electricity.

In vain: Without success.

Estray: Someone who wanders about without purpose or destination.

Flotsam: Floating wreckage or cargo from a shipwreck.

Jetsam: Part of a ship that is tossed overboard to lighten its load.

Not a **Polish Jew fresh from Warsaw or Cracow** ... but had a keener instinct, an intenser energy, and a freer hand than he—American of Americans, with Heaven knew how many **Puritans** and **Patriots** behind him, and an education that had cost a civil war. He made no complaint and found no fault with his time; he was no worse off than the Indians or the buffalo who had been ejected from their heritage by his own people. . . .

One comfort he could enjoy to the full. Little as he might be fitted for the work that was before him, he had only to look at his father and Motley to see figures less fitted for it than he. All were equally survivors from the forties—**bric-á-brac** from the time of **Louis Philippe**; stylists; **doctrinaires; ornaments** that had been more or less suited to the colonial architecture, but which never had much value in Desbrosses Street or Fifth Avenue [New York City streets]. They could scarcely have earned five dollars a day in any modern industry. The men who commanded high pay were as a rule not ornamental. Even Commodore Vanderbilt and Jay Gould lacked social charm. Doubtless the country needed ornament—needed it very badly indeed—but it needed energy still more, and **capital** most of all, for its supply was ridiculously out of proportion to its wants. On the new scale of power, merely to make the continent habitable for civilized people would require an **outlay** that would have **bankrupted** the world. As yet, no portion of the world except a few narrow stretches of western Europe had ever been tolerably provided with the essentials of comfort and convenience; to fit out an entire continent with roads and the **decencies of life** would exhaust the credit of the entire planet. . . . From the moment that railways were introduced, life took on extravagance. . . .

The new Americans, of whom he was to be one, must, whether they were fit or unfit, create a world of their own, a science, a society, a philosophy, a universe, where they had not yet created a road or even learned to dig their own iron. They had no time for thought; they saw, and could see, nothing beyond their day's work. . . .

Having cleared its path so far, society went back to its work, and threw itself on that which stood first—its roads. The field was vast; altogether beyond its power to control **offhand**; and society dropped every thought of dealing with anything more than the single fraction called a railway system. This relatively small part of its task was still so big as to need the energies of a generation, for it required all the new machinery to be created—capital, banks, mines, furnaces, shops, power-houses, technical knowledge, mechanical population,

Polish Jew fresh from Warsaw or Cracow: Adams was referring to the large population of Jews from Poland that immigrated to the United States at the end of the nineteenth century to escape religious persecution at home.

Puritans: Protestants who advocated strict morals.

Patriots: Ones who love and support their country.

Bric-á-brac: Collection of small items, usually of sentimental value.

Louis Philippe: The king of France from 1830 to 1848.

Doctrinaires: People who focus on abstract theories.

Ornaments: People with appealing social skills.

Capital: Accumulated wealth or goods devoted to the production of other goods.

Outlay: Payment.

Bankrupted: Reduced to financial ruin.

Decencies of life: Conditions or services considered essential for a proper standard of living.

Offhand: Without preparation.

*together with a steady remodeling of social and political habits, ideas,
and institutions to fit the new scale and suit the new conditions. The
generation between 1865 and 1895 was already **mortgaged** to the
railways, and no one knew it better than the generation itself.*

What happened next . . .

Adams had *The Education of Henry Adams* privately printed
in 1907 and distributed it to friends. He even allowed some of
the people he had criticized within its pages to read the book
and make any corrections they felt were necessary. Among
these readers were U.S. president Theodore Roosevelt (1858–
1919; served 1901–9) and politician Henry Cabot Lodge
(1850–1924). Adams was never satisfied with his book and it
was not published until after his death in 1918. In 1919 *The
Education of Henry Adams* was awarded the Pulitzer Prize for
autobiography.

The building of U.S. railroads continued at a fast pace. The
length of the U.S. rail network grew from 35,000 miles in 1865
to 93,000 miles in 1880. By 1890 there were more than 164,000
miles of railroad lines in use. The railroads were essential to
American industry. Busy towns and cities arose along the railways and were dependent on them for shipments of food and
goods. Building railroads also created huge new industries in
steel, iron, and coal used in construction.

Did you know . . .

- Henry Adams's older brother, Charles Francis Adams Jr.
  (1835–1915), was also a historian and journalist. He
  began writing about the railroads after the Civil War, focus-
  ing in particular on the battle for the Erie between Jay
  Gould and Cornelius Vanderbilt. At that time Henry
  Adams was beginning his career and chose to write about
  Jay Gould and his gold conspiracy. Three long essays by the
  brothers appeared in a collection called *A Chapter of Erie*
  (1869). The articles were considered early examples of
  muckraking—a type of journalism that exposed dishonesty
  and injustices in business and government.

Consider the following . . .

- In the excerpt Henry Adams described coming home to a country that had changed so much he could barely recognize it. What are some of the changes he mentioned in this excerpt?

- Adams described himself as the "American of Americans, with Heaven knew how many Puritans and Patriots behind him." How do you think he felt about coming from such a famous and socially powerful family? Why did he compare himself and his family to the Indians and buffalo?

For More Information

Books

Adams, Henry. *The Education of Henry Adams: An Autobiography.* New York: Time Inc., 1964.

Rowe, John Carlos, ed. *New Essays on "The Education of Henry Adams."* Cambridge, U.K.: Cambridge University Press, 1996.

Smith, Page. *The Rise of Industrial America: A People's History of the Post-Reconstruction Era.* Vol. VI. New York: McGraw-Hill, 1984.

Web Sites

Adams, Charles Francis. "A Chapter of Erie." *Chapters of Erie and Other Essays.* Boston, MA: James R. Osgood and Co., late Ticknor & Fields, and Fields, Osgood, & Co., 1871. http://yamaguchy.netfirms.com/adams/erie_01.html (accessed on July 6, 2005).

"Henry Adams: Teacher Resource: The Education of Henry Adams." *C-Span's New History Series: American Writers.* http://www.americanwriters.org/classroom/resources/tr_adams.asp (accessed on July 6, 2005).

"Ulysses S. Grant. People and Events: Henry Adams, 1838–1918." *American Experience: PBS.* http://www.pbs.org/wgbh/amex/grant/peopleevents/p_adams.html (accessed on July 6, 2005).

Memorial of the Chinese Six Companies

"Memorial of the Chinese Six Companies to U.S. Grant, President of the United States"

Written in 1876
Reprinted in *The Power of Words: Documents in American History,*
vol. II: 35–37, 1996

In the mid-nineteenth century, industrialization began to spread across the United States at a rapid rate, and factories began searching for large quantities of new workers to help meet the production demands. In the 1840s businesses started recruiting workers from European countries, and by the end of the decade immigrants began to form a significant part of the industrial workforce. Life in the United States was difficult for these newcomers, and they were often the victims of discrimination by their employers. They were paid the lowest wages and were forced to work in jobs that Americans did not want. After a few generations in the country, however, most immigrants from Europe found acceptance in American society. This was not the situation with the Chinese, who began arriving in small numbers on the West Coast around the same time as Europeans were arriving on the East Coast. The Chinese workers were essential in the building of railroads and roads and they supplied the necessary workforces for many U.S. industries. Despite this, some of the worst anti-immigrant discrimination was directed at them, and this situation did not improve for many decades.

"At the present time an intense excitement and bitter hostility against the Chinese in this land, and against further Chinese emigration, has been created in the minds of the people...."

Some Chinese immigrants were attacked as they arrived in San Francisco.

(Bancroft Library. University of California.)

Before the 1860s there were about forty-one thousand Chinese people in the United States, most of whom had moved to California during the gold rush of 1848 and remained in the state. (After gold was discovered in California in 1848 there was a rapid migration to the state. California's population grew from about 14,000 in 1848 to almost 100,000 by 1850.) Discrimination against the Chinese began shortly after their arrival based mainly on prejudices and fears that the Chinese might take work away from European immigrants. In 1852 the California legislature passed the Foreign Miner's Tax, a tax on the earnings of Chinese and Mexican prospectors, making it impossible for them to compete financially with the white miners. The state also imposed an alien poll tax—a tax of a fixed amount, in this case $2.50 per month—on each Chinese adult working in the country. Additionally, the Chinese were often allowed to seek gold only in mines that had already been abandoned by white prospectors. Because of the actions taken against them by the state government, most Chinese miners during the gold rush were forced to work as cooks and launderers.

Anti-Asian sentiment led the state of California to rule in 1854 that no person of Chinese descent could testify in court. Chinese immigrants were robbed, beaten, and even killed and their attackers were not punished because neither the victims nor any other Chinese witnesses could give evidence against them. After the gold rush, most Chinese workers headed for the Chinatowns of California cities, where they hoped they would be safer surrounded by their fellow countrymen.

In 1862 a new employment opportunity arose when the federal government helped finance the construction of a transcontinental railroad (one that spanned the North American continent from the Atlantic Ocean to the Pacific Ocean). Two railroad companies were chosen for the job. The Union Pacific was to lay tracks westward from Omaha, Nebraska, and the Central Pacific was to begin laying tracks in Sacramento, California, and work eastward. At some point in between, the two companies, and their sets of tracks, would meet. A problem occurred, however, when after two years the Central Pacific had only laid fifty miles of tracks in northern California, mainly because it could not find or keep laborers. The work that lay ahead, such as cutting tracks through the steep Sierra Nevada mountain range in northern California, was dangerous and difficult, and many refused the job or were not skilled enough to do it. Finally, the company decided to try using Chinese laborers. Although some managers were unsure about the idea, once they had seen the Chinese immigrants at work Central Pacific quickly hired 12,500 Chinese employees. Chinese laborers leveled ground, laid track, and blasted the tunnels through which the railroad would run. Chinese construction crews became known for their reliable and cheap labor, their lack of complaints, and repeatedly risking their lives to get the job done. By 1867 the Chinese represented 90 percent of the Central Pacific Railroad workforce. In just two years' time, the Chinese workers laid track through canyons and over land that many had thought was impassable.

On July 28, 1868, the United States and China signed the Burlingame Treaty. The treaty called for the free emigration (the process of leaving one's country to live elsewhere) of the citizens of both countries. It also acknowledged rights of freedom of worship and gave the Chinese "all privileges of the public educational institutions under the control of the government of the United States." The United States entered the treaty because Chinese laborers were necessary to the building of the transcontinental railroad and it wished to encourage more workers to move to the country to help finish the job. Less than a year after the Burlingame Treaty's signing, on May 10, 1869, at Promontory Point, Utah, workers of the Central Pacific and Union Pacific railroads met and the nation's first transcontinental railroad was completed. After this success, the nation's debt to the Chinese workers and the promises of the Burlingame Treaty were quickly forgotten.

After the railroad was finished, Chinese workers took up factory, handicraft, and retail work in cities such as San Francisco. In 1870 the majority of all Chinese immigrants in the United States still lived in California. Ninety-five percent of those who arrived in the state in the late nineteenth century were young males. So few of the immigrants were females because the Chinese believed that respectable women did not leave their parents' or in-laws' homes. The Chinatowns established bachelor societies in which men lived, socialized, and worked. Most were waiting either to go back to China or to raise enough money to bring their families to the United States.

Chinese immigrants tended to rely on family, or clan, associations for community support. When the young men of China arrived in the United States, they immediately began to form associations in the new country by grouping themselves by their family names. For example, there was a Yee association for all Yees, a Moy association for all Moys, and so forth. Members gave these associations the loyalty one would give to extended family. Fellow members were seen as cousins, whether or not there was any blood relation. In San Francisco each of the family associations belonged to one of six larger district associations. At the head of all six associations was the Chinese Consolidated Benevolent Association, also known as the Chinese Six Companies.

San Francisco was the center of Chinese society. The city's district associations provided aid and advice to the immigrants. Typically, upon arrival in San Francisco newcomers were met by members of their district, people from their region in China who spoke the same dialect (a variety of a language spoken in a particular region). They were housed at district headquarters and worked where their kinsmen had employment contracts or connections. The district associations provided loans and protection to the recent arrivals and helped them with legal problems. The associations also loaned the money to travel to the United States to potential immigrants in China. When an immigrant arrived in the United States, he had to pay the association back from his first earnings, and so the Six Companies often put the new arrivals to work in labor gangs. The Six Companies thus gained great power over many Chinese immigrants, who were not allowed to look for their own jobs and had to follow the companies' rules and regulations.

To white Californians, the Chinese immigrants appeared to be little more than slaves who often arrived already in debt to the merchants of the Six Companies. The non-Asian settlers were also suspicious of them because they were members of a racial minority and they practiced religions unfamiliar to Europeans. The Chinese also looked different from other immigrants. All Chinese males at that time were required by Chinese law and tradition to wear their hair in a long braid called a queue. For many young Chinese men, the queue was important because without it they could never go home to be reunited with their families. Their clothes, too, differed greatly from those of Westerners, and they ate very different foods, including rice, fish, and vegetables. Because many of the Chinese workers planned to return home eventually to their families, they did not try to adopt American ways.

In 1873 the U.S. economy experienced a decline. Businesses and banks failed and jobs became hard to find. The anti-Asian movement in California grew in response to these troubles. Non-Asian workers began to speak out against what they referred to as the Yellow Peril, claiming that the Chinese workers were taking jobs away from Americans. Many newspapers, eager to make money from the sensational stories, joined in the out-cry against the Asians who, they declared, had invaded the nation. Middle-class Californians, disturbed by tales of drug abuse and prostitution in the Chinese community, supported the protesters. Many Californians refused to buy or use Chinese goods and services. Gangs stormed Chinatowns, destroying homes and property and physically attacking the residents. Employers were pressured to fire their Chinese workers, and, now that they no longer needed armies of unskilled laborers, even the railroads did not defend the immigrants.

Things to remember while reading "Memorial of the Chinese Six Companies to U.S. Grant, President of the United States":

- The Chinese Consolidated Benevolent Association, more commonly known as the Chinese Six Companies, was established in San Francisco during the 1850s and quickly became the most powerful organization among the Chinese in the United States. It was formed when the Ning Yuen, Hop Wo, Kong Chow, Yeung Wo, Sam Yup, and Yan Wo district associations created a mutual board of directors to represent the Chinese people of San Francisco and elsewhere in the nation.

- The Chinese Six board of directors consisted of wealthy merchants. They attempted to avoid discrimination by hiring a non-Asian attorney to serve as the group's spokes-person outside of Chinatown. The Chinese Six Companies addressed local, state, and federal governments regarding issues of immigration and harassment.

- Chinese immigrants had good reason to feel unsafe in their new country. In one of many instances of anti-Asian vio-lence, a riot broke out in Los Angeles in 1871. A mob of about five hundred people attacked the city's Chinatown, burning houses and dragging Chinese people from their homes.

Some were beaten; others were hanged or burned to death. Nineteen Chinese men died in the riot and countless others were injured.

- In the 1870s Irish immigrant and labor leader Denis Kearney (1847–1907) became the head of the Workingman's Party. Kearney, who campaigned under the slogan "The Chinese Must Go!" was a powerful force in the anti-Asian movement. He and his followers were responsible for the hanging of Chinese people and the burning and bombing of their businesses and homes. In the most well-known instance, the San Francisco Riot of 1876, Kearney encouraged a mob of several hundred unemployed workers to roam the streets in search of Chinese workers to attack. People were hurt and terrorized, and homes and businesses were destroyed. The governor of California finally called out the National Guard and several warships to stop the rioting.

Denis Kearney, head of the Workingman's Party, opposed Chinese immigration. *(Library of Congress/Corbis. Reproduced by permission.)*

- In 1876 the anti-Chinese movement succeeded in forcing a congressional investigation into Chinese immigration. The investigation was conducted in San Francisco and thousands of people were interviewed. Some San Franciscans told the committee that Chinese workers had made a valuable contribution to the transcontinental railroad and to agriculture. But several public officials attacked the Chinese immigrants for practicing unfamiliar religions, eating strange foods, and not having their wives in the country with them, all of which they considered uncivilized behavior. Angry labor leaders said that the Chinese accepted lower wages, which put white men out of work. The memorial to U.S. president Ulysses S. Grant (1822–1885; served 1869–77) was a response to these charges prepared by the Chinese Six Companies, which represented the Chinese people.

- At the time the memorial was written, no immigrants had ever been blocked from entering the United States.

"Memorial of the Chinese Six Companies to U.S. Grant, President of the United States"

To His Excellency U.S. Grant, President of the United States of America

*Sir: In the absence of any **Consular representative**, we, the undersigned, in the name and in behalf of the Chinese people now in America, would most respectfully present for your consideration the following statements regarding the subject of Chinese emigration to this country:*

*We understand that it has always been the settled policy of your honorable Government to welcome emigration to your shores from all countries, without **let or hindrance**. The Chinese are not the only people who have crossed the ocean to seek a residence in this land. . . .*

*American steamers, **subsidized** by your honorable Government, have visited the ports of China, and invited our people to come to this country to find employment and improve their condition. Our people have been coming to this country for the last twenty-five years, but up to the present time there are only 150,000 Chinese in all these United States, 60,000 of whom are in California, and 30,000 in the city of San Francisco.*

*Our people in this country, for the most part, have been peacable, law-abiding, and industrious. They performed the largest part of the unskilled labor in the construction of the Central Pacific Railroad, and also of all other railroads on this coast. They have found useful and **remunerative** employment in all the manufacturing establishments of this coast, in agricultural pursuits, and in family service. While benefiting themselves with the honest reward of their daily toil, they have given satisfaction to their employers and have left all the results of their industry to enrich the State. They have not **displaced** white laborers from these positions, but have simply multiplied the industrial enterprises of the country.*

Consular representative: Person appointed by the government of one nation to represent that country in another nation.

Let or hindrance: Obstacles.

Subsidized: Paid for.

Remunerative: Profitable.

Displaced: Taken the place of.

The Chinese have neither attempted nor desired to interfere with the established order of things in this country, either of politics or religion. They have opened no whiskey saloons for the purpose of dealing out poison and **degrading** their fellow-men. They have promptly paid their **duties**, their taxes, their rents, and their debts. . . .

At the present time an intense excitement and bitter hostility against the Chinese in this land, and against further Chinese emigration, has been created in the minds of the people, led on by His Honor the Mayor of San Francisco and his associates in office, and approved by His Excellency the Governor, and other great men of the State. These great men gathered some 20,000 of the people of this city together on the evening of April 5, and adopted an address and resolutions against Chinese emigration. . . .

It is charged against us that not one **virtuous** Chinawoman has been brought to this country, and that here we have no wives nor children. The fact is, that already a few hundred Chinese families have been brought here. These are all **chaste**, pure, keepers-at-home, not known on the public street. There are also among us a few hundred, perhaps a thousand, Chinese children born in America. The reason why so few of our families are brought to this country is because it is contrary to the custom and against the **inclination** of virtuous Chinese women to go so far from home, and because the frequent outbursts of popular indignation against our people have not encouraged us to bring our families with us against their will. . . .

It is charged against us that we have purchased no real estate. The general tone of public sentiment has not been such as to encourage us to invest in real estate, and yet our people have purchased and now own over $800,000 worth of real estate in San Francisco alone.

It is charged against us that we eat rice, fish, and vegetables. It is true that our diet is slightly different from the people of this honorable country; our tastes in these matters are not exactly alike, and cannot be forced. But is that a sin on our part of sufficient **gravity** to be brought before the President and Congress of the United States?

It is charged that the Chinese are no benefit to this country. Are the railroads built by Chinese labor no benefit to the country? Are the manufacturing establishments, largely worked by Chinese, no benefit to this country? Do not the results of the daily toil of a hundred thousand men increase the riches of this country? Is it no benefit to this country that the Chinese annually pay over $2,000,000 duties at the Custom

Degrading: Dragging down in moral or intellectual character.

Duties: Taxes, usually on imports.

Virtuous: Morally excellent.

Chaste: Innocent.

Inclination: Natural character or attitude.

Gravity: Seriousness.

Mercantile: Trade.

house of San Francisco? Is not the $200,000 annual poll-tax paid by the Chinese any benefit? And are not the hundreds of thousands of dollars [in] taxes on personal property, and the foreign miners' tax, annually paid to the revenues of this country, any benefit?...

It is charged that all Chinese laboring men are slaves. This is not true in a single instance. Chinamen labor for bread. They pursue all kinds of industries for a livelihood. Is it so then that every man laboring for his livelihood is a slave? If these men are slaves, then all men laboring for wages are slaves.

*It is charged that the Chinese commerce brings no benefit to American bankers and importers. But the fact is that an immense trade is carried on between China and the United States by American merchants, and all the carrying business of both countries, whether by steamers, sailing vessels or railroads, is done by Americans. No China ships are engaged in the carrying traffic between the two countries. Is it a sin to be charged against us that the Chinese merchants are able to conduct their **mercantile** business on their own capital? And is not the exchange of millions of dollars annually by the Chinese with the banks of this city any benefit to the banks?*

We respectfully ask a careful consideration of all the foregoing statements. The Chinese are not the only people, nor do they bring the only evils that now afflict this country.

What happened next ...

Anti-Chinese violence and discrimination continued. Mobs attacked Chinese immigrants in Colorado, Washington, Alaska, Oregon, and Wyoming, killing and injuring many.

Americans on the East Coast viewed the controversy as a West Coast problem since few Chinese had settled in the East. In 1870, however, when seventy-five Chinese workers were hired at a shoe factory in North Adams, Massachusetts, labor groups throughout the East predicted the arrival of large numbers of Chinese workers and hostilities increased.

When California adopted its state constitution in 1879, one-third of the document's authors were members of Kearney's

Workingman's Party. Not surprisingly, the constitution was strongly anti-Chinese. According to the law, Chinese workers could not be hired in any public jobs, and cities and towns had the power to relocate Chinese people outside the town limits. The constitution declared the Chinese "to be dangerous to the well-being of the state," calling on the legislature to "discourage their immigration by all means within its power."

In the mid-nineteenth century, politicians from the West introduced many acts to Congress in an effort to keep Chinese immigrants from entering the country. These acts had been repeatedly vetoed (rejected) by the president, but in 1882 the Westerners and others who feared Chinese immigration succeeded in getting the Chinese Exclusion Act passed. The act, which banned Chinese laborers from entering the country, was the first major restriction on immigration to the United States, and it was the first time anyone had been denied entry to the country because of race.

The anti-Chinese riot of 1880, in Denver, Colorado.
(© Bettmann/Corbis.)

The Exclusion Act was extended for ten more years after its initial ten-year term, and in 1904 it was extended indefinitely. Since under the act it was not possible for Chinese men to bring their families to the United States or to go back to China to marry, the population of Chinese in the country dropped significantly.

By the late 1930s Japan had become a strong military power and sought to expand its empire by invading China in 1937. When the United States entered World War II (1939–45; a war in which Great Britain, France, the United States, and their allies defeated Germany, Italy, and Japan), China and the United States became allies in their fight against the Japanese. Chinese immigrants joined the U.S. military and fought alongside American soldiers. In 1943, in an effort to encourage further friendly relations between the two countries, the Chinese

Exclusion Act was finally repealed. Immigration from China was still limited, but the Chinese were no longer subjected to the kinds of discrimination as they had been in the past.

Did you know . . .

- The Naturalization Act of 1790 stated that only "free white persons" could become citizens. This was widened to include African Americans under the Fourteenth Amendment in 1870, but Asians were still excluded. Thus, unlike most other immigrants in the nineteenth century, the Chinese were not eligible for U.S. citizenship. This law remained in place until 1952.

- Between 1820 and 1880, three million Irish and three million German immigrants entered the United States. In 1900 there were only an estimated ninety thousand people of Chinese descent in the country.

Consider the following . . .

- Why do you think labor organizations, charitable groups, and federal or state laws failed to help the Chinese immigrants in the nineteenth century?

- What tone does the memorial to the president set? What do you think the Chinese Six Companies intended this document to accomplish?

For More Information

Books

Chan, Sucheng. *Asian Americans: An Interpretive History.* Boston, MA: Twayne Publishers, 1991.

The Chinese Six Companies. "Memorial of the Chinese Six Companies to U.S. Grant, President of the United States." In *The Power of Words: Documents in American History.* Edited by T. H. Breen. New York: HarperCollins College Publishers, 1996.

McCunn, Ruthanne Lum. *Chinese American Portraits: Personal Histories, 1828–1988.* San Francisco: Chronicle Books, 1988.

Saxton, Alexander. *The Indispensable Enemy: Labor and the Anti-Chinese Movement in California.* Berkeley: University of California Press, 1971.

Takaki, Ronald. *Strangers from a Different Shore.* New York: Penguin Books, 1991.

Web Sites

"The Chinese Experience: Eyewitness Accounts." *A Bill Moyers Special: Becoming American, the Chinese Experience: PBS.* http://www.pbs.org/becomingamerican/ce_witness.html (accessed on July 6, 2005).

"A History of Chinese Americans in California." *National Park Service.* http://www.cr.nps.gov/history/online_books/5views/5views3.htm (accessed on July 6, 2005).

The Concentration of Wealth

Excerpt from "The Concentration of Wealth: Its Economic Justification"

By William Graham Sumner
Written in the 1880s
Reprinted in *Social Darwinism: Selected Essays of William Graham Sumner,* **1963**

"The millionaires are a product of natural selection, acting on the whole body of men to pick out those who can meet the requirement of certain work to be done."

William Graham Sumner (1840–1910) was one of the leading social philosophers during the period of the Industrial Revolution known as the Gilded Age, which began in the early 1860s and extended to the turn of the century. The Gilded Age was marked by a rapid growth of industrialism and big business throughout the United States. Many Americans objected to the political and financial power the industrialists and big corporations gained during these years and were concerned that some businessmen were becoming very wealthy while a large number of workers were barely able to live on their wages. By the 1880s citizens were demanding the government regulate big business in order to lessen the influence of the giant corporations and their leaders. Sumner spoke with passion and intelligence against this call for reform. He strongly opposed government intervention in the economy and workplace. He believed that the possible effects of such interference were not understood by those requesting it and could damage the progress of the nation through a lack of understanding of possible consequences.

William Graham Sumner disapproved of the decadence of lavish parties such as this. *(© Bettmann/Corbis.)*

Sumner was born into a modest home in Paterson, New Jersey, to parents who had emigrated from England. His father, an uneducated machinist, loved reading and believed deeply in the value of education. Sumner went to public schools in Hartford, Connecticut, and in 1859 he entered Yale University. After graduation he went to Germany and England to study for the Episcopal priesthood, and in 1870 he became rector of a church in New Jersey. However, he soon found that his interests lay in social and economic matters rather than religion. Sumner left the ministry in 1872 when Yale invited him to accept a newly created position as the head of political and social science at the university. During his employment at Yale he helped develop the new field of sociology (the scientific study of human behavior), which had been founded several decades earlier in Europe. Sumner helped set the framework for the study of sociology in the United States, replacing philosophical contemplation of human behavior with scientific analysis. He became known as one of the college's most effective educators.

Sumner was greatly influenced by the writings of English philosopher Herbert Spencer. *(© Michael Nicholson/Corbis.)*

While he was a student Sumner read a series of articles by English philosopher Herbert Spencer (1820–1903) that were later collected in the book *The Study of Sociology* (1873). Spencer first used the phrase "the survival of the fittest" and argued that the wealthy and powerful took their place at the top of society because they were the best adapted to their environment, while those who did not compete well became poor and eventually died out. He developed his theory based in part on the work of biologist Charles Darwin (1809–1882) and the theory of evolution, which stated that all plant and animal species changed over time because of biological differences passed from one generation to the next. Spencer's social Darwinism, which promoted the idea that people succeeded or failed due to certain natural laws (principles that originated only in nature and governed human interactions) was considered by many to promote a laissez-faire system, or one in which the government did not interfere with commerce and industry beyond the minimum necessary. Sumner was particularly drawn to Spencer's view that natural laws dictated human survival, and the philosopher's ideas about society remained a strong influence on Sumner over the years.

Sumner considered himself to be a scientist of society. He took some of the most well-loved American concepts—democracy, equality, rights, duty, liberty—and examined them in their purest forms, without the emotions people usually attached to them. In his writings he tried to base his search for truths about the world on factual evidence rather than on feelings, reasoning, or imagination. Sumner believed social progress could only be determined in this way, and that investigation using only ideas and theories rather than hard evidence lacked practical use. In his early years as a professor at Yale, he was fascinated by the social and economic aspects of the industrializing nation. He measured the success of the new society in material terms, particularly in how effectively its technology and industry had transformed the nation's resources to make human life better. During the 1880s, when Sumner wrote his article "The Concentration of Wealth," industrialization had brought about an overall rise in the national earnings and placed more products on the market. The average standard of living had been raised, which Sumner believed proved his theories to be correct.

Reformers, socialists, and labor leaders, however, disagreed with Sumner's positive view of society and spoke out against the majority of the nation's wealth being held by just a few people. In 1860, 2 percent of the U.S. population owned one-third of the nation's riches. This state of economic distribution was called concentration of wealth, which meant that most of the nation's capital (wealth or goods devoted to the production of other goods) belonged to a very small portion of its people. In contrast, by 1890 eleven million of the country's twelve million families earned less than $1200 per year. For this eleven million, the average annual income was $380, well below the poverty line. Industrial workers lived in overcrowded cities, received low wages, and worked long hours in dangerous and unhealthy conditions. Young children worked in factories. Many of the nation's laborers were victims of racial and gender discrimination. A large number of people believed that the democratic ideal pictured by the men who had written the U.S. Constitution had been destroyed by the rise of huge corporations. While a small group of Americans became rich and passed their money from generation to generation, others were born into poverty they could not rise out of. The reformers believed this went against the American notion that all men were created equal.

In the late nineteenth century, corporate monopolies were on the rise. A monopoly is the exclusive possession or right to produce a particular good or service, or the ownership of all companies producing a certain product. When corporations found that competition among them was driving prices down and lowering their profits, the largest companies began to work together, dividing up territories to limit competitors within an area. Without competition, the companies could set higher prices for their goods. The combined businesses became large and powerful creations that could remove unwanted competition. The first trusts were also being organized in this period. A trust was formed when several companies in the same industry joined their properties and stocks together under a single board of trustees who then ran all the companies. As the trusts got bigger and stronger, they were able to buy out more and more of their competitors, and it became nearly impossible for new companies to get started. Capital became concentrated in just a few huge corporations, particularly transportation and heavy industry, which includes industries such as steel and oil refining that convert large volumes of raw materials into products of higher value, usually requiring a very large investment in large machinery.

William Graham Sumner. *(Photo by Hulton Archive/Getty Images.)*

The monopolies produced millions of dollars for a few industrialists, such as financier J. P. Morgan (1837–1913), steel businessman Andrew Carnegie (1835–1919), and oil refiner John D. Rockefeller (1839–1937), who became a billionaire by the early twentieth century. J. P. Morgan's United States Steel Corporation was the nation's first billion-dollar enterprise. Some Americans saw these industrialists as robber barons, ruthless men who cared only about their own fortunes, but others, including Sumner, considered them captains of industry and credited the progress and financial health of the country to their daring, if often dishonest, business deals. But it is worthy to note that Sumner did not like or trust the robber barons of his day. He was a very proper man who, on a personal level, found their corruption contemptible. But he did not believe it was the place of the government to interfere with their work, and he feared that the government was more likely to become corrupted by business than to eliminate the corruption.

Things to remember while reading the excerpt from "The Concentration of Wealth: Its Economic Justification":

- Sumner was highly influenced by Darwin's theory of evolution, especially his thoughts on natural selection. Darwin concluded that some individuals in a species were better equipped to find food, survive disease, and escape predators than others. He reasoned that these individuals were more likely to survive, mate, and produce offspring, while those that were not as well adapted to their environment were less likely to prosper. As a result, each generation of a population would consist of individuals that were better and better adapted to their environment, and the characteristics of the population would change to reflect this. Darwin believed these changes took place at a biological level, however, and had nothing to do with human social organization.

- In "The Concentration of Wealth," Sumner argues against the belief system of the Enlightenment, a philosophical movement that arose in seventeenth- and eighteenth-century Europe. The Enlightenment, also called the Age of Reason, celebrated the rational powers people used to help them understand the universe. Enlightenment philosophers believed that through self-examination and the use of reason, humans could achieve their highest goals: knowledge, freedom, and happiness. Sumner did not believe these goals were necessarily something that could, or should, be pursued, and he maintained that no human being who worked for a living was truly free.

- Toward the end of the excerpt Sumner defends the industrialists by comparing the telegraph system, which was created before the rise of big business, and the telephone system, which was invented after corporate practices were in use. Samuel F. B. Morse (1791–1872) first demonstrated his telegraph machine in 1837, but it was not until 1843 that he succeeded in convincing Congress to pay for a test line to be installed between Baltimore, Maryland, and Washington, D.C. Although the experimental line worked, communication remained limited to stations linked by a cable, and few people had the money or technical

Befooled: Deceived.

Deductions: Conclusions reached through reasoning.

Dogmas: Ideas that are widely held to be true but are not proven by facts or evidence.

Analogies: Comparisons based on things resembling each other.

Republican: Characteristic of a state in which the supreme power lies in the body of citizens who vote for the officers and representatives of their government.

Democratic: Characteristic of a state in which the majority rules and social equality is in some way enforced. A democracy is governed by its people, usually through a system of representation involving regular free elections.

Joint-stock companies: Groups that form business organizations and sell shares of the organizations to people who then claim part of the profits as well as the business risks.

Oligarchies: Ruled by a small, powerful group.

Monarchies: Ruled by a single person who rules with absolute authority.

Vigor: Intensity.

knowledge to attempt to build lines to cross the entire country. By the 1850s a small number of promoters and stockholders began to organize local companies to install cables. A line was completed in California, and gradually investors ran cables to other locations. Despite the country's great need for a communications system, progress remained slow, and it was not until 1866 that the first successful transatlantic telegraph connection was established between Europe and the United States.

- When Alexander Graham Bell (1847–1922) invented the telephone, however, U.S. businessmen moved quickly. Bell patented his design in 1876, and the Bell Telephone Company was formed within a year. By 1880 there was already one telephone for every one thousand people in the United States. Theodore N. Vail (1845–1920), Bell's operations director, built the American Telephone and Telegraph Company (AT&T) to provide long-distance calling to Bell customers. The first long-distance lines from New York City to Albany, New York, and Boston, Massachusetts, were built in 1887, and new lines began to open steadily thereafter, offering instant communications nationwide and eventually worldwide. By 1899 the net worth of AT&T was approximately $120 million, and the company had essentially monopolized U.S. long-distance service.

Excerpt from "The Concentration of Wealth: Its Economic Justification"

*Every age is **befooled** by the notions which are in fashion in it. Our age is befooled by "democracy"; we hear arguments about the industrial organization which are **deductions** from democratic **dogmas** or which appeal to prejudice by using **analogies** drawn from democracy to affect sentiment about industrial relations. Industry may be **republican**; it never can be **democratic**, so long as men differ in productive power and in industrial virtue. In our time **joint-stock companies**, which are in form republican, are drifting over into **oligarchies** or **monarchies** because one or a few get greater efficiency of control and greater **vigor** of administration. They direct the enterprise in a way which* produces more, or more economically. This is the purpose for which the organization exists and success in it outweighs everything else. We see the competent men refuse to join in the enterprise, unless they can control it, and we see the stockholders willingly put their property into the hands of those who are, as they think, competent to manage it successfully. The strongest and most effective organizations for industrial purposes which are formed nowadays are those of a few great **capitalists**, who have great personal confidence in each other and who can bring together adequate means for whatever they desire to do. Some such **nucleus** of individuals controls all the great joint-stock companies.

It is obvious that the "concentration of wealth" can never be anything but a **relative** term. Between 1820 and 1830 Stephen Girard [1750–1831; a wealthy banker, merchant, and philanthropist] was a **proverb** for great wealth; to-day a man equally rich would not be noticed in New York for his wealth. In 1848 John Jacob Astor [1763–1848; a fur trader whose real estate investments made him the first known millionaire in the United States] stood alone in point of wealth; to-day a great number **surpass** him. A fortune of $300,000 was then regarded as **constituting** wealth; it was taken as a minimum above which men were "rich." It is certain that before long some man will have a billion. It is impossible to criticize such a **moving notion.** The concentration of capital is also necessarily relative to the task to be performed; we wondered lately to see a corporation formed which had a capital of a billion. No one will wonder at such a corporation twenty-five years **hence.**

There seems to be a great readiness in the public mind to take alarm at these **phenomena** of growth—there might rather seem to be reason for public congratulation. We want to be provided with things abundantly and cheaply; that means that we want increased economic power. . . .

In fact, there is true **correlation** between (a) the great productiveness of modern industry and the **consequent** rapid accumulation of capital from one period of production to another and (b) the larger and larger **aggregations** of capital which are required by modern industry from one period of production to another. We see that the movement [toward increasing industrialization] is constantly accelerated, that its **scope** is all the time widening, and that the masses of material with which it deals are greater and greater. The dominant cause of all this is the application of steam and electricity to transportation, and the communications of intelligence—things which we boast about as great triumphs of the nineteenth century. They have made it possible to extend efficient control, from a given central point,

Capitalists: People who put their wealth to use in business and industry in order to make more wealth.

Nucleus: Central, controlling group.

Relative: Comparative.

Proverb: Popular truth.

Surpass: Become greater than.

Constituting: Composing.

Moving notion: Changeable value.

Hence: From this time.

Phenomena: Observable events.

Correlation: Similar or parallel meaning.

Consequent: Following as a result of.

Aggregations: Gatherings of all parts of something into a whole.

Scope: Area covered.

over operations which may be carried on at a great number of widely separated points, and to keep up a close, direct, and intimate action and reaction between the central control and the distributed agents. That means that it has become possible for the organization to be extended in its scope and complexity, and at the same time intensified in its activity. Now whenever such a change in the societal organization becomes possible it also becomes inevitable, because there is economy in it. . . . The highest degree of organization which is possible is the one that offers the maximum of profit; in it the economic advantage is greatest. There is therefore a **gravitation** toward this degree of organization. . . .

In the **classical** states with slavery and in the **medieval** states with **serfdom,** the great achievements which realized the utmost that the system was capable of were attained only where wealth was concentrated in productive enterprises. . . . If we could get rid of some of our notions about liberty and equality, and could lay aside eighteenth century philosophy according to which human society is to be brought into a state of blessedness, we should get some insight into the might of the societal organization; what it does for us, and what it makes us do. Every day that passes brings us new phenomena of struggle and effort between parts of the societal organization. What do they all mean? They mean that all the individuals and groups are forced against each other in a ceaseless war of interests, by their selfish and mutual efforts to fulfill their career on earth within the conditions set for them by the state of the arts, the facts of the societal organization, and the current dogmas of world philosophy. As each must win his living, or his fortune, or keep his fortune, under these conditions, it is difficult to see what can be meant in the sphere of industrial or economic effort by a "free man". . . .

It is interesting to compare the **exploitation** of the telephone with that of the telegraph fifty years earlier. The latter was, in its day, a far more wonderful invention, but the time and labor required to **render** it generally available were far greater than what has been required for the telephone, and the fortunes which were won from the former were insignificant in comparison with those which have been won from the latter. Both the public and the promoters acted very differently in the two cases. In these later times promoters seize with **avidity** upon an enterprise which contains promise, and they push it with energy and **ingenuity,** while the public is **receptive** to "improvements"; hence the modern methods offer very great opportunities, and the rewards of those men with **sagacity** and good judgment, are very great. It is well that they are so, because these rewards stimulate to the utmost all the ambitious and able men, and they make it certain that great and useful inventions will not long remain unexploited as they did formerly. . . .

Gravitation: Natural movement.

Classical: Of or relating to the ancient Greeks or Romans.

Medieval: Relating to the Middle Ages (c. 500 CE–c. 1500 CE).

Serfdom: A system in which a person is attached to land owned by a lord and must perform labor for the lord in return for certain rights.

Exploitation: Using something to the greatest possible advantage.

Render: Make.

Avidity: Eagerness.

Ingenuity: Cleverness.

Receptive: Ready or willing to receive favorably.

Sagacity: Wisdom.

What matters it then that some millionaires are idle, or silly, or **vulgar***; that their ideas are sometimes* **futile** *and their plans* **grotesque***, when they turn aside from money-making? How do they differ in this from any other class? The millionaires are a product of natural selection, acting on the whole body of men to pick out those who can meet the requirement of certain work to be done. In this respect they are just like the great statesmen, or scientific men, or military men. It is because they are thus selected that wealth—both their own and that intrusted to them—aggregates under their hands. Let one of them make a mistake and see how quickly the concentration gives way to* **dispersion***. They may fairly be regarded as the naturally selected agents of society for certain work. They get high wages and live in luxury, but the bargain is a good one for society. There is the intensest competition for their place and occupation. This assures us that all who are competent for this function will be employed in it, so that the cost of it will be reduced to the lowest terms; and furthermore that the competitors will study the proper conduct to be observed in their occupation. This will bring discipline and the correction of arrogance and* **masterfulness.**

Vulgar: Lacking good taste.

Futile: Having no useful result.

Grotesque: Outlandish.

Dispersion: The state of being scattered.

Masterfulness: Having an overbearing nature.

What happened next . . .

Sumner's beliefs were based largely on his distrust of government and its interference with the economy. He was not a supporter of big business. As years passed, he observed with great unease the influence of the industrialists and capitalists on the government, and he remained uncertain about the possibility of human progress throughout his life. Late in Sumner's career he began exploring the evolution of social institutions such as religion, marriage, and family. His most famous work, *Folkways* (1907), was about social customs and mores, the informal group habits that emerged and shaped society.

Despite Sumner's assurances that the general public was better off with a market free from government interference, during his life the nation experienced three economic depressions, one in 1873, one in 1884, and the last, which was especially destructive, in 1893. Many labor strikes against large corporations and railroads ended in violence during these years.

Observers such as newspaper editor Henry Demarest Lloyd (1847–1903) disagreed with Sumner's philosophy. Lloyd was an early reformer who fought against the concentration of wealth. He became one of the leading journalists of the late nineteenth century after writing an article criticizing the Standard Oil monopoly for the *Atlantic Monthly* in 1881. With this article he became the first, and one of the best-known, muckrakers, journalists who investigated and exposed the dishonesty and misconduct of corporations and their leaders. His attack on Standard Oil and other monopolies was the focus of his 1894 book *Wealth Against Commonwealth.*

The national protest against big business finally moved the U.S. government to attempt to restrain the monopolies, although few politicians wanted to fight against the powerful corporations. The Sherman Antitrust Act was passed by Congress in 1890 in an attempt to break up corporate trusts that limited competition or restrained trade. The language of the act, though, lacked a clear explanation of what exactly restraint of trade was, which meant the nation's courts had to try to define the term themselves. Federal judges were as reluctant as Congress to challenge big business. In the decade after the act's passage, the federal government prosecuted only eighteen antitrust cases, and court decisions did little to break up monopolies. The demands of the reformers did not lessen, however, and at the beginning of the twentieth century, government began to strongly regulate business. In 1911 the U.S. Justice Department won important victories against two monopolies, breaking up John D. Rockefeller's Standard Oil Company of New Jersey and James B. Duke's American Tobacco Company. These decisions demonstrated a new national intolerance toward monopolistic trade practices.

Did you know . . .

- Sumner's belief in the concentration of wealth in the hands of the few was complicated by the fact that some of the millionaires he defended were not behaving very gracefully at that time. A description from "Andrew Carnegie: The Gilded Age," in *American Experience: PBS,* describes the upper-class New York scene: "Americans who achieved wealth celebrated it as never before. In New York, the opera, the theatre, and lavish parties consumed the ruling class' leisure hours. Sherry's Restaurant hosted formal horseback dinners for the New York Riding Club. Mrs. Stuyvesant Fish once threw a dinner party to honor her dog who arrived sporting a $15,000 diamond collar." Sumner himself was a very moral and economical man who disapproved of such wasteful spending.

- Although Sumner's beliefs were highly varied he was generally considered to be a follower of conservatism, a political philosophy that valued traditions and institutions that were already established and sought to avoid sudden changes.

Consider the following ...

- Was the concentration of wealth during the Gilded Age a positive or negative factor in the development of the American society? Prepare yourself to participate on either side of a debate on this issue. List at least five arguments for the reformers who sought government regulation over the corporations and more equality in the economic system. Then list five or more arguments for the laissez-faire policy and the social Darwinists.

- In the excerpt Sumner questioned the ideas of democracy, liberty, and freedom in the industrial organization, and perhaps in human society in general. Does his questioning of these concepts seem shocking? What do you think he is trying to say about the way Americans tend to use these concepts?

For More Information

Books

Cashman, Sean Dennis. *America in the Gilded Age: From the Death of Lincoln to the Rise of Theodore Roosevelt.* New York and London: New York University Press, 1984.

"The Concentration of Wealth: Its Economic Justification." In *Social Darwinism: Selected Essays of William Graham Sumner.* Englewood Cliffs, NJ: Prentice-Hall, Inc., 1963, pp. 150–57.

Smith, Page. *The Rise of Industrial America: A People's History of the Post-Reconstruction Era.* Vol. VI. New York: McGraw-Hill, 1984.

Web Sites

"Andrew Carnegie: The Gilded Age." *The American Experience: PBS.* http://www.pbs.org/wgbh/amex/carnegie/gildedage.html (accessed on July 6, 2005).

On Liberty, Society, and Politics: The Essential Essays of William Graham Sumner. Edited by Robert C. Bannister. Liberty Fund Press, 1992. http://www.swarthmore.edu/SocSci/rbannis1/AIH19th/WGS1.html (accessed on July 6, 2005).

How the Other Half Lives

Excerpt from How the Other Half Lives: Studies Among the
Tenements of New York
By Jacob A. Riis
Originally published in 1890
Reprinted in 1957 by Hill and Wang

Newspaper reporter and photojournalist Jacob Riis (1849–1914) was one of the earliest social reformers to use his work to document the effects of industrialization on the lower-class citizens of the United States. Riis's articles, books, and photographs helped focus public attention on the unhealthy living and working conditions experienced by many of his fellow New Yorkers, and he was credited for bringing about many governmental reforms in the city.

Riis was born in Ribe, Denmark, and received most of his early schooling from his father, a teacher who also worked for a local weekly paper. As a young man Riis trained to be a carpenter, but at the age of twenty-one he decided to immigrate to New York. He arrived in the city in 1870, a period when jobs were hard to find and competition for them was fierce. For years Riis was forced to take any temporary job he could find, including farm work, brickmaking, and peddling. He even tried mining in Pennsylvania for a short time. Riis was so poor that several times he was forced to stay in the police department lodging houses of the city—filthy, crowded, noisy basement rooms run by the city police for the needy,

"'Crazy old buildings, crowded rear tenements in filthy yards, dark, damp basements, leaking garrets, shops, outhouses, and stables converted into dwellings, though scarcely fit to shelter brutes, are habitations of thousands of our fellow-beings in this wealthy, Christian city.'"

Jacob Riis photographed the poor of New York and wrote about their plight.
(© Bettman/Corbis.)

which lacked toilets, baths, or bedding. Experiencing such poverty during his first years in the United States made a powerful impression on Riis that lasted the rest of his life.

In 1878 Riis found work as a reporter at the *New York Tribune.* He was assigned to the police beat and began to write highly detailed accounts of the city's most violent crimes. At the same time he began to report on the harmful environments in which many New Yorkers lived and worked. His tiny downtown office was surrounded by tenements, rundown, overcrowded apartment buildings that barely meet minimum health standards. As Riis wandered

the poor, mainly immigrant neighborhoods gathering material for his
stories, he became determined to try
to bring about positive change.

At the time Riis began writing, most
wealthy New Yorkers believed the poor
were responsible for their own problems, judging them either too weak or
too immoral to escape from poverty and
slum life. Riis argued that it was not the
people, but the slums themselves, that
were the social problem. He saw that
many of the city's lower-class citizens
were not criminals or drunkards, but
normal people struggling to overcome
the terrible circumstances in which
they lived. He was certain that most
New Yorkers simply failed to understand the troubles of the poor and
decided to use journalism to communi-
cate to his readers what it was like to live
in the city's tenements.

Jacob Riis. *(© Corbis)*

Riis worked tirelessly in his efforts to
report the horrors of the tenement districts, but he quickly found that not
everyone believed his descriptions were factual. Frustrated by
the limits of the written word, he began to use photography to
convey the misery of daily life in the slums. Riis hoped his stories
would have a far greater effect on the public if they were accompanied by pictures. The technology to print his photographs
was not yet available, however, so what appeared with his articles at first were drawings based on his pictures.

In 1888 Riis began to work for the *New York Sun*. In that year
the paper printed an article called "Flashes from the
Slums," which was accompanied by twelve drawings based
on Riis's photographs. The article described what strange
figures Riis and his assistants made in the city streets in the
dead of night, as they quickly approached the tenement dwell-
ers with their odd-looking equipment, snapped the photograph in a blinding flash, and ran away, capturing candid
shots of the real life on the streets without stopping to ask

Jacob Riis photographed this poor family in their tenement apartment.
(© Bettmann/Corbis.)

permission. Riis displayed his photographs in slide shows that he delivered in churches and schools. Many people were so overwhelmed by his shows that they spoke out loud directly to the images of people in the slides.

As Riis continued his work for the *Sun,* he investigated many aspects of the city's slums: sanitary conditions, disease, crime, safety, family life, the fate of women and children, and even the treatment of the bodies of those who died from hunger or cold. In 1890 Riis published his first book, *How the Other Half Lives: Studies Among the Tenements of New York,* sections of which had already appeared in *Scribner's* magazine. The book contained seventeen of his photographs, but the reproduction quality was poor due to the technological limitations of the time. Riis's book was widely read and had an intense effect on New Yorkers, moving many to pity and a few to take action to help.

Things to remember while reading the excerpt from *How the Other Half Lives: Studies Among the Tenements of New York*:

- In the late eighteenth century, 95 percent of the U.S. population lived in rural areas. There were only five cities with more than ten thousand people and no city as large as fifty thousand. With industrialization, however, came urbanization. By 1870 almost 170 cities had populations over 10,000 and 15 cities had more than 100,000 people.

- In 1890, the year Riis's book was published, New York City had a population of 1.5 million and was the nation's largest city and port. The city continued to grow, and in 1900, only ten years later, its population had nearly doubled at 3.4 million. Most of the huge increase was due to the large number of immigrants arriving from Europe.

- From the 1820s to the 1880s, most immigrants that came to the United States were from England, Scotland, Scandinavia, Germany, and Ireland. Poor economic and political conditions in Germany and Ireland during those years caused about three million people from each country to move to America in search of better lives. The Great Migration of 1880 to 1920 that followed brought twenty-seven million immigrants to the country, mainly from the eastern European nations of Russia, Poland, Italy, Greece, and Austria-Hungary.

- At the turn of the twentieth century, the highest immigrant populations in the nation resided in four of its largest cities: New York; Boston, Massachusetts; Pittsburgh, Pennsylvania; and Chicago, Illinois. Some nationalities were more likely than others to settle in the urban areas. It was estimated that five out of every six Irish and Russian travelers and three out of four Italian and Hungarian immigrants chose to live in cities.

- The nation's cities were not prepared for the large inflow of people, most of whom were poor, unskilled, and did not speak English. Resourceful city-dwellers began to convert older houses into tenement buildings to rent to the newcomers at high prices. Because rental space was so limited and the demand was so great, landlords and real estate developers cut the buildings up into tiny, dark, stuffy living areas. Closets became bedrooms for multiple people. Small houses built for one family often became the residence for ten or more families, all of which were paying high rents.

- By the early 1900s, 1.2 million people were crowded into thirty-seven thousand overcrowded tenement buildings in New York. The tenements did not provide adequate water, air, or sewage or garbage removal systems. Many people who lived in the slums became victims of crime or disease.

- Riis quotes heavily throughout his book from the many reports he had researched before writing it.

Excerpt from How the Other Half Lives: Studies Among the Tenements of New York

Chapter 1: Genesis of the Tenement

*The first tenement New York knew bore the **mark of Cain** from its birth, though a generation passed before the writing was **deciphered**. It was the "**rear house**," infamous ever after in our city's history. There had been tenant-houses before, but they were not built for the purpose. Nothing would probably have shocked their original owners more than the idea of their harboring a **promiscuous** crowd; for they were the **decorous** homes of the old **Knickerbockers**, the proud aristocracy of Manhattan in the early days.*

*It was the stir and bustle of trade, together with the tremendous immigration that followed upon the war of 1812 that **dislodged**, them. In thirty-five years the city of less than a hundred thousand came to harbor half a million souls, for whom homes had to be found ... [The original owners'] comfortable dwellings in the once fashionable streets along the East River front fell in to hands of real estate agents and boarding-house keepers.... As business increased, and the city grew with rapid strides, the necessities of the poor became the opportunities of their wealthier neighbors, and the stamp was set upon the old houses, suddenly become valuable.... [According to a report to the Legislature of 1857] "their large rooms were partitioned into several smaller ones, without regard to light or **ventilation**, the rate of rent being lower in proportion to space or height from the street; and they soon became*

Mark of Cain: Image from the Old Testament referring to Cain's murder of his brother, Abel. Cain was sentenced to a lifetime of exile by God, who then placed a mark on his face.

Deciphered: Read or explained.

Rear house: Building erected on the lot of an existing residence for the purpose of housing tenants.

Promiscuous: Not selective.

Decorous: Proper.

Knickerbockers: Descendants of the early Dutch settlers of New York.

Dislodged: Forced out.

Ventilation: Air circulation.

*filled from cellar to **garret** with a class of tenantry living from hand to mouth, loose in morals, **improvident** in habits, degraded, and **squalid** as beggary itself.".* . .

Still the pressure of the crowds did not abate, and in the old garden where the stolid Dutch **burgher** grew his tulips or early cabbages a rear house was built, generally of wood, two stories high at first. Presently it was carried up another story, and another. Where two families had lived ten moved in. The front house followed suit, if the brick walls were strong enough. The question was not always asked, judging from complaints made by a contemporary witness, that the old buildings were "often carried up to a great height without regard to the strength of the foundation walls." It was rent the owner was after; nothing was said in the contract about either the safety or the comfort of the tenants. . . .

Worse was to follow. It was "soon perceived by estate owners and agents of property that a greater percentage of profits could be realized by the conversion of houses and blocks into **barracks,** and dividing their space into smaller proportions capable of containing human life within four walls. . . . Blocks were rented of real estate owners, or '**purchased on time,**' or **taken in charge at a percentage,** and held for **under-letting.**" With the appearance of the middleman, wholly irresponsible, and utterly reckless and unrestrained, began the era of tenement building which turned out such blocks as Gotham Court, where, in one **cholera epidemic** that scarcely touched the clean wards, the tenants died at the rate of one hundred and ninety-five to the thousand of population; which forced the general **mortality** of the city up from 1 in 41.83 in 1815, to 1 in 27.33 in 1855, a year of unusual freedom from epidemic disease, and which wrung from the early organizers of the Health Department this wail: "There are numerous examples of tenement-houses in which are lodged several hundred people that have a **pro rata** allotment of ground area scarcely equal to two square yards upon the city lot, court-yards and all included." The tenement-house population had swelled to half a million souls by that time, and on the East Side, in what is still the most densely populated district in all the world, China not excluded, it was packed at the rate of 200,000 to the square mile, a state of affairs wholly unexampled. The utmost **cupidity** of other lands and other days had never **contrived** to herd much more than half that number within the same space. The greatest crowding of Old London was at the rate of 175,816. **Swine** roamed the streets and gutters as their principal **scavengers.** The death of a child in a tenement was registered at the Bureau of Vital Statistics as "plainly due to suffocation in the foul air of an unventilated apartment, and the Senators, who had come down from Albany to find out what

Garret: Room on the top floor of a house, typically under a sloped roof.

Improvident: Rash.

Squalid: Dirty and wretched.

Burgher: Solid middle class citizen.

Barracks: Plain structures usually used for temporary shelter.

Purchased on time: Bought with the understanding that the purchaser will pay the owner back in installments over time.

Taken in charge at a percentage: Managed by a third party for a percentage of the profits.

Under-letting: Rented by a third party for the purpose of renting it out again at a higher rate.

Cholera epidemic: The spread of sometimes fatal infectious bacterial disease of the gastrointestinal tract, usually the result of drinking water contaminated by poor sanitation.

Mortality: Death rate.

Pro rata: In proportion.

Cupidity: Greed.

Contrived: Planned.

Swine: Pigs.

Scavengers: Animals that eat garbage.

was the matter with New York, reported that 'there are annually cut off from the population by disease and death enough human beings to people a city, and enough human labor to sustain it.'" And yet experts had testified that, as compared with uptown, rents were from twenty-five to thirty percent higher in the worst slums of the lower wards, with such accommodations as were enjoyed, for instance, by a "family with boarders" in Cedar Street, who fed hogs in the cellar that contained eight or ten loads of manure; or "one room 12 x 12 with five families living in it, comprising twenty persons of both sexes and all ages, with only two beds, without partition, screen, chair, or table." The rate of rent has been successfully maintained to the present day, though the hog at least has been eliminated.

Lest anybody flatter himself with the notion that these were evils of a day that is happily past and may safely be forgotten, let me mention here three very recent instances of tenement-house life that came under my notice. One was the burning of a rear house in Mott Street, from appearances one of the original tenant-houses that made their owners rich. The fire made homeless ten families, who had paid an average of $5 a month for their mean little cubby-holes. The owner himself told me that it was fully insured for $800, though it brought him in $600 a year rent. He evidently considered himself especially entitled to be pitied for losing such valuable property. Another was the case of a hard-working family of man and wife, young people from the old country, who took poison together in a Crosby Street tenement because they were "tired." There was no other explanation, and none was needed when I stood in the room in which they had lived. It was in the attic with sloping ceiling and a single window so far out on the roof that it seemed not to belong to the place at all. With scarcely room enough to turn around in they had been compelled to pay five dollars and a half a month in advance. There were four such rooms in that attic, and together they brought in as much as many a handsome little cottage in a pleasant part of Brooklyn. The third instance was that of a colored family of husband, wife, and baby in a wretched rear **rookery** in West Third Street. Their rent was eight dollars and a half for a single room on the top-story, so small that I was unable to get a photograph of it even by placing the camera outside the open door. Three short steps across either way would have measured its full extent.

There was just one excuse for the early tenement-house builders, and their successors may plead it with nearly as good right for what it is worth. "Such," says an official report, "is the lack of house-room in the city that any kind of tenement can be immediately crowded with lodgers, if there is space offered." Thousands were living in cellars.

Rookery: Crowded tenement building.

There were three hundred underground lodging-houses in the city when the Health Department was organized. Some fifteen years before that the old Baptist Church in Mulberry Street, just off Chatham Street, had been sold, and the rear half of the frame structure had been converted into tenements that with their swarming population became the scandal even of that reckless age. The wretched pile harbored no less than forty families, and the annual rate of deaths to the population was officially stated to be 75 in 1,000. These tenements were an extreme type of very many, for the big barracks had by this time spread east and west and far up the island into the sparsely settled wards. . . .

The climax had been reached. The situation was summed up by the Society for the Improvement of the Condition of the Poor in these words: "Crazy old buildings, crowded rear tenements in filthy yards, dark, damp basements, leaking garrets, shops, outhouses, and stables converted into dwellings, though scarcely fit to shelter brutes, are habitations of thousands of our fellow-beings in this wealthy, Christian city." . . .

What happened next . . .

Not long after *How the Other Half Lives* was published, Riis made an important friend and ally in his mission to help the poor. In his autobiography, *Making of an American* (1901), Riis explained how future president Theodore Roosevelt (1858–1919; served 1901–9), then the police commissioner of New York City, suddenly appeared in his life:

> It could not have been long after I wrote 'How the Other Half Lives' that he came to the Evening Sun office one day looking for me. I was out and he left his card merely writing on the back of it that he had read my book and had 'come to help.' That was all, and it tells the whole story of the man. I loved him from the day I first saw him; nor ever in all the years that have passed has he failed of the promise made then. No one ever helped as he did.

Greatly moved by Riis's book, Roosevelt began to accompany him on many of his nightly journeys through the slums of New York. Roosevelt admired Riis, and when he became president he offered Riis government positions. Riis refused, however, claiming his work was in the city.

Developments in Photography

Jacob Riis lived in a time when the art of photography was beginning to grow. In 1871 the dry plate process was invented. In this method the basis of the photograph was an emulsion, or a suspended mix of silver salts, which formed a coating on a glass plate on which an image is captured as a negative. The dry plate process replaced portable darkrooms, which had been used in the past to develop negatives immediately after the picture was taken. This allowed a photographer to travel to take pictures, rather than the subjects having to come to him. By 1878 dry plates were being manufactured commercially, and in 1881 George Eastman (1854–1932) founded the Eastman Dry Plate Company. The company went on to develop flexible film so that photographic negatives would be less likely to break. By 1888 Eastman's company had developed roll film and immediately came out with a box camera already loaded with enough film for one hundred pictures that could be developed at its Rochester, New York, location. Eastman-Kodak became incorporated in 1892. It would eventually become the world's largest photography company and it still is today.

By the turn of the twentieth century, Riis's work had started to take effect and improvement began to occur. New Yorkers demanded action to renovate the city's slums. School playgrounds and boys' and girls' clubs were established. The city water was purified, which reduced epidemics of yellow fever, smallpox, and cholera. The police station lodging houses for the homeless were eliminated and more humane shelters were created. Riis helped force the destruction of overcrowded rear-tenements and demanded light for dark tenement hallways. One of the most notable victories in his career was the demolition of Mulberry Bend, the worst tenement block in the city, which was replaced by Mulberry Bend Park.

Riis continued to write and lecture frequently on the problems of the poor. He published over a dozen books and many articles. He died in Massachusetts at the age of sixty-five.

Riis was well-known by the time of his death, but his photography had been mostly forgotten. A collection of his photographs lay hidden in the attic of his family's home in Long Island for decades. In 1946 the photographs were found, restored, and placed on display in the Museum of the City of New York.

Did you know . . .

- Many of Riis's photographs were taken at night so he needed an artificial lighting system. His technique was still in the experimental stages, consisting of an open flash set against a frying pan. It did not always work well; he almost blinded himself once, and twice he set fire to the immediate surroundings while taking his pictures. On another occasion he set fire to his own clothes.

- Riis and photographer Lewis Hine (1874–1940) are credited with a style known as social reform photography. Both used the camera to document the problems of the poor and to try to bring about social changes.

- In his preface to Alland Alexander Sr.'s 1993 book, *Jacob A. Riis: Photographer and Citizen,* noted photographer Ansel Adams (1902–1984) praised Riis's work: "The factual and dated content of subject has definite historic importance, but the larger content lies in Riis's expression of people in misery, want and squalor. These people live again for you in the print—as intensely as when their images were captured on the old dry plates of ninety years ago. . . . I have thought much about this intense, living quality in Riis's work; I think I have an explanation of its compelling power. It is because in viewing those prints I find myself identified with the people photographed. I am walking in their alleys, standing in their rooms and sheds and workshops, looking in and out of their windows. And they in turn seem to be aware of me. . . ."

Consider the following . . .

- Read the previous entry, Chapter 9, which contains the excerpt from William Graham Sumner's "The Concentration of Wealth: Its Economic Justification." Sumner believed that charity was to be avoided because it interfered with the natural social process in which the people best adapted to their environment succeeded and the weak lived in poverty or eventually died out. Riis disagreed with Sumner's theory. If he were talking to Sumner, what do you think his argument would have been?

- Look at the photographs by Riis in this chapter. Write down in detail what you see, what you particularly notice about each picture, and how it makes you feel.

For More Information

Books

Alexander, Alland Sr. *Jacob A. Riis: Photographer and Citizen.* New York: Aperture Book, 1993.

Riis, Jacob A. *How the Other Half Lives: Studies Among the Tenements of New York.* New York: Hill and Wang, 1957.

Riis, Jacob. *Making of An American.* New York: Harper & Row, 1901.

Periodicals

"Work Among the Poor." *New York Times* 8 (10 April 1895): 4.

Web Sites

"Jacob Riis." *Masters of Photography.* http://www.masters-of-photography.com/R/riis/riis_articles.html (accessed on July 6, 2005).

Random Reminiscences

Excerpt from **Random Reminiscences of Men and Events**
By John D. Rockefeller
Published in 1909

John D. Rockefeller (1839–1937) was the founder and driving force behind the Standard Oil Company, one of the largest corporations of the late nineteenth and early twentieth centuries. The company's spectacular rise to domination of the oil industry in a few short decades was largely the result of Rockefeller's foresight and vision, his hard work, his demand for efficiency, and his mission to cut out competition by whatever means was available. It was Rockefeller's goal to control every aspect of the oil business, from taking it out of the earth to shipping it, refining it, selling it, and even delivering it to its end users. During Rockefeller's years as the company's president, Standard Oil was often criticized by the public for being a monopoly, which meant that the corporation had almost exclusive control of the nation's oil refining business, making it nearly impossible for other businesses to compete in the industry.

Standard Oil developed a bad reputation early in its rise. The press frequently printed stories about the underhanded tactics used by the company to squash its rivals and force small business owners to sell or give way to its

"It is a common thing to hear people say that this company has crushed out its competitors. Only the uninformed could make such an assertion. It has and always has had, and always will have, hundreds of active competitors."

A Standard Oil refinery. *(© Corbis.)*

steady advancement toward monopoly. Political cartoons about Rockefeller appeared in newspapers and magazines (see Chapter 13). Two best-selling books attacked Standard Oil, monopolies, and Rockefeller himself. For many years Rockefeller made it a policy never to publicly respond to any of the many accusations made against his company, but he made his views on business known. Rockefeller claimed that his company set a valuable standard for American business. Rockefeller believed that by combining the many competing refineries and associated businesses under Standard Oil's control, he had provided Americans with a ready supply of affordably priced oil and thus considerably raised the quality of life in the nation. He also argued that Standard Oil's operating practices, which included ruling its industries with scientific efficiency on a large scale and having almost unrestrained power over them, represented the future of business. Still, the papers were full of his misdeeds. In his memoirs of 1909, *Random Reminiscences of Men and Events,* he wrote a defense of his company and his life's work.

Although he later became one of the nation's richest men, Rockefeller was born into a modest home in Richford, New York, in 1839. He took his first job at the age of sixteen as a bookkeeper for a merchant company in Cleveland, Ohio, saving enough money to go into business on his own in just a few years. He was very successful in his wholesale grocery business, and when he saw an opportunity arise in the new industry of oil refining in 1863, he had the means to invest in it. By 1865 Rockefeller and a partner had opened a refinery and within a couple of years, thanks to the business skills of Rockefeller and his associates, Cleveland became the major center for crude oil refining. Rockefeller's refineries produced at least twice as much as any other of Cleveland's nearly thirty refineries, and it continued to grow under Rockefeller's astute supervision.

John D. Rockefeller. (© *Bettmann/Corbis.*)

In 1870 the Standard Oil Company was chartered as a corporation in the state of Ohio. At that time, the company controlled one-tenth of American refining. Competition in the oil industry was disordered, with dramatic rises and falls occurring in the price of oil. In times when oil prices were high, hundreds of businessmen rushed to establish new production and refining businesses. With so many people producing oil, an excess of supply flooded the market, driving prices down, often to levels at which there was no longer any profit to be made. When prices continued to stay low, the small companies began to collapse. Larger companies with more money could afford to hold out longer, which had the unintended effect of keeping prices down for long periods. Thus, the industry's extreme price variations hurt even the healthiest companies.

Standard Oil survived the hard times partly because it had a supply of capital reserves (investment funds) and was able to borrow heavily from them. Rockefeller also ran a highly efficient business, cutting production costs and doing away with unnecessary expenses so he could profit at lower prices than other refiners. Despite this, he sought to stop the chaos affecting the market by gaining control of it. Rockefeller thought that free market competition—a situation in which businesses competed against each other without outside controls—was inefficient. He thought it was particularly harmful in the oil industry, with its mix of large, prosperous companies and small, weak newcomers. Rockefeller believed that the less successful companies, in their attempts to survive, drove prices down, which hurt big, efficient firms like Standard Oil.

One of the primary expenses in the oil industry was transportation. In the early years of the oil boom, oil was transported in barrels, usually by railroad or boat, from well to refinery and then again from refinery to market. By 1868 Rockefeller had figured out how to profit from this system. He made a deal with Jay Gould (1836–1892), owner of the Erie Railroad, promising him that Standard Oil would consistently ship a specific volume of oil on his railroad in return for rebates (the return of part of his freight charge payments). Rockefeller went on to make many similar deals with other shippers, forcing the rail and steamboat companies to compete with each other to offer him the lowest shipping rates.

In 1872 Rockefeller participated in the South Improvement Company scheme, a secret alliance between the railroads and a small group of the most successful Cleveland oil refiners. The railroads agreed to post their freight rates at a standard price, but then to quietly pay rebates to the large refiners participating in the agreement. The railroads would also pay the member refiners drawbacks, which were fees charged to nonmembers to ship their freight. High shipping costs would make the nonmembers unable to compete with the larger refineries, and most would go out of business.

When news of the South Improvement scheme got out, the excluded oil producers and refiners protested, and the state of Pennsylvania outlawed the agreement before it went into effect. Even though Rockefeller had not initiated the pact, his public image was badly damaged by his involvement in it. The bad press did not slow down his efforts to control the oil market. Early in 1872 he went to the owners of twenty-six Cleveland oil refineries and offered to buy them out by determining the value of their businesses and giving them stock in Standard Oil equal to that value. The rival owners would then become partners in Standard Oil, or, if they preferred, they could choose payment in cash. Twenty-one refiners sold out within three months in what came to be called the Cleveland Massacre. Some claimed they had been pressured into selling at prices less than their businesses were worth. The state had not yet overturned the South Improvement Company pact when he approached the other refineries and some feared their businesses would be worthless if the pact was in place. Though many considered his tactics ruthless, evidence shows that Rockefeller paid generously for the companies he bought, and those who chose to accept payment in Standard Oil stock became very wealthy. Rockefeller added the productive refineries to his business and closed down the weaker ones.

In the early days of oil refining, the oil from the oil fields was shipped to refiners in barrels carried by railroad. In order to cut costs, Rockefeller bought factories that made barrels and he bought acres of timberland to obtain his own wood. It soon became apparent, though, that oil pipelines, a system of underground pipes that would conduct oil from the fields directly to the refineries without railroads or barrels, were the way of the future. Standard Oil began to build an extensive pipeline system and they soon controlled almost all of the pipelines of the industry. If they dominated the pipelines, then all independent oil producers would be forced to go through Standard Oil. People who worked in the oil industry independently of Standard Oil were desperate to find ways to compete. Under the name of the Tidewater Pipe Line Company, independent oilmen got together to build two major pipelines that would allow oil producers to bypass Standard's pipeline network. Tidewater found financial backing from some of the top institutions of Wall Street.

Standard then entered an industrial war against Tidewater, a bitter and expensive push by both companies to set pipeline routes from fields to refineries and draw customers to use them. Standard bought a charter from the state of Maryland granting the company the exclusive right to build pipelines for a season, but the Tidewater group simply shifted its focus to Pennsylvania. Rockefeller sent out his agents to warn companies not to use Tidewater pipes; he bought up the lands in the path of their pipelines; he bought out the refineries that might use their services. According to Ron Chernow, author of *Titan: The Life of John D. Rockefeller, Sr.*, he also planted stories in local newspapers warning farmers about oil leaks from Tidewater's pipes that would destroy their crops. He used his powerful connections with the railroads to push them to forbid Tidewater from crossing their tracks and to stop them from carrying necessary building supplies to the Tidewater construction sites. Standard also spent huge amounts in bribing state legislators to maintain right-of-way systems that were costly to Tidewater. When Tidewater got past all the obstacles Rockefeller had set in its path and started up its pipeline business, Standard dropped its pipeline rates so low that most of Tidewater's potential customers chose to use Standard instead. In the end, Tidewater entered into a pact, agreeing to cooperate with Standard in order to raise pipeline rates. Tidewater was then slowly absorbed into the company, and Standard Oil had the monopoly on pipelines.

By 1879 Standard Oil Company controlled between 90 and 95 percent of the American refining capacity, dominating the country's petroleum industry. Because all the transactions had been done in secret, many people were surprised to suddenly find that Standard Oil had become an industrial giant. Standard Oil continued to grow during the 1880s. Under the direction of Rockefeller's brother, William (1841–1922), the firm also expanded into the international market. Standard Oil products became well-known in Asia, Africa, South America, and even Central Europe, where Standard Oil encountered stiff competition from cheap Russian oil. By the 1890s Standard Oil had pioneered a nationwide system to deliver oil directly to homes and businesses in almost every American town. Although consumers benefited greatly from this practice, which made heating fuel and gasoline for their cars affordable and easy to get, criticism of Standard Oil's business tactics increased. One major complaint was that the company required the stores that sold its products to agree to sell only Standard products.

The Standard Oil Company (Ohio) was the center of the richest and most powerful industrial organization in the nation. Under its charter with the state of Ohio, however, it had no legal right to own property or stock beyond the state's borders. To get around this limitation, between 1873 and 1879 Standard Oil bought stock in other companies, often buying enough to own or control the companies, or to get a seat on their boards of directors. The Standard Oil partners, such as Rockefeller, Henry M. Flagler (1830–1913), and William Rockefeller, then acted as trustees of the new stocks. Each of them sat on the boards of the companies Standard had purchased or had a controlling interest in, and thus they were able to dictate the company's practices so that all would cooperate with Standard Oil, reducing competition. In effect, all companies were part of the same organization. This trustee device gave the company a flexible means of expanding well beyond the borders of Ohio and also permitted Rockefeller and his associates to hide their activities. Holding to a strict legal interpretation of the nature of the trustees, which stated that they were acting on behalf of the stockholders and not the Standard Oil Company, Standard Oil officials, including Rockefeller himself, repeatedly denied publicly and under oath that the company owned or controlled certain companies that they did in fact hold.

By 1879 Standard Oil had outgrown this informal arrangement, and in 1882 the Standard Oil Trust was created. Under this agreement all properties owned or controlled by the Standard Oil Company were placed in the hands

Henry W. Flagler was one of Rockefeller's early partners.
(© Bettmann/Corbis. Reproduced by permission.)

of a board of nine trustees, one of which was John D. Rockefeller. Standard Oil Company (Ohio) stock was exchanged for trust certificates. The nine trustees exercised general supervision over all Standard Oil companies and the many other Standard organizations whose stock was held in the trust. This included the assets of all regional Standard Oil companies, one of which was Standard Oil of New Jersey, the third largest U.S. refinery at the time. The Standard Oil Trust created a giant new centralized company and gave Rockefeller and his associates the administrative flexibility to operate and to direct their worldwide activities effectively.

By the late 1880s, the public had become uncomfortable with the power that big business held over the nation and soon the Standard Oil monopoly gained attention. The New York legislature investigated the company's holdings and practices in 1879 and again in 1888. Editorial writer Henry Demarest

Lloyd (1847–1903) fought a lifelong campaign against monopolies, starting with Standard Oil. His 1881 *Atlantic Monthly* article, "Story of a Great Monopoly," focused the attention of the nation on the company's questionable business methods. In writing this article Lloyd became one of the first muckrakers, journalists who investigated and exposed business or government misconduct in order to promote reform. Lloyd's most important book, *Wealth Against Commonwealth* (1894), spoke strongly against Standard Oil. The best-known critical work about the company, however, was Ida M. Tarbell's (1857–1944) *History of the Standard Oil Company,* written in 1904 (see Chapter 12). Rockefeller refused to respond directly to these attacks, believing the quality of his products was good enough to justify Standard's operating practices.

In 1890 Congress passed the Sherman Antitrust Act, which made unfair restraint of trade illegal and outlawed monopolies. On March 2, 1892, the Ohio Supreme Court convicted Standard Oil of violating the Sherman Act. The court decision led to the breaking up of the Standard Oil Trust back into its independent parts. Standard responded by taking advantage of favorable state laws in New Jersey, and the New Jersey refinery became the trust's parent holding company, a company whose primary function is to own the stocks of other corporations. Rockefeller remained president, and the management of the trust was joined together under the same directors sitting on the boards of the more than thirty subsidiary companies (companies that were controlled by the parent company). The supposedly separate companies were therefore able to act as a single unit.

Rockefeller retired from Standard Oil in 1896 at the age of fifty-six. After that he gave over the daily management of the company to his successor and remained president in name only. Because of this, the criticisms that were aimed at Standard Oil continued to be directed at him. All his life, Rockefeller had been strongly tied to his church and the Baptist religion. He was a very moral man in his personal dealings, and a proud and caring husband and father. He led a fairly modest life (for being the richest man in the world); he did not drink alcohol or have expensive hobbies. He managed to separate his ruthless business dealings from his personal life. In several interviews he stated his belief that he was selected by God to become extremely wealthy and powerful. And he believed that monopolies such as the one he had built were the most efficient form of business and that they could make the American standard of living higher. In these respects, it is clear he felt that he was doing constructive work rather than being greedy and brutal to other business owners. Rockefeller never dealt with the many specific accusations of his underhanded methods of advancing his monopoly; in the excerpt from *Random Reminiscences,* the reader can sense his pride as well as his defensiveness when he speaks of his company in very general and glowing terms.

Things to remember while reading the excerpt from *Random Reminiscences of Men and Events*:

- Economic conditions in the post–Civil War United States were extremely favorable for the rise of giant, powerful corporations that made their executives very wealthy. There were no federal income taxes, few corporate taxes, and almost no regulation of business. Many of the country's leaders had adopted the views of English economist Adam Smith (1723–1790), who, in his noted book *An Inquiry into the Nature and Causes of the Wealth of Nations* (1776), reasoned that economies should be regulated only by competition among businesses, without interference from the government. This hands-off policy of the government was called laissez-faire, an economic doctrine that opposes government regulation of commerce and industry beyond the minimum necessary.

- Many industrialists of the period regularly purchased the favors of elected officials either with money, gifts, or more often, with shares of their company stock.

- Although in *Random Reminiscences* Rockefeller claimed Standard Oil was not a monopoly, in other discussions he freely acknowledged his efforts to gain control over the industry by combining companies. In an interview quoted by biographer Ron Chernow in *Titan: The Life of John D. Rockefeller, Sr.,* Rockefeller stated: "The oil business was in confusion and daily growing worse. Someone had to take a stand.... This movement was the origin of the whole system of economic administration. It has revolutionized the way of doing business all over the world.... The day of the combination is here to stay."

- Rockefeller was not the first to try to form a business combination, or to merge leading companies into an organization that could take control of an entire industry. Corporate combinations had begun during the 1860s with business pools—agreements among rivals within an industry to share their profits or divide up territories in order to avoid destructive competition and maintain higher prices. Salt producers were among the first to create a successful pool in the United States. Under the Michigan Salt Association, formed in 1869, the salt companies agreed to divide up their territories. Since there were no other competitors within these assigned territories, they were immediately able to double the price of salt, and all participating companies profited. Other industries soon formed similar pools. The lack of competition in the market hurt consumers, who had to pay higher prices.

- From the 1870s on, the trend in business was toward consolidation, a process in which companies purchased other companies and folded them into one large combination. There were two general ways to consolidate. One was horizontal expansion, in which the primary company purchased as many of its rival companies as possible. The end result would be a monopoly, or ownership of all companies in the industry. The other way to consolidate was vertical expansion, in which the primary company bought up the companies that provided the services it needed, thus avoiding paying competitive prices for equipment, transportation, and manufacturing. Rockefeller expanded Standard Oil both horizontally, by buying his competitors, and vertically, by buying businesses that made barrels, provided oil transportation, and built pipelines.

- By 1890 monopolies and trusts controlled the production of such products as whiskey, sugar, cigarettes, and lead, as well as dominating the nation's railroad industry. Citizens of the United States were divided between two very different views of these corporate organizations. Some accepted trusts as a natural result of modern industry. Among those who were in favor of trusts, some wanted general government oversight of the large monopolies, while others preferred no interference outside the market. A second group of Americans believed monopolies were unfair and hurt the country by concentrating wealth and political power in the hands of only a few businessmen. This group called for the dissolution (breaking apart) of all monopolies in the interest of restoring and preserving a competitive market system.

Excerpt from Random Reminiscences of Men and Events

The Standard Oil Company

*For years the Standard Oil Company has developed step by step, and I am convinced that it has done well its work of supplying to the people the products from **petroleum** at prices which have decreased as the efficiency of the business has been built up. It gradually extended its services first to the large centers, and then to towns, and on to the smallest places, going to the homes of its customers, delivering the oil to suit the convenience of the actual users. This same system is being followed out in various parts of the world.... Do you think this trade has been developed by anything but hard work?*

*This plan of selling our products direct to the consumer and the exceptionally rapid growth of the business bred a certain **antagonism** which I suppose could not have been avoided....*

I have often wondered if the criticism which centred upon us did not come from the fact that we were among the first, if not the first, to work out the problems of direct selling to the user on a broad scale. This was done in a fair spirit and with due consideration to every one's rights. We did not ruthlessly go after the trade of our competitors and attempt to ruin it by cutting prices or instituting a spy system. We had set ourselves the task of building up as rapidly and as broadly as possible the volume of consumption. Let me try to explain just what happened.

*To get the advantage of the facilities we had in manufacture, we sought the utmost market in all lands—we needed **volume**. To do this we had to create selling methods far in advance of what then existed; we had to dispose of two, or three, or four gallons of oil where one had been sold before, and we could not rely upon the usual trade channels then existing to accomplish this. It was never our purpose to interfere with a*

Petroleum: Oil and oil products.

Antagonism: Opposition.

Volume: Large quantities.

dealer who adequately **cultivated** his field of operations, but when we saw a new opportunity or a new place for extending the sale by further and effective facilities, we made it our business to provide them. In this way we opened many new lines in which others have shared. In this development we had to employ many comparatively new men. The ideal way to supply material for higher positions is, of course, to recruit the men from among the youngest in the company's service, but our expansion was too rapid to permit this in all cases. That some of these employees were **over-zealous** in going after sales it would not be surprising to learn, but they were acting in violation of the expressed and known wishes of the company. But even these instances, I am convinced, occurred so seldom, by comparison with the number of transactions we carried on, that they were really the exceptions that proved the rule.

Every week in the year for many, many years, this **concern** has brought into this country more than a million dollars gold, all from the products produced by American labour. I am proud of the record, and believe most Americans will be when they understand some things better. These achievements, the development of this great foreign trade, the owning of ships to carry the oil in bulk by the most economical methods, the sending out of men to fight for the world's markets, have cost huge sums of money, and the vast capital employed could not be raised nor controlled except by such an organization as the Standard is to-day. . . .

The 60,000 men who are at work constantly in the service of the company are kept busy year in and year out. The past year has been a time of great **contraction**, but the Standard has gone on with its plans **unchecked**, and the new works and buildings have not been delayed on account of lack of capital or fear of bad times. It pays its workmen well, it cares for them when sick, and pensions them when old. It has never had any important strikes, and if there is any better function of business management than giving profitable work to employees year after year, in good times and bad, I don't know what it is. . . .

It is a common thing to hear people say that this company has crushed out its competitors. Only the uninformed could make such an assertion. It has and always has had, and always will have, hundreds of active competitors; it has lived only because it has managed its affairs well and economically and with great **vigor.** To speak of competition for a minute: Consider not only the able people who compete in refining oil, but all the competition in the various trades which make and sell by-products—a great variety of different businesses. And perhaps of even more importance is the competition in foreign lands. The Standard is always fighting to sell the American product against the oil produced

Cultivated: Prepared to be productive.

Over-zealous: Too eager.

Concern: Rockefeller refers here to his company, Standard Oil.

Contraction: Decrease in the country's business activity and economic growth.

Unchecked: Unrestrained.

Vigor: Strength.

from the great fields of Russia, which struggles for the trade of Europe, and the Burma oil, which largely affects the market in India. . . . Every time we succeeded in a foreign land, it meant dollars brought to this country, and every time we failed, it was a loss to our nation and its workmen. . . .

I think I can speak thus frankly and enthusiastically because the working out of many of these great plans has developed largely since I retired from the business fourteen years ago.

*The Standard has not now, and never did have a royal road to supremacy, nor is its success due to any one man, but to the multitude of able men who are working together. If the present managers of the company were to relax efforts, allow the quality of their product to **degenerate**, or treat their customers badly, how long would their business last? About as long as any other neglected business. To read some of the accounts of the affairs of the company, one would think that it had such a hold on the oil trade that the directors did little but come together and declare **dividends**. It is a pleasure for me to take this opportunity to pay tribute to the work these men are doing, not only for the company they serve, but for the foreign trade of our country; for more than half of all the product that the company makes is sold outside of the United States. If, in place of these directors, the business were taken over and run by anyone but experts, I would sell my interest for any price I could get. To succeed in a business requires the best and most earnest men to manage it, and the best men rise to the top.*

Degenerate: Decline.

Dividends: Shares in the company's surplus or income.

What happened next . . .

In November 1906 the Federal Circuit Court of the Eastern District of Missouri brought charges against Standard Oil for creating a monopoly and restraining trade. In 1909 the Missouri court found Standard Oil guilty of violating the Sherman Antitrust Act in two ways: by forming a holding company and by restraining competition by fixing transportation rates, supply costs, and output prices. Standard Oil appealed the decision, but in 1911 the Supreme Court upheld the Missouri decision and ordered the Standard Oil Trust to be broken up, separating the parent holding company, Jersey Standard, from its thirty-three major subsidiaries. Many of the individual companies continued to operate under the name Standard Oil. These included the Standard Oil Company of Indiana (later American), the Standard Oil Company (Ohio), Standard Oil Company of California (later Chevron), Standard Oil of New Jersey (later Exxon), and Standard Oil of New York (later Mobil).

The Standard Oil case of 1911 significantly changed the course of American business history. The victory of the government against a powerful trust proved that regulation could be accomplished. Although the successor companies to the trust, particularly the New Jersey unit, maintained considerable market power in their regional territories, the dissolution of Standard Oil into many independent companies effectively increased competition in the oil industry. Companies that were able to share in the oil profits included Shell, Gulf, and Sun.

Did you know . . .

- When Rockefeller retired from the daily management of Standard Oil in 1896, his personal fortune was an estimated $900 million. (This was after he had already donated hundreds of millions in his efforts to promote human welfare and the arts; thus he was often considered America's first billionaire.) His interests turned toward philanthropy (the voluntary giving of money or other assets by an individual or group to promote the good of others). He became one of the great leaders in American philanthropy as well as in business. He virtually created the University of Chicago with a founding donation in 1889 of $600,000 and later gifts (some from his son) totaling $80 million. He founded the Rockefeller Institute for Medical Research in 1901 and the General Education Board in 1902. His philanthropy was further regulated with the creation of the Rockefeller Foundation in 1913. At the time of his death, he had given away more than $500 million, and the influence of his philanthropic institutions was still growing.

- The Rockefellers never let the public see any of the harmful effects that the constant public criticism of Rockefeller had on their family. Ron Chernow notes: "Rockefeller, his wife, his son, and two of his three daughters were afflicted by serious medical problems or nervous strain" due to the public exposure of Rockefeller as a corporate criminal and the attacks on him personally.

Consider the following . . .

- John D. Rockefeller's Standard Oil monopoly introduced many new business practices to the United States and changed the nature of commerce in the country forever. In this excerpt, what arguments does he make for being viewed as an American hero? Do you believe he was a heroic captain of industry, an unscrupulous robber baron only interested in his own profits, or both?

- Why do you think free market competition has been considered so important in American history? Should monopolies exist to organize the various industries?

For More Information

Books

Chernow, Ron. *Titan: The Life of John D. Rockefeller, Sr.* New York: Vintage Books, 2004.

Lloyd, Henry Demarest. *Wealth Against Commonwealth.* New York: 1894.

Nevins, Allan. *John D. Rockefeller: The Heroic Age of American Enterprise.* New York: Charles Scribner's Sons, 1940.

Rockefeller, John D. *Random Reminiscences of Men and Events.* New York: Doubleday, Page & Company, 1909.

Web Sites

Poole, Keith. "John D. Rockefeller Senior, 1839–1937: The Rockefellers." *American Experience, PBS.* http://www.pbs.org/wgbh/amex/rockefellers/peopleevents/p_rock_jsr.html (accessed on July 6, 2005).

12

The History of Standard Oil

Excerpt from **The History of the Standard Oil Company**
By Ida M. Tarbell
Published in book form in 1904

Writer and editor Ida M. Tarbell (1857–1944) was one of the first great female journalists in the United States. Her best-known work, *The History of the Standard Oil Company* (1904), exposed the questionable business practices of John D. Rockefeller's Standard Oil Trust, which had been formed when Rockefeller combined all his corporations in an attempt to reduce competition and control prices in the oil industry. When Tarbell began researching the enormous company in 1902, it had already survived more than thirty years of criticism, state and federal investigation, and legal actions against it (see Chapter 11). The publication of her book helped result in a 1911 Supreme Court decision to dissolve Standard Oil and altered the future course of business in the country, surprising many who had underestimated her influence since she was a woman reporter and a newcomer in the field.

Tarbell was born in 1857 in Hatch Hollow, one of the oilfield towns of Erie County, Pennsylvania. During the 1850s vast numbers of oil wells were being built across the county, transforming the poor, rural region into one of the centers of

Ida Tarbell, author of *The History of the Standard Oil Company.* *(© Bettmann/Corbis.)*

the new oil industry. When the oil wells began producing in Pithole Creek, an area near Tarbell's home, her father, Frank, rushed to start a wooden barrel shop there. The wells at Pithole quickly dried up, however, and the family moved to Titusville. Bad fortune followed the family to the new town, and Frank Tarbell's business failed when iron tanks came into use for oil storage. Like many other hopefuls, he then attempted to become an independent oil producer.

In 1872 news reached Titusville that the Standard Oil Company and several other wealthy oil refiners (people who ran factories in which oil in its natural state was broken down into commercial products such as oil lamp fuel or kerosene) had entered into a secret pact with the railroads that served the oil industry. The pact was known as the South Improvement Company and its purpose was to keep shipping rates low for its members and high for nonmembers. The higher shipping rates would effectively close down many of the smaller independent producers, such as Ida Tarbell's father, since they would not be able to compete with the South Improvement members. Soon after the citizens of Titusville heard about the planned agreement, the railroads posted their new rates, which were double what they had been the week before. Tarbell, who was fifteen at the time, witnessed the gatherings of the angry independent oilmen when they learned about the rates. Speeches were made encouraging the hanging of South Improvement Company members and the burning of their oil tanks. The oilmen of Titusville refused to sell their oil to the member refiners, beginning a standoff that probably hurt them more than it did the refiners. Eventually, in response to the public uproar, the South Improvement Company was shut down by the state, although Standard Oil did go on to eliminate many independent companies in Titusville. Over the years Tarbell's father and brother—along with most independent oil producers in the town—were ruined by Standard Oil's schemes to gain control of the entire industry.

After the South Improvement controversy, Tarbell enrolled in high school, where she excelled in the sciences. She entered Allegheny College as the only female in a class of forty, graduating with a degree in biology in 1880. She taught school in Ohio for a couple of years after college but soon returned home in search of more challenging work. She took a job writing for the *Chautauquan,* a monthly continuing education magazine published by the Methodist church, and eventually became its managing editor. After eight years this, too, lost her interest and Tarbell moved to Paris with some friends. There she studied history at the Sorbonne and the University of Paris from 1891 to 1894, making her living by writing articles for American magazines. While in Paris she read Henry Demarest Lloyd's *Wealth Against Commonwealth* (1894), a five-hundred-page criticism of monopolies (corporations that had exclusive possession or control of a product), in particular the Standard Oil Company. Reading Lloyd's work renewed the anger she had felt against John D. Rockefeller and his oil monopoly when it put her family out of business.

Tarbell worked for publisher Samuel McClure's magazine.
(© Bettmann/Corbis.)

During her years in Paris, Tarbell's writing was gaining an audience in the United States. It caught the attention of Samuel S. McClure (1857–1949), who had founded the popular monthly magazine *McClure's* in 1893. He hired her to write an eight-part biographical series on the French emperor Napoleon Bonaparte (1769–1821; ruled 1804–15). The series raised *McClure's* circulation from 24,500 readers to 100,000 readers. When Tarbell returned to New York in 1894, McClure hired her as an editor. Over the next four years she wrote a very popular biographical series on the life of President Abraham Lincoln (1809–1865; served 1861–65), which caused the magazine's circulation to rise again to 300,000 readers.

As the twentieth century began, a new kind of journalist, called a muckraker, was becoming popular. Muckrakers sought out and exposed the misconduct of well-known people or high profile organizations. Muckraking journalists wrote articles about injustices or abuses, hoping the information they provided would stimulate the public to demand reform. McClure, who was at the forefront of the new journalistic movement, began to restructure the format of his magazine to include coverage of social issues, particularly dishonesty in government and misconduct in the business world. Unlike some of the other magazine owners of the period, McClure demanded from his writers accurate, well-researched reporting and clear, logical analysis.

In 1902 Tarbell persuaded McClure to let her do a three-part series on the business practices of Standard Oil and began two years of deep investigation into the giant corporation. Rockefeller had always attempted to keep a low profile, and most of his complex business dealings and transactions had been conducted in secret. Because the company had recently been under federal investigation, however, Tarbell found volumes of public records to examine. Using her extraordinary gifts for absorbing and organizing hundreds of factual details, she put together the most thorough record of the company in existence up until the early twenty-first century. Tarbell wove the history of Rockefeller and Standard Oil into a fascinating story and explained the complicated business practices of the corporation in terms that were easy to understand. Critics agreed that her research was extremely thorough, and that, despite her personal dislike of Standard Oil (which she openly acknowledged throughout the book), her work was highly accurate. Although intended as an attack on Rockefeller, the information the series revealed about him was well-supported by papers that became available after his death and has stood up well over time. Tarbell even wrote at length about the excellence of the company, praising its management and efficiency. But the work's overall effect was to reveal the ruthless practices of Standard Oil. Her readers responded with enthusiasm, and the original plan for three articles turned into a nineteen-article series that ran from 1902 to 1904. *McClure's* readership soared and the series of articles was published in book form in 1904 as *The History of the Standard Oil Company*.

In her work Tarbell carefully acknowledged the genius and hard work with which Rockefeller handled Standard Oil. She made it clear that Rockefeller's corporation had acquired its power and wealth through his unusual business talent and drive, and his choice of associates who had the same top skills and motivations. Tarbell did not oppose large corporations that followed honest policies. Her point was, rather, that Rockefeller was already so successful that he did not need to ruthlessly destroy the independents and small business owners. In her 1939 book *All in a Day's Work,* she observed of Standard Oil: "They had never played fair, and that ruined their greatness for me."

Things to remember while reading the excerpt from *The History of the Standard Oil Company*:

- Tarbell began writing her articles about Standard Oil at the close of an American era of politics that had become known for its dishonesty and greed. Throughout the Gilded Age (the era of industrialization from the early 1860s to the turn of the century in which a few wealthy individuals gained tremendous power and influence), the great industrialists rarely answered to the public for their conduct. A famous example of the attitude of the top industrialists and railroad owners of the time was reported to have occurred sometime in the 1880s, when a reporter asked railroad tycoon William Henry Vanderbilt (1821–1885) if his business should be accountable to the public. Vanderbilt is said to have shouted "The public be damned!" (cited in *Trivia-Library.com*).

- The Progressive Era began around the end of the nineteenth century and lasted roughly through 1918. During this period, farmers, industrial workers, artisans, small business owners, and an increasing number of middle-class citizens joined forces in opposition to the power that the giant corporations wielded over the American government and economy.

- Ida Tarbell was not the only one to begin an examination of the Standard Oil monopoly in 1902. President Theodore Roosevelt (1858–1919; served 1901–9) started a federal investigation the same year.

- In *The History of the Standard Oil Company,* Tarbell described the way the South Improvement Company pact was planned among the refiners and railroads. Although Rockefeller participated in the South Improvement plan, it was probably not his idea. However, Tarbell showed throughout her book that this kind of scheme was a common method used by Standard Oil to eliminate competition. Historians who later gained access to Rockefeller's private papers agreed that he and his associates acquired businesses using similar secret manipulation of transportation systems and other essential resources and services. The documentation showed that Rockefeller made many deals with railroads and other shippers and had inside information about the shipments of rival oil producers and refiners.

- Tarbell focused her writings on John D. Rockefeller although many of the dishonorable practices she described were carried out by the corporation's other partners. By the time the articles were published, Rockefeller had retired and was no longer involved in the daily management of the company. Because he was still the president of the company in name, however, the public continued to hold him accountable for its actions.

Excerpt from **The History of the Standard Oil Company**

*Something more than local troubles occupied [the elite group of Cleveland oil refiners]. This was the condition of the refining business as a whole. It was unsatisfactory in many particulars. First, it was overdone. The great profits on refined oil and the growing demand for it had naturally caused a great number to rush into its manufacture. . . . There was . . . a much larger amount of refining actually done than the market demanded. The result was that the price of refined oil was steadily falling. Where Mr. Rockefeller had received on an average $58\frac{3}{4}$ cents a gallon for the oil he exported in 1865, the year he went into business, in 1870 he received but $26\frac{3}{8}$ cents. In 1865 he had a **margin** of forty-three cents, out of which to pay for transportation, manufacturing,*

Margin: Difference between the net sales and the net costs of producing a product. Net refers to the amount remaining after the deduction of all expenses or loss.

barrelling and marketing and to make his profits. In 1870 he had but 17$\frac{1}{8}$ cents with which to do all this. To be sure his expenses had fallen enormously between 1865 and 1870, but so had his profits. The **multiplication** *of refiners with the intense competition threatened to cut them down still lower. Naturally Mr. Rockefeller and his friends looked with dismay on this lowering of profits through gaining competition. . . .*

In the fall of 1871, while Mr. Rockefeller and his friends were occupied with all these questions, certain Pennsylvania refiners, it is not too certain who, brought to them a remarkable scheme, the gist of which was to bring together secretly a large enough body of refiners and shippers to persuade all the railroads handling oil to give to the company formed special **rebates** *on its oil, and* **drawbacks** *on that of other people. If they could get such rates it was evident that those outside of their* **combination** *could not compete with them long and that they would become eventually the only refiners. They could then limit their output to actual demand, and so keep up prices. This done, they could easily persuade the railroads to transport no* **crude** *for exportation, so that the foreigners would be forced to buy American refined. They believed that the price of oil thus exported could easily be advanced fifty percent. The control of the refining interests would also enable them to fix their own price on crude. As they would be the only buyers and sellers, the* **speculative** *character of the business would be done away with. In short, the scheme they worked out put the entire oil business in their hands. It looked as simple to put into operation as it was dazzling in its results. . . .*

With [a new] charter in hand Mr. Rockefeller and **Mr. Watson** *and their associates began to seek* **converts.** *In order that their great scheme might not be injured by* **premature** *public discussion they asked of each person whom they approached a pledge of secrecy. . . .*

[At a meeting on January 2, 1872, in Philadelphia] a discussion came up as to what refiners were to be allowed to go into the new company. Each of the men represented had friends whom he wanted taken care of, and after considerable discussion it was decided to take in every refinery they could get hold of. This decision was largely due to the railroad men. . . . That is, while the **incorporators** *had intended to kill off all but themselves and their friends, the railroads refused to go into a scheme which was going to put anybody out of business—the plan if they went into it must cover the refining trade as it stood. It was enough that it could prevent any one in the future going into the business. . . .*

Multiplication: Great increase.

Rebates: Return of part of the shipping charges.

Drawbacks: Extra fees charged to nonmembers for shipping their freight that were payable to the South Improvement Company.

Combination: The South Improvement Company, a secret agreement between certain successful refiners and railroads.

Crude: Crude oil; oil as it comes from the ground, before refining.

Speculative: Financially insecure.

Mr. Watson: P. H. Watson of Ashtabula, Ohio, the president of the South Improvement Company and a business representative of Rockefeller's.

Converts: People to join the South Improvement Company.

Premature: Early.

Incorporators: Oil refiners who had initially created the alliance.

It has frequently been stated that the South Improvement Company represented the bulk of the oil-refining interests in the country. The incorporators of the company in approaching the railroads assured them that this was so. As a matter of fact, however, the thirteen gentlemen above named, who were the only ones ever holding stock in the concern, did not control over one-tenth of the refining business of the United States in 1872.... In assuring the railroads that they controlled the business, they were dealing with their hopes rather than with facts....

By the 18th of January the president of the Pennsylvania road, J. Edgar Thompson, had put his signature to the contract, and soon after **Mr. Vanderbilt** and **Mr. Clark** signed for the Central system, and **Jay Gould** and **General McClellan** for the Erie. The contracts to which these gentlemen put their names fixed **gross rates** of freight from all common points, as the leading shipping points within the Oil Regions were called, to all the great refining and shipping centers—New York, Philadelphia, Baltimore, Pittsburgh and Cleveland. For example, the open rate on crude to New York was put at $2.56. On this price the South Improvement Company was allowed a rebate of $1.06 for its shipments; but it got not only this rebate, it was given in cash a like amount on each barrel of crude shipped by parties outside the combination.

The open rate from Cleveland to New York was two dollars, and fifty cents of this was turned over to the South Improvement Company, which at the same time received a rebate enabling it to ship for $1.50. Again, an independent refiner in Cleveland paid eighty cents a barrel to get his crude from the Oil Regions to his works, and the railroad sent forty cents of this money to the South Improvement Company. At the same time it cost the Cleveland refiner in the combination but forty cents to get his crude oil. Like drawbacks and rebates were given for all points—Pittsburgh, Philadelphia, Boston and Baltimore.

An interesting **provision** in the contracts was that full **waybills** of all petroleum shipped over the roads should each day be sent to the South Improvement Company. This, of course, gave them knowledge of just who was doing business outside of their company—of how much business he was doing, and with whom he was doing it. Not only were they to have full knowledge of the business of all shippers—they were to have access to all books of the railroads....

The reason given by the railroads in the contract for granting these extraordinary privileges was that the "magnitude and extent of the business and operations" purposed to be carried on by the South Improvement Company would greatly promote the interest of the railroads and make it desirable for them to encourage their

Mr. Vanderbilt: Cornelius "Commodore" Vanderbilt (1794–1877), an extremely wealthy and powerful railroad industrialist.

Mr. Clark: Horace Clark (1815–1873), president of the Lake Shore and Michigan Southern Railroad, the Northern Indiana Railroad, and the Union Pacific Railroad.

Jay Gould: (1836–1892) Financier and owner of the Erie Railroad.

General McClellan: George B. McClellan (1826–1885), president of the Atlantic & Great Western Railroad.

Gross rates: Rates consisting of an overall total not counting deductions.

Provision: Condition.

Waybills: Documents prepared by the carrier of a shipment of goods providing details of the shipment, route, and charges.

undertaking. The evident advantages received by the railroad were a regular amount of freight—the Pennsylvania was to have forty-five percent of the Eastbound shipments, the Erie and Central each $27\frac{1}{2}$ percent, while West-bound freight was to be divided equally between them—fixed rates, and freedom from the system of **cutting** which they had all found so harassing and disastrous. That is, the South Improvement Company, which was to include the entire refining capacity of the company, was to act as the evener of the oil business.

[By February 1872] Mr. Rockefeller had the charter and contracts of the South Improvement Company in hand, and was ready to see what they would do in helping him carry out his idea of wholesale combination in Cleveland. There were at that time some twenty-six refineries in the town—some of them very large plants. All of them were feeling more or less the discouraging effects of the last three or four years of railroad discriminations in favour of the Standard Oil Company. To the owners of these refineries Mr. Rockefeller now went one by one, and explained the South Improvement Company. "You see," he told them, "this scheme is bound to work. It means an absolute control by us of the oil business. There is no chance for anyone outside. But we are going to give everybody a chance to come in. You are to turn over your refinery to my appraisers, and I will give you Standard Oil Company stock or cash, as you prefer, for the value we put upon it. I advise you to take the stock. It will be for your good." Certain refiners objected. They did not want to sell. They did want to keep and manage their business. Mr. Rockefeller was regretful, but firm. It was useless to resist, he told the hesitating; they would certainly be crushed if they did not accept his offer, and he pointed out in detail, and with gentleness, how **beneficent** the scheme really was—preventing the **creek refiners** from destroying Cleveland, ending competition, keeping up the price of refined oil, and eliminating speculation. Really a wonderful **contrivance** for the good of the oil business.

Cutting: Lowering shipping charges in order to keep business from going to a competitor.

Beneficent: Producing good.

Creek refiners: Independent oil refiners in Titusville and other parts of Pennsylvania.

Contrivance: Arrangement.

What happened next . . .

The Standard Oil Company, always private and secretive, never publicly responded to Tarbell's articles. This hurt the company's reputation deeply.

Tarbell's articles and book focused public resentment on the Standard Oil Trust at a time when the corporation could not afford the attention. Within one year of the book's release, the federal courts brought charges against Standard Oil for being a monopoly and restraining trade (limiting free market competition). In 1911 the Supreme Court ordered the Standard Oil Trust to be dissolved. Most historians credited Tarbell's book as being responsible for the breaking up of the trust and for later laws passed to regulate the giant corporations and monopolies.

Ida Tarbell and several other famous muckrakers left *McClure's* in 1906 and started their own publication, *American Magazine.*

In 1999 the Journalism Department at New York University created a list of the best one hundred works of twentieth-century American journalism. Ida Tarbell's *History of the Standard Oil Company* was ranked number five.

Did you know . . .

- Ida Tarbell's father tried to persuade her not to write about Standard Oil. He was convinced the huge and powerful company would destroy *McClure's* or even seek to physically harm his daughter. Nothing of the sort occurred.

- Ida Tarbell was the most successful female journalist of her time. When the women's suffrage (right to vote) movement began to increase, suffragists called for her support, but Tarbell would not endorse their cause. Although she had been publicly and successfully competing in the largely male-dominated field of journalism for decades, she believed that women should play a domestic role in society and that voting and working in the public world might drain them of the moral force that she believed was natural to them. Her views seemed to contradict her own life, since she was one of the country's most successful women, but she felt that because she had never married she was different than most women.

- By the time Tarbell's book was published, John D. Rockefeller was becoming one of the most influential philanthropists (people who give their money and time to charitable causes for the good of others) of his time.

Consider the following ...

- How did the South Improvement Company pact hurt refiners who were not members of the pact? How did it favor members? Why do you think secret railroad rates were considered so important?

- Tarbell's book about Standard Oil is considered a classic piece of muckraking journalism. Do you think this kind of reporting is valuable to U.S. society? Why or why not?

For More Information

Books

Brady, Kathleen. *Ida Tarbell: Portrait of a Muckraker.* New York: Putnam, 1984.

Chernow, Ron. *Titan: The Life of John D. Rockefeller, Sr.* New York: Vintage Books, 2004.

Tarbell, Ida M. *All in the Day's Work: An Autobiography.* New York: Macmillan, 1939.

Tarbell, Ida M. *The History of the Standard Oil Company.* New York: McClure, Phillips and Co., 1904.

Web Sites

"Ida Tarbell." *Pennsylvania Historical and Museum Commission.* http://www.phmc.state.pa.us/ppet/tarbell/page1.asp?secid=31 (accessed on July 6, 2005).

"Origins of Sayings—'The Public Be Damned.'" *Trivia-Library.com.* http://www.trivia-library.com/b/origins-of-sayings-the-public-be-damned.htm (accessed on July 6, 2005).

"The Rockefellers: People and Events: Ida Tarbell, 1857–1944." *American Experience, PBS.* http://www.pbs.org/wgbh/amex/rockefellers/peopleevents/p_tarbell.html (accessed on July 6, 2005).

Antitrust Political Cartoons

"A Trustworthy Beast"
Originally published in *Harper's Weekly* (October 20, 1888)
William A. Rogers, artist

"A Trust Giant's Point of View"
Originally published in *The Verdict* (January 22, 1900)
Horace Taylor, cartoonist

"A society in which a few men are the employers and the great body are merely employees or servants, is not the most desirable in a republic."

Ohio Supreme Court.

In the latter part of the Gilded Age (the era of industrialization from the early 1860s to the turn of the century in which a few wealthy individuals gained tremendous power and influence), a growing number of the American population became alarmed about the increasing power of big business. Of particular concern were the giant trusts, which were groups of companies within an industry that joined together under one board of directors—called trustees—in order to reduce competition and control prices. As the trusts got bigger and stronger, they were able to buy out more and more of their competition, and the wealth became concentrated in just a few huge corporations, especially in transportation and heavy industry (industries that manufactured on a large scale with the use of complex and expensive machinery). To most people it seemed that there was no law or organization strong enough to break the trusts. Though many state governments tried to regulate business, the trusts could avoid the state regulations by moving their headquarters to another state, and the federal government continued to follow its long-standing policy of not interfering.

Public dissatisfaction with the power of the giant trusts was vividly and intensely expressed in political cartoons, which were extremely popular during the Gilded Age. Political cartoons have their roots in fifteenth-century Italy, where artists drew caricatures of important political and religious figures. These drawings exaggerated their subjects' prominent physical characteristics or personality traits in a humorous way that tended to ridicule the subject, affectionately or with malice. By the eighteenth century, political cartoons had become an established means of commenting on many kinds of political issues, as well as people, in Europe. The first political cartoon in the United States is thought to be Benjamin's Franklin's drawing called "Join or Die," published in his Philadelphia newspaper, the *Pennsylvania Gazette,* in 1754. The cartoon depicts a snake divided into eight parts, each representing one of the colonies. It urged the colonies to join together to fight against common enemies and would eventually become a symbol for the American Revolution (1775–83), when the American colonists fought England to win their independence.

During the Gilded Age, political cartoons became a popular means of expression. This was partly because of new publishing technology that allowed them to be produced for mass circulation in inexpensive weekly or monthly magazines. But it was also due to the intensity of political feelings and conflicts at the time. The most noted of the political cartoonists of the time was Thomas Nast (1840–1902; see "Did you know . . ." section) who was especially noted for his cartoon attack on the political corruption in New York City. There were many other popular cartoonists, representing all sides of each political issue. Most cartoonists were associated with a particular magazine, such as *Puck, Harper's Weekly,* or *The Verdict.* The political cartoons show some of the frustrations and fears of everyday people living in the time of rapid industrialization.

Two of the largest trusts of the Gilded Age, Carnegie Steel, formed by Andrew Carnegie (1835–1919), and the Standard Oil Company Trust, created by John D. Rockefeller (1839–1937), were frequently targets of political cartoons. Public opinion was divided as to whether these two hugely successful industrialists were robber barons—men who ruthlessly destroyed smaller businesses for their own profit—or captains of industry—men who courageously forged the way for industrialism (the development of industry) and made the United States the richest country in the world. The political cartoons of the era clearly expressed the uneasiness of those who viewed Carnegie and Rockefeller as robber barons and the government as a weak force that was powerless to stop them.

Andrew Carnegie and Carnegie Steel

Andrew Carnegie was born in Dunfermline, Scotland, in 1835. His father was a skilled weaver, but by the 1840s hand weaving had been replaced by machines, and Carnegie's father could no longer make a living at his craft. The family immigrated to the United States in 1848, and both Carnegie and his father found jobs in a cotton factory in Pennsylvania. Andrew worked as a bobbin boy, carrying the spools on which the yarn or threads were held, for $1.20 a week.

The young Carnegie hoped to someday have a successful career so he studied on his own during his free time to make up for his lack of formal education. At the age of fourteen he became a messenger boy in the Pittsburgh, Pennsylvania, telegraph office and within two years was promoted to a telegraph operator position. He was such a quick and responsible worker that within two more years he became the secretary to Thomas A. Scott, the superintendent of the western division of the Pennsylvania Railroad. During the American Civil War (1861–65; a war between the Union [the North], who were opposed to slavery, and the Confederacy [the South], who were in favor of slavery), Carnegie was promoted to Scott's position while Scott served in the Union army. By the end of the war, Carnegie was a reasonably wealthy young man. He left the railroad in 1865 and made a large fortune by buying and selling investments in England and the United States.

Around 1865 steel slowly began to replace iron as the building material of choice for many projects in the United States. Steel was an alloy (a compound made up of two or more metals) of carbon and iron that was harder and stronger than iron. Before the 1860s it had been too expensive to produce steel in large quantities, but in 1856 British inventor Henry Bessemer (1813–1898) invented a machine that was able to mass-produce steel cheaply. Carnegie observed the exciting new changes taking place in the English iron industry as a result of the adoption of Bessemer's system, and in the early 1870s he began building the largest steel mill in the United States.

Carnegie found talented partners, and by using the latest technology and keeping costs down, his company produced steel more efficiently than its rivals and was able to sell at the lowest prices on the market. In 1881 he combined his company with several others, naming it the Carnegie Steel Company. Carnegie obtained vast acres of coalfields and iron-ore deposits that furnished the raw materials needed to make steel. Then he purchased the ships and railroads needed to transport these supplies to the mills. Carnegie was able to consistently defeat his competitors by always having the lowest prices and the highest profits. By the end of the nineteenth century, the Carnegie Steel Company controlled all the elements it used in its production process and was producing one-fourth of the nation's steel.

Although he became one of the wealthiest men in the nation, Carnegie never forgot his humble beginnings. He was one of the few industrialists of his time to consider the unfortunate situation of his workers in public writings, initially arguing for their right to form labor unions in order to bargain collectively for better wages and working conditions. In spite of these views, conflict with a union arose at his plant in Homestead, Pennsylvania. In 1892, even though he knew that trouble was coming, Carnegie went overseas, leaving his strongly anti-union business partner in charge. When a strike began at the mill, the partner brought in outsiders to forcefully remove the workers, starting a violent confrontation that led to military intervention and the breaking of the union in Carnegie's steel mills. By not speaking up on behalf of the workers, Carnegie accepted his partner's actions, allowing his company to remain strongly antiunion for many years to come.

John D. Rockefeller and the Standard Oil Trust

John D. Rockefeller was born in New York state. His father was a trader who traveled frequently, disappearing for months and even years. He eventually married another woman, leaving Rockefeller's mother solely responsible for the family. The

Rockefellers moved from one home to another, often without a steady income, until they reached Cleveland, Ohio. Rockefeller attended school for two years, then, at sixteen, he went to work as an accountant for a wholesale trading company. Even as a very young man, Rockefeller was serious, hardworking, religious, and had an overwhelming desire to succeed. Though he was very careful in planning his future, he made some daring moves. The first was to leave his job and invest $2,000 of his savings in a partnership in a wholesale grocery business. During the first years of the Civil War, Rockefeller's business did extremely well, and he earned a small fortune that was very useful as he moved into the oil business.

Prior to the 1850s, crude oil (liquid petroleum in its natural state) could be refined into kerosene for lighting lamps, but it was not a practical fuel because it could only be obtained by a difficult process of skimming it off the top of pond water. When the first modern oil well was drilled in Pennsylvania in 1859, crude oil suddenly became available in large quantities. In 1861 the first oil refinery (an industrial plant where crude oil is processed to remove impurities and create oil products) opened in the United States. In 1865 Rockefeller decided to get involved in oil refining as a side business, even though few thought there was much of a future in it. By the end of the year, his Cleveland oil refinery was producing at least twice as much as any other refinery in the city.

Since Rockefeller's refinery was not close to the oil wells in Pennsylvania or to many of its consumers, he and the other refiners in Cleveland shipped massive quantities of oil on a regular basis. Low shipping rates were essential to maintaining competitive prices and high profits. Railroads at the time commonly gave rebates, or partial refunds of payment, to favored shippers. The larger the shipper, the higher the rebate they received. Rockefeller skillfully controlled the railroads to get the lowest rates possible, offering them large amounts of consistent business in return. This allowed him to sell for a lower price than his competitors.

Rockefeller invested in the best machinery and often altered his manufacturing processes in order to save a few cents per step. Standard Oil began making its own barrels to ship oil, and, since the company needed wood for the barrels,

Rockefeller bought his own timber tracts (wooded areas used for logging). He owned his own warehouses, bought his own tank cars, and owned or produced a large portion of the raw materials and transportation he needed to operate.

Early in 1872 Rockefeller decided to buy out most of the twenty-six other Cleveland oil refineries. The owners were offered either cash or Standard Oil stock in exchange for their companies. If they did not sell, they risked being driven out of business by the powerful Standard Oil Company. Twenty-one refiners sold out within three months. Some claimed they had been pressured into selling at prices less than their businesses were worth, while others said they felt threatened by Standard Oil's railroad rate advantages. Rockefeller merged the stronger companies he had purchased into Standard Oil and shut down the weaker ones.

Rockefeller pursued a similar course in all of the refining centers of the country. He developed a bad reputation with the public for the distasteful methods he used, which sometimes included sending thugs to physically intimidate competitors into selling. By the end of 1872, Rockefeller and his associates controlled all the major refineries in Cleveland, New York City, Pittsburgh, and Philadelphia, Pennsylvania. Over the next decade, the Standard Oil Company developed a pipeline system, purchased new oil-bearing lands, acquired extensive oil shipping facilities, and constructed an efficient marketing system.

In the process of buying up its competition, Standard Oil acquired stock in other companies, which was illegal in Ohio. To get around the law, the stocks were simply purchased in the names of various stockholders acting as trustees. A more formal arrangement was needed, so in 1882 the Standard Oil Trust was created by an agreement that placed all properties owned or controlled by the Standard Oil Company in the hands of nine trustees, including Rockefeller. The trustees exercised general supervision over all forty companies in the trust. Standard Oil became one of the biggest companies in the United States, and by 1899 it controlled between 90 and 95 percent of the American oil refining capacity, dominating the country's petroleum industry. The trust was the first of its kind and became a model for U.S. business despite the constant complaints about Rockefeller's ruthless elimination of his competitors.

In 1892 the Ohio Supreme Court found Standard Oil to be an illegal monopoly and forbade the trust to operate in that state, leading to the dissolution, or breaking up, of the Standard Oil trust back into its independent companies. The court declared, declaring in its ruling that "Monopolies have always been regarded as contrary to the spirit and policy of the common law. . . . A society in which a few men are the employers and the great body are merely employees or servants, is not the most desirable in a republic" (*Ohio v. Standard Oil Co. 49 Ohio, 137 [1892]*). Standard Oil responded by shifting its central holding company from Ohio to New Jersey, where state laws governing business combinations were looser, and restructuring and enlarging its other properties. To most people, there seemed to be no way to limit its domination of the industry.

The artists of the two cartoons in this chapter have captured the sense of helplessness of the nation against the seemingly unstoppable forces of these two businessmen and their monopolies. Like most forms of political expression, the cartoons' purpose is not simply to reflect the views of the artists and their readers, but also to urge the American public to rally for reform.

Things to remember while viewing these political cartoons:

- The first cartoon, "A Trustworthy Beast," presents a well-dressed and smiling Andrew Carnegie talking to an upset Uncle Sam (a figure representing the United States). Behind Carnegie is a many-headed monster, complete with horns and tongues. Each of the heads of the monster represents one of the major trusts of the Gilded Age: salt, lumber, sugar, oil, and steel. The caption quotes a newspaper interview of Carnegie that had appeared a few weeks earlier.

- The second cartoon, "A Trust Giant's Point of View," shows John D. Rockefeller holding the U.S. capitol building in the palm of his hand. A huge spread of Standard Oil buildings and refineries looms in the background. Rockefeller is viewing the capitol through what appears to be a jeweler's microscope, as if the government was a diamond that he is considering purchasing. He also appears to be removing coins from it as if it were a piggy bank.

"A Trustworthy Beast"

A TRUSTWORTHY BEAST.

The public may regard trusts or combinations with serene confidence."—ANDREW CARNEGIE, in an interview in *N. Y. Times*, Oct. 9.

"A Trustworthy Beast." *(Provided courtesy of HarpWeek, LLC.)*

"A Trust Giant's Point of View"

"A Trust Giant's Point of View." *(© Snark/Art Resource, NY.)*

What happened next . . .

Concern among the American public about trusts finally convinced Congress to pass the Sherman Antitrust Act in 1890. The act barred any "contract, combination in the form of trust or otherwise, or conspiracy, in restraint of trade" and made it a federal crime "to monopolize [dominate by excluding others] or attempt to monopolize, or combine or conspire . . . to monopolize any part of the trade or commerce among the several states." Despite the act's passage, however, the government still preferred not to interfere in business. In fact, more combinations and trusts were formed between 1897 and 1901 than at any other time in American history.

In 1901 investment banker J. P. Morgan (1837–1913) bought Carnegie Steel, paying Carnegie the extremely high price of $480 million for his company. Morgan merged Carnegie Steel with ten other steel companies, naming the new company U.S. Steel. It was the world's first billion-dollar company. U.S. Steel operated with expenses and revenues greater than all but a few of the world's governments, and was responsible for about 80 percent of the nation's steel production by 1910.

In *Standard Oil v. United States,* decided on May 15, 1911, the U.S. Supreme Court found the Standard Oil Trust guilty of violating the Sherman Antitrust Act of 1890. The court declared the trust had restricted trade by buying out small independent oil companies and cutting prices in selected areas to force out rivals. The case resulted in the separating of the parent Standard Oil from its thirty-three branch companies.

In 1920 the U.S. Supreme Court dismissed an antitrust suit against U.S. Steel. The court explained that U.S. Steel was not formed with the intent to monopolize or restrain trade or to restrict competition, and that the formation of the steel trust was a natural result of the existing industrial technology. Despite its gigantic size, the corporation did not abuse its market power to increase profits by reducing the wages of its employees or lowering product quality or output. The court did not find any evidence of unfair practices or trade restraints.

Did you know . . .

- Political cartoons were a popular and influential form of political expression during the Gilded Age. Sometimes cartoons were more powerful than newspaper articles. Thomas Nast, a German immigrant who served as staff artist for *Harper's Weekly* from 1862 to 1886, was the most popular political cartoonist of the time. In 1869 Nast began a crusade against the dishonest New York political machine (an unelected governing system) run by William Marcy "Boss" Tweed (1823–1878), who was stealing millions from the city. Nast ran a year-long series of cartoons presenting Tweed as a thief and mocking his crooked associates. Nast's readers were outraged at Tweed's actions. Tweed reportedly told Nast: "Let's stop those damned pictures. I don't care so much what the papers write about me—my constituents [voters] can't read, but damn it, they can see pictures" (as quoted in *HarpWeek*).

- Carnegie and Rockefeller spent much of their vast fortunes on philanthropy, the desire or effort to help humankind, as by making charitable donations. Andrew Carnegie gave away huge amounts of money long before his retirement in 1901 and pursued philanthropy full-time thereafter. He disliked the idea of charity, and only put his money into institutions that helped people to improve themselves. Carnegie funded 2,509 public libraries, built Carnegie Hall in New York City, and founded the Carnegie Institute of Technology, which later became Carnegie-Mellon University. In 1905 he established the Carnegie Foundation for the Advancement of Teaching and in 1910 the Carnegie Endowment for International Peace. In 1911 he founded the Carnegie Corporation of New York. In his lifetime he gave away an estimated $350 million.

- John D. Rockefeller retired from Standard Oil Company in 1896 at the age of fifty-six and then devoted his time and fortune to philanthropy. He practically created the University of Chicago by donating gifts and money that totaled $80.6 million. He created the Rockefeller Institute for Medical Research in 1901 and the General Education Board in 1902. In 1913 he formed the giant Rockefeller Foundation. During his lifetime he gave away an estimated $500 million.

Consider the following . . .

- Satire is a technique of writing or art that makes fun of or attacks its subject in a humorous or witty manner in order to provoke change. Explain the way that each of these cartoons uses satire to make its point. Do you find these cartoons funny? Do they change the way you feel about Carnegie and Rockefeller and their trusts?

- How is the U.S. government portrayed in each of the cartoons? How do these representations of the government compare to the images of Carnegie and Rockefeller? Look at facial expressions, size, positions, and any other details that distinguish these figures.

For More Information

Books

Cashman, Sean Dennis. *America in the Gilded Age: From the Death of Lincoln to the Rise of Theodore Roosevelt.* New York and London: New York University Press, 1984.

Chernow, Ron. *Titan: The Life of John D. Rockefeller, Sr.* New York: Vintage Books, 1998.

Smith, Page. *The Rise of Industrial America: A People's History of the Post–Reconstruction Era.* Vol. VI. New York: McGraw-Hill, 1984.

Periodicals

"A Trustworthy Beast." *Harper's Weekly* (October 20, 1888). William A. Rogers, artist. This article can also be found online at http://www.harpweek.com/09Cartoon/BrowseByDateCartoon.asp?Month=October&Date=20 (accessed on July 6, 2005).

"A Trust Giant's Point of View." *The Verdict* (January 22, 1900). Horace Taylor, cartoonist. This article can also be found online at *The Authentic History Center.* http://www.authentichistory.com/images/postcivilwar/cartoons/pcw_cartoons02.html (accessed on July 6, 2005).

Web Sites

Adler, John. "Background: Harper's Weekly." *HarpWeek.* http://www.harpweek.com/02About/about.asp (accessed on July 6, 2005).

"The Richest Man in the World: Andrew Carnegie." *American Experience: PBS.* http://www.pbs.org/wgbh/amex/carnegie/ (accessed on July 6, 2005).

"The Rockefellers: John D. Rockefeller Sr. 1839–1937." *American Experience: PBS.* http://www.pbs.org/wgbh/amex/rockefellers/peopleevents/p_rock_jsr.html (accessed on July 6, 2005).

Federal Antitrust Legislation

Excerpt from the Interstate Commerce Act of 1887

Public Law 49–41, February 4, 1887
Enrolled Acts and Resolutions of Congress, 1789–
General Records of the United States Government, 1778–1992
Record Group 11
National Archives

Excerpt from the Sherman Antitrust Act of 1890

U.S. Code, Title 15, Chapters 1–7
Published by the Office of the Law Revision Counsel of the U.S. House of Representatives

> "Corporations, which should be the carefully restrained creatures of the law and the servants of the people, are fast becoming the people's masters."
>
> *President Grover Cleveland.*

In the second half of the nineteenth century, the largest industries in the United States enjoyed tremendous growth under the direction of a few very rich and powerful men. Financial investors J. P. Morgan (1837–1913) and Jay Gould (1836–1893), oil businessman John D. Rockefeller (1839–1937), railroad chief Cornelius Vanderbilt (1794–1877), and steel boss Andrew Carnegie (1835–1919) all built huge, highly profitable corporations that were more extensive and complex than any that had previously existed in the country. These men exercised a great amount of influence over the business world and national affairs, and the American public opinion of them was strongly divided. Those who applauded the manufacturing advances the wealthy businessmen introduced to the country referred to them as captains of industry, while those who criticized them for their dishonest business practices and poor treatment of workers called them robber barons.

Competition was fierce among the industrialists. When two companies produced the same product or service, each was forced to lower their prices or improve their product in order to keep their customers. This greatly reduced profits and created unstable market conditions. As the industrialists built their businesses, therefore, the strongest among them tried to gain control over their competition. Sometimes they started price wars by setting their own prices very low, forcing others in the industry to reduce prices as well. Eventually, the lack of profit caused smaller businesses to collapse. In some instances the large corporations made agreements with other well-established businesses, dividing up territories between them or merging so they could set higher prices without interference. In this environment only the largest corporations could survive, and thus most of the nation's money and power came to rest in the hands of a small group of elite businessmen.

By the 1880s the big industrialists were, in many ways, more powerful than the state and federal governments. Because there was no central banking system to control the nation's economy, the industrialists and financial investors had the power to cause financial panics and change the prices of gold and other commodities with their buying and selling. When the industrialists joined together, they could name their own prices for their services, such as railroad shipping rates, or goods, such as oil or steel. Sometimes their joint efforts destroyed independent businesses, farmers, and labor unions. The government had almost no power to stop the big corporations. It had long held a laissez-faire (non-interfering) attitude toward the economy, and almost all large corporations invested in large gifts of stock or money to influential politicians to keep them pro-business. The U.S. public became alarmed. Nineteenth-century Americans considered free market competition an essential part of a democracy (government by the people). They demanded that the government and courts take action to block single businessmen from gaining so much control over the industries. The first two federal legislations that resulted from this call for reform were the Interstate Commerce Act of 1887, which regulated businesses that spanned across state lines, and the Sherman Antitrust Act of 1890, which prohibited monopolies and any unreasonable limiting of competition within an industry.

Many Americans believed the railroad industry presented the biggest problem. During the 1880s new railroad construction occurred at a very fast pace. Competing lines raced to put down track in order to lay claim to the best areas of the country, whether railroad service was needed in them or not. The railroad network became overbuilt, with more trains running than there were freight and passengers to travel on them. The cost of railroad operations was high, and as the companies could not afford to lose customers to competitors, they often used dishonest means to stay in business. There was little governmental control over the industry, and, since the railroads usually let legislators and politicians ride the trains for free, many feared the officials would not be inclined to enforce any order.

Railroad rates were extremely unstable. In regions where there was little competition and one company dominated, that company often charged its customers very high rates. In areas where competition was intense, the railroads reduced their rates and then raised rates in other less competitive areas to compensate. They offered rebates (return of part of the payment) to large-volume shippers, which hurt the smaller businesses that did not get money back. Often the railroads entered into agreements among themselves to fix rates at a high level. They also sometimes charged more to ship freight a short distance in order to offer lower rates to big shippers for longer hauls.

The lack of railroad regulation especially hurt farmers who relied on the railways to carry their crops to urban markets. The high cost of shipping could use up their entire profit on a crop and put them into deep debt. In 1867 angry farmers banded together to found an organization known as the Grange, and in the 1870s they convinced five states to pass what were called Granger laws, regulating railroad rates through state commissions, groups of people appointed to carry out the laws. These state commissions, however, were ineffective against the powerful railroads because, as railway networks continued expanding their services across state lines, an individual state's power to regulate the railroads lessened. and the federal government did not regulate interstate commerce (trade that crosses the borders between two or more states).

Other industries also had to deal with the issue of competition. Some businesses merged, or joined together, with their

Grange members gathered at a convention in Chicago. The Grange was a group of angry farmers working for railroad regulation. *(© Corbis.)*

competitors to set prices and control production. In the 1860s a number of pools were formed. Pools were agreements among rivals to share profits or divide up territories in order to maintain higher prices. The major trend in the 1870s was toward combining—a process in which companies purchased other companies and folded them into one large organization.

Most state laws strictly controlled mergers, forbidding companies to own stock in other companies. In order to get around these laws, trusts were created in the early 1880s. A trust was an agreement made between stockholders in several companies to transfer the shares they owned of their company to a set of trustees who represented the entire group of companies. In return, the stockholders received a document promising them a certain share of the combined earnings of the jointly managed companies. In effect, the trust became one central company composed of all the participating companies. By controlling most or all of an industry, trusts could set prices and drive out new competition through price wars. The first trust was established by John D. Rockefeller's Standard Oil Company in 1882. The Standard Trust was so successful that trusts in many other industries soon followed. As many of these trusts succeeded in taking over most of the business within their industry, eventually the term came to be applied to national monopolies (a monopoly is the exclusive possession of, or right to, manufacture a product or provide a service).

By the 1890s, after hundreds of mergers and combinations, there were only six huge railroad systems left out of the hundreds that had been formed and J. P. Morgan owned four of them. Morgan also put together a huge steel combination, U.S. Steel, the largest corporation the country had ever seen. Standard Oil took over hundreds of smaller companies and folded them into its trust. Public resentment against these and similar actions grew. In 1889 Kansas enacted the first state antitrust legislation, and the effort soon spread across the South and West. By 1900 twenty-seven states had created laws prohibiting or regulating trusts, but many trusts dealt in interstate commerce and thus could not be controlled by the state commissions. For example, when the state of Ohio moved against the Standard Oil Company in 1892, the trust simply re-formed under the more business-friendly laws of New Jersey. Pressure mounted for the federal government to take action, but the trusts donated heavily to political campaigns, bribed legislators, and were in a position to help or harm many politicians. Additionally, many politicians believed the big corporations did the nation an important service and hesitated to impose any restrictions on them.

Things to remember while reading the excerpts from the Interstate Commerce Act and the Sherman Antitrust Act:

- It was not fully clear who had the authority to regulate the interstate commerce of the railroads, but the U.S. Constitution offered some guidance. Although it gave the states the power to regulate trade within their own borders, the so-called "commerce clause" of Article I gave Congress the power to "regulate Commerce ... among the several states." The idea of federal regulation was not easily accepted. In 1877 the Supreme Court ruled in the case *Munn v. Illinois* that the state regulatory boards had jurisdiction over the railroads. But less than a decade later, in the case of *Wabash, St. Louis and Pacific Railway Company v. Illinois,* the high court overturned its earlier decision and proclaimed that only the U.S. Congress had the right to regulate interstate commerce, as stated in the commerce clause from the Constitution.

John Sherman, the U.S. senator who sponsored the Sherman Antitrust Act.

- After the *Wabash* decision, Congress passed one of the most important legislative measures of the era, the Interstate Commerce Act of 1887. This act created the first federal regulatory agency, a five-person Interstate Commerce Commission (ICC), to oversee passenger and freight charges on any railroad that operated in more than one state. The commission was also authorized to hear public testimony on violations, to examine company records, and in general to oversee law enforcement as it applied to railroads.

- Responding at last to the public outrage against corporate trusts and monopolies, in 1888 Senator John Sherman (1823–1900) of Ohio introduced an antitrust measure in the U.S. Senate. However it was only after another two years and considerable revision that Congress passed the act. The Sherman Antitrust Act of 1890 barred any excessive attempts to eliminate competition in an industry and made it a federal crime to create a monopoly. Enforcement of the act was supervised by the U.S. attorney general, who was the chief law officer of the nation.

- The wording of the Interstate Commerce Act and the Sherman Antitrust Act was vague and many politicians and legal experts noted that it was not specific enough to be enforceable. Some suspected that the congressmen who wrote these acts did not truly support business regulation. As you read the acts, take note of some of the terms that might be considered unclear when it came to making a charge against a railroad or a trust.

Excerpt from the Interstate Commerce Act of 1887

Be it enacted . . . That the **provisions** *of this act shall apply to any common* **carrier** *or carriers engaged in the transportation of passengers or property wholly by railroad, or partly by railroad and partly by water when both are used, under a common control, management, or arrangement, for a continuous carriage or shipment, from one State or Territory of the United States, or the District of Columbia, or from any place in the United States through a foreign country to any other place in the United States, and also to the transportation in like manner of property shipped from any place in the United States to a foreign country and carried from such place to a port of* **transshipment,** *or shipped from a foreign country to any other place in the United States, and also to the transportation in like manner of property shipped from any place in the United States to a foreign country and carried from such place to a port of entry either in the United States or an* **adjacent** *foreign country:* Provided, however, *That the provisions of this act shall not apply to the transportation of passengers or property, or to the receiving, delivering, storage, or handling of property, wholly within one State, and not shipped to or from a foreign country from or to any State or Territory as* **aforesaid.** . . .

All charges made for any service **rendered** *or to be rendered in the transportation of passengers or property as aforesaid, or in connection therewith, or for the receiving, delivering, storage, or handling of such property, shall be reasonable and just; and every unjust and unreasonable charge for such service is prohibited and declared to be unlawful.*

Provisions: Conditions.

Carrier: Transportation line that carries passengers or freight for a fee.

Transshipment: Transfer from one carrier to another for further transportation.

Adjacent: Having a common border.

Aforesaid: Previously mentioned.

Rendered: Given in exchange for payment.

Sec. 2. That if any common carrier subject to the provisions of this act shall, directly or indirectly, by any special rate, **rebate, drawback,** or other device, charge, demand, collect, or receive from any person or persons a greater or less **compensation** for any service rendered, or to be rendered, in the transportation of passengers or property, subject to the provisions of this act, than it charges, demands, collects, or receives from any other person or persons for doing for him or them a like and **contemporaneous** service in the transportation of a like kind of traffic under substantially similar circumstances and conditions, such common carrier shall be deemed guilty of unjust **discrimination,** which is hereby prohibited and declared to be unlawful. . . .

Sec. 5. That it shall be unlawful for any common carrier subject to the provisions of this act to enter into any contract, agreement, or **combination** with any other common carrier or carriers for the **pooling** of freights of different and competing railroads, or to divide between them the **aggregate** or **net proceeds** of the earnings of such railroads, or any portion thereof; and in any case of an agreement for the pooling of freights as aforesaid, each day of its continuation shall be deemed a separate offense.

Sec. 6. That every common carrier subject to the provisions of this act shall print and keep for public inspection schedules showing the rates and fares and charges for the transportation of passengers and property which any such common carrier has established and which are in force at the time upon its railroad, as defined by the first section of this act. . . .

Sec. 11. That a Commission is hereby created and established to be known as the Inter-State Commerce Commission, which shall be composed of five Commissioners, who shall be appointed by the President, by and with the advice and consent of the Senate. . . .

Sec. 12. That the Commission hereby created shall have authority to inquire into the management of the business of all common carriers subject to the provisions of this act, and shall keep itself informed as to the manner and method in which the same is conducted, and shall have the right to obtain from such common carriers full and complete information necessary to enable the Commission to perform the duties and carry out the objects for which it was created; and for the purposes of this act the Commission shall have power to require the attendance and testimony of witnesses and the production of all books, papers, **tariffs,** contracts, agreements, and documents relating to any matter under investigation, and to that end may call upon the aid of any court of the United States in requiring the attendance and testimony of

Rebate: Return of a part of the payment.

Drawback: Partial refund.

Compensation: Payment.

Contemporaneous: Occurring at the same time.

Discrimination: Partiality or prejudice.

Combination: An organization formed when companies buy other companies and fold them into one large company.

Pooling: Combining in a common effort.

Aggregate: Total of all parts.

Net proceeds: The remainder of earnings after costs and expenses are deducted.

Tariffs: Taxes on imported products.

witnesses and the production of books, papers, and documents under the provisions of this section. . . .

Excerpt from the Sherman Antitrust Act of 1890

*Sec. 1. Every contract, combination in the form of trust or otherwise; or **conspiracy**, in **restraint** of trade or commerce among the several States, or with foreign nations, is hereby declared to be illegal. Every person who shall make any such contract or engage in any such combination or conspiracy, shall be deemed guilty of a **misdemeanor**, and, on conviction thereof, shall be punished by a fine not exceeding five thousand dollars, or by imprisonment not exceeding one year, or by both said punishments, in the **discretion** of the court.*

Sec. 2. Every person who shall monopolize, or attempt to monopolize, or combine or conspire with any other person or persons, to monopolize any part of the trade or commerce among the several States, or with foreign nations, shall be deemed guilty of a misdemeanor, and, on conviction thereof, shall be punished by fine not exceeding five thousand dollars, or by imprisonment not exceeding one year, or by both said punishments, in the discretion of the court.

Conspiracy: Secret plot among members of a group to achieve a joint result.

Restraint: Limitation.

Misdemeanor: Minor crime.

Discretion: Judgment.

Invested with jurisdiction: Given the authority to apply the law.

District attorneys: Prosecuting officers of a court district.

Institute proceedings in equity: Request a court to force a party to act in compliance with the law.

Petition: Formal written request made to the court.

Enjoined: Prohibited by judicial order.

Sec. 3. Every contract, combination in form of trust or otherwise, or conspiracy, in restraint of trade or commerce in any Territory of the United States or of the District of Columbia, or in restraint of trade or commerce between any such Territory and another, or between any such Territory or Territories and any State or States or the District of Columbia, or with foreign nations, or between the District of Columbia and any States or States or foreign nations, is hereby declared illegal. Every person who shall make any such contract or engage in any such combination or conspiracy, shall be deemed guilty of a misdemeanor, and, on conviction thereof, shall be punished by fine not exceeding five thousand dollars, or by imprisonment not exceeding one year, or by both said punishments, in the discretion of the court.

*Sec. 4. The several circuit courts of the United States are hereby **invested with jurisdiction** to prevent and restrain violations of this act; and it shall be the duty of the several **district attorneys** of the United States, in their respective districts, under the direction of the Attorney General, to **institute proceedings in equity** to prevent and restrain such violations. Such proceedings may be by way of **petition** setting forth the case and praying that such violation shall be **enjoined** or otherwise prohibited. When the parties complained of shall have been duly notified of such petition the courts shall proceed, as soon as may be, to the hearing and determination of the case; and pending such petition and* *before final **decrees**, the court may at any time make such temporary **restraining order** or prohibition as shall be deemed just in the **premises**.*

*Sec. 5. Whenever it shall appear to the court before which any proceeding under Section four of this act may be pending, that the ends of justice require that other parties should be brought before the court, the court may cause them to be summoned, whether they reside in the district in which the court is held or not; and **subpoenas** to that end may be served in any district by the **marshal** thereof. . . .*

Decrees: Judicial decisions.

Restraining order: Legal order issued before the final decision of the case that keeps the situation unchanged until the decision is made.

Premises: Case set forth.

Subpoenas: Documents ordering a person to appear in court.

Marshal: Officer of the court acting in a role similar to a sheriff.

What happened next . . .

There was little enforcement of the Interstate Commerce Act in the first decades after its creation. The Interstate Commerce Commission (ICC) and the courts seemed to favor the interests of the railroads. From 1887 to 1911, the ICC brought railroads to court on only sixteen occasions, and the railroads won fifteen of those cases.

During the administration of President Theodore Roosevelt (1858–1919; served 1901–9), the ICC's authority was greatly strengthened. Discriminatory practices against short haul routes were ruled illegal in 1903, and in 1906 the ICC received the authority to enforce approved rates without first getting court orders. Aside from stabilizing railroad rates, the Interstate Commerce Act was important because it was the first federal intervention in business and provided the basis for federal regulation of commerce in the twentieth century.

By the 1960s the railroads were losing customers to other forms of transportation, particularly cars, trucks, and airlines, and they no longer posed much threat to free market competition. In December 1995 the ICC Sunset Act dissolved the ICC.

The Sherman Act was not enforced at all in the early years after its passage. The attorneys general at the end of the nineteenth century tended to be pro-trust and the courts were not inclined to rule against private industry. From 1890 to 1901 only eighteen antitrust suits were filed, and four of them were actually against labor unions said to be plotting to restrain free competition. In fact, more combinations and trusts were formed between 1897 and 1901—after the passage of the Sherman Antitrust Act—than at any other time in American history. By 1901 a few hundred large companies controlled almost half of U.S. manufacturing and greatly influenced almost all key industries.

The trust-busting movement began in 1904 with the Supreme Court's decision in *Northern Securities Co. v. U.S.* to break up a railroad trust. Over forty antitrust lawsuits were filed during Theodore Roosevelt's administration. Roosevelt and his successor, William Howard Taft (1857–1930; served 1909–13), used the Sherman Act to make businesses more responsible to the greater good of society.

In 1914 Congress passed the Clayton Antitrust Act, which prohibited companies from charging different buyers different prices for the same products, contracts restricting business with competitors, mergers between competing companies, and companies buying stock in competing companies.

Did you know . . .

- Many railroad companies, big and small, actually welcomed federal oversight by the ICC. They would rather fight one regulator, the federal government, than fighting the same war in all the state legislatures. In addition, the railroads had a lot to lose in an unregulated environment in which they were forced to pay rebates and drop their prices in order to compete. Far from being free market capitalists, most railroads favored government regulations that would ensure them a rational process of setting rates and a guaranteed profit.

- The Sherman Antitrust Act was amended several times over the years and was still in use in the early twenty-first century. One well-known violation occurred in November 1999, when a federal judge determined that computer software company Microsoft had used its monopolistic market position to restrict competition and harm consumers. Microsoft controlled more than 90 percent of the computer software market and had a market value of $470 billion, but that was not the problem. The judge's report alleged that Microsoft restricted the market access of its web browser competitor Netscape by bundling (making it an automatic part of the purchase) its own browser, Microsoft Internet Explorer, with the popular computer operating system Microsoft Windows. This meant that all computer systems that used Windows contained Microsoft's browser, thereby making the Netscape browser technically unnecessary. The court also found that Microsoft used intimidation so Apple Computers would use its browser and bullied Intel, a company that made computer chips, into staying out of the software market, threatening to work with computer chip companies that were Intel's rivals to damage Intel's business if Intel did not comply. The court ordered Microsoft to be broken into smaller companies to dissolve its monopoly. Microsoft appealed the decision, and in 2001 the U.S. Court of Appeals upheld the ruling that Microsoft was a monopoly but overturned the order to break up the company, mainly because it found fault with the first judge's handling of the case.

Consider the following ...

- Imagine that you own a small farm in Illinois in 1890. In what ways would your life and income be affected by the railroad competition, and by the pools, trusts, and giant corporations? How do you think you would feel about the powerful industrialists?

- Legislation for regulating the big businesses was demanded by the public long before the federal government acted. Why do you think the members of Congress and the courts were so slow to create the laws?

For More Information

Books

Cashman, Sean Dennis. *America in the Gilded Age: From the Death of Lincoln to the Rise of Theodore Roosevelt.* New York and London: New York University Press, 1984.

Smith, Page. *The Rise of Industrial America: A People's History of the Post-Reconstruction Era.* Vol. VI. New York: McGraw-Hill, 1984.

Swisher, Karl Brent. *American Constitutional Development.* Boston, MA: Houghton Mifflin, 1954.

Web Sites

"Interstate Commerce Act. The People's Vote: 100 Documents That Shaped America." *U.S. News and World Report.* http://www.usnews.com/ usnews/documents/docpages/document_page49.htm (accessed on July 6, 2005).

"Sherman Act, 1890: Defining Documents of the United States." *Class Brain.com.* http://www.classbrain.com/artteenst/publish/ article_127.shtml (accessed on July 6, 2005).

Other Sources

Interstate Commerce Act. Public Law 49–41, February 4, 1887; Enrolled Acts and Resolutions of Congress, 1789– General Records of the United States Government, 1778–1992; Record Group 11; National Archives.

Sherman Antitrust Act of 1890. U.S. Code, Title 15, Chapters 1–7. Published by the Office of the Law Revision Counsel of the U.S. House of Representatives.

15

Letters to Michael and Hugh

Excerpt from Letters to Michael and Hugh [Owens] from
P. M. Newman

By P. M. Newman
Written in May 1951
Located in the International Ladies' Garment Workers'
Union Archives, Kheel Center for Labor-Management
Documentation and Archives
Available online at http://www.ilr.cornell.edu/trianglefire/texts/
letters/newman_letter.html

Labor organizer Pauline M. Newman (c. 1888–1986) and her family immigrated to New York in 1901 from Lithuania. Although she was only thirteen years old and did not speak English, Newman immediately began to look for work so she could help with the family's expenses. She held temporary jobs for a couple of months before getting hired at the Triangle Shirtwaist Factory, where she worked until 1909. Labor conditions at the factory were dangerous and unhealthy, which was typical of the garment industry during this period. After she left the Triangle factory, Newman spent the rest of her life fighting so that others would not be forced to work in similarly poor environments.

Around the turn of the twentieth century, an estimated eighteen thousand immigrants arrived in New York City each month. Newman's family was among the hundreds of thousands of Eastern European Jews who settled in about one square mile of the city's Lower East Side. This area was one of the most densely populated districts in the world, packed with tenements (urban dwellings rented by impoverished families that barely meet or fail

> "We were not organized and we knew that individual protest amounted to the loss of one's job. . . . Therefore, we were, due to our ignorance and poverty, helpless against the power of the exploiters."

Many immigrant women worked in sweatshops like this one. *(© Corbis.)*

to meet the minimum standards of safety, sanitation, and comfort), factories, banks, synagogues, and shops of all kinds.

Many of the new immigrants who lived in the Lower East Side, especially the women and girls, went to work in the garment industry. There were about six hundred garment factories in New York City during the early 1900s. Most were small, consisting of an attic or a floor or two of a commercial building, and had been rapidly established to fill the growing national demand for inexpensive ready-made clothes. Enterprising immigrants could start up one of these shops without much investment cash. Unlike other industries, clothing manufacturing did not require expensive or bulky machinery, but it did require a lot of human labor. To keep costs down, workers in the garment industry were paid as little as possible and almost no money went into making the workplace safe, healthy, or comfortable. Many shop owners set up their businesses in basements or tiny, airless tenement apartments, crowding in as many sewing machines as would fit. The result was a sweatshop, a place where women and children were employed to work long hours in crowded, dangerous conditions. Infectious diseases spread rapidly among workers, even sometimes passing to customers on the clothing they purchased. Poor lighting hurt workers' eyes, and sitting in cramped positions for long hours was physically damaging, particularly to children. Few employers gave much thought to fire prevention or safe exits in case of fire.

About 75 percent of the garment workers in New York during the late nineteenth and early twentieth centuries were Jewish immigrant women and children. It is estimated that in 1880 there were between 60,000 and 100,000 children ranging in age from eight to sixteen working in the city's factories. The exact number was unknown because the city's laws against child labor were poorly enforced and commonly ignored, and few factories kept records of the underage laborers they hired.

Although labor unions were rising in other industries to help people negotiate for better working conditions with their employers, most of them would not organize women or unskilled labor, partly because they did not like the extra competition for their jobs and partly because many of the labor leaders did not approve of women working at all. Few public agencies or government regulations existed to provide protection and fair treatment for the garment workers. Employers were not required to pay a minimum wage, offer health insurance, provide pensions for old age or illness, help widows and orphans, or meet many safety or health requirements. The conduct of the factory owners angered the laborers, who did not like receiving wages that were not enough to live on and working long hours every day of the week. The garment workers also had no guarantee that their jobs would not suddenly disappear. As unpleasant as their work was, most dreaded the frequent slow periods in the business, when they could be out of a job for four or five months.

The women and children who worked in the sweatshops of New York at the turn of the century were uneducated. Many did not speak English. They were unlikely to leave behind them records of their experience, like memoirs, art, or letters. For the most part, their experiences have been lost to later generations.

Pauline Newman was one of the few who went on to other things after her early years at the Triangle factory, and fortunately, many years later, she chose to write about it. Her letters to friends Michael and Hugh Owens, in which she looks back to her teenage days at the factory, provide a personal view of life in the sweatshops.

Things to remember while reading the excerpt from the Letters to Michael and Hugh [Owens] from P. M. Newman:

- Hundreds of the clothing shops produced the popular shirtwaist. This was a form-fitting, long-sleeved, high-necked blouse designed to be worn with an ankle-length skirt. Both working women and middle-class women appreciated this new style, which was more comfortable than earlier women's garments.

- The nation's largest shirtwaist factory was the Triangle Company, owned by two wealthy men named Max Blanck and Isaac Harris. In 1906 the company moved to the eighth, ninth, and tenth floors of the new Asch Building in New York City's Greenwich Village. The company had between five hundred and six hundred employees, almost all immigrant women and girls, and was able to produce about two thousand garments each day to ship to markets all over the United States. This amounted to about $1 million in business each year.

- In 1900 a group of male cloak makers formed the International Ladies' Garment Workers Union (ILGWU). The term "ladies" referred to the kind of clothes being made—as opposed to men's garments—rather than the gender of the group members. But since about 70 percent of the women's clothing industry workforce was made up of immigrant women, the union did have a female majority.

- By 1909 about 150 Triangle employees had joined the ILGWU against the wishes of Blanck and Harris. In September the owners labeled the union members troublemakers and fired them. Workers from Triangle went on strike in protest. In November, ILGWU joined Triangle, calling a general strike involving laborers from hundreds of garment factories who demanded better wages and more predictable working hours. The strike became known as the Uprising of 20,000, with the number representing the estimated turnout of garment industry workers. It lasted until February 1910, when 339 of the companies agreed to some of the improvements called for by the workers. Triangle was one of the thirteen companies that refused to negotiate.

- Pauline Newman was one of the speakers at the Triangle strikes. Her participation impressed the ranking members of ILGWU, and in 1910 she left Triangle to become the nation's first female full-time labor organizer. In letters to her acquaintances forty years after her time at Triangle, Newman recounted what it was like to work at the factory. Like most of the women and children who worked in the garment industry, Pauline Newman left few records behind and little is known about her life. Her letters have been printed in many history collections because they provide a voice for the thousands who worked in the infamous sweatshops of New York in the first years of the twentieth century.

Excerpt from Letters to Michael and Hugh [Owens] from P. M. Newman

*One day a relative of mine who was employed by the now infamous Triangle Shirt Waist Co., the largest manufacturers of shirt waists in New York City, got me a job with that firm. The day I left the Jackson street shop the foreman told me that I was very lucky to have gotten a job with that **concern** because there is work all year round and that I will no longer have to look for another job. I found later that workers were actually eager to work for this company because there was steady employment. For me this job differed in many respects from the previous ones. The Triangle Waist Co. was located at Green Street and Washington Place. This was quite a distance from my home. Since the day's work began at seven thirty it meant that I had to leave home at six forty, catch the horse car—yes, boys, there were horse cars in those days, then change for the electric trolley at Duane and Broadway and get off at Washington Place. You will be interested to know that both rides cost only a nickel and if I remember a-right the service was much better than it is to-day when we pay fifteen ["fifteen" is crossed out and hand written above it is "20"] cents for a single ride!*

Concern: Business.

*The day's work was supposed to end at six in the afternoon. But, during most of the year we youngsters worked overtime until 9 PM every night except Fridays and Saturdays. No, we did not get additional pay for overtime. At this point it is worth recording the generocity (sic) of the Triangle Waist Co. by giving us a piece of apple pie for supper instead of additional pay! Working men and women of today who receive **time and one half** and at times double time for overtime will find it difficult to understand and to believe that the workers of those days were evidently willing to accept such conditions of labor without protest. However, the answer is quite simple—we were not organized and we knew that individual protest amounted to the loss of one's job. No one in those days could afford the luxory (sic) of changing jobs—there was no unemployment insurance, there was nothing better than to look for another job which will not be better than the one we had. Therefore, we were, due to our ignorance and poverty, helpless against the power of the exploiters.*

*As you will note, the days were long and the wages low—my starting wage was just one dollar and a half a week—a long week—consisting more often than not, of seven days. Especially was this true during the **season**, which in those days were longer than they are now. I will never forget the sign which on Saturday afternoons was posted on the wall near the elevator stating—"if you don't come in on Sunday you need not come in on Monday"!. . . We did not like it. As a matter of fact we looked forward to the one day on which we could sleep a little longer, go to the park and get to see one's friends and relatives. It was a bitter disappointment.*

*My job, like that of the other kids was not **strenous** (sic). It consisted of trimming off the threads left on the shirt waists by the **operators.** We were called "cleaners." Hundreds of dozens of shirt waists were carried from the machines to the "children's corner" and put into huge cases. When these were trimmed they were put in similar empty case ready for the examiners to finish the job. By the way, these cases were used for another purpose which served the employers very well indeed. You see, boys, these cases were high enough and deep enough for us kids to hide in, so that when a factory inspector came to inspect the factory he found no violation of the child labor law, because he did not see any children at work—we were all hidden in the cases and covered with shirt waists! Clever of them, was it not? Somehow the employers seemed to have known when the inspector would come and had time enough to arrange for our hiding place.*

*As I said before, the job was not strenous (sic). It was **tedious.** Since our day began early we were often hungry for sleep. I remember a song we used to sing which began with "I would rather sleep than eat." This*

Time and one half: An increased rate of pay for overtime equaling one and a half times the full hourly pay.

Season: Period in the year when business is at its peak.

Strenous: Strenuous; difficult.

Operators: The people who handled the sewing machines.

Tedious: Boring.

*song was very popular at that time. But there were conditions of work which in our ignorance we so patiently tolerated such as **deductions** from your **meager** wages if and when you were five minutes late—so often due to transportation delays; there was the constant watching you lest you pause for a moment from your work; (rubber heels had just come into use and you rarely heard the foreman or the employer sneak up behind you, watching.) You were watched when you went to the lavatory and if in the opinion of the forelady you stayed a minute or two longer than she thought you should have you were threatened with being fired; there was the searching of your purse or any package you happen to have lest you may have taken a bit of lace or thread. The deductions for being late was stricktly (sic) enforced because deductions even for a few minutes from several hundred people must have meant quite a sum of money. And since it was money the Triangle Waist Co. employers were after this was an easy way to get it. That these deductions meant less food for the worker's children bothered the employers not at all. If they had a conscience it apparently did not function in that direction. As I look back to those years of actual slavery I am quite certain that the conditions under which we worked and which existed in the factory of the Triangle Waist Co. were the **acme** of exploitation perpetrated by humans upon defenceless (sic) men women and children—a sort of punishment for being poor and **docile**.*

Despite these inhuman working conditions the workers—including myself—continued to work for this firm. What good would it do to change jobs since similar conditions existed in all garment factories of that era? There were other reasons why we did not change jobs—call them psychological, if you will. One gets used to a place even if it is only a work shop. One gets to know the people you work with. You are no longer a stranger and alone. You have a feeling of belonging which helps to make life in a factory a bit easier to endure. Very often friendships are formed and a common understanding established. These among other factors made us stay put, as it were.

Deductions: Amounts taken out of one's pay.

Meager: Small.

Acme: Highest point.

Docile: Easily led or managed.

What happened next ...

On Saturday afternoon, March 25, 1911, the Triangle factory workers were shutting down operations for the night when a fire broke out near a corner of the eighth floor. Its cause has never been determined. Although the Asch building itself was believed to be fireproof, the interior of the Triangle Company on the upper three floors was packed with flammable objects such as clothing products, bolts of cloth, and linen and cotton cuttings littering the floors. Gas was used in some of the machines. Company management had a policy of locking most exits from the outside so that their workers could not take unnoticed breaks or steal lace or cloth. Additionally, the exits were only twenty inches wide, designed to restrict access to one person at a time.

Within minutes the fire spread to the two higher floors. The company's one shaky fire escape led nowhere and collapsed when several workers climbed onto it. When fire crews arrived they discovered their ladders were several stories too short to reach the top three floors of the Asch building and the water pressure was insufficient for the hoses to reach that height. As the fire engulfed the upper portion of the building, forty-seven of the trapped workers jumped to their deaths, some already on fire. In total 146 workers died and 70 were seriously injured.

Triangle owners Blanck and Harris were charged with manslaughter for locking the exit doors in their factory, but they were cleared of all charges within eight months. Families of some of the Triangle victims brought civil suits against the two owners but ended up receiving only about $75 for each of their loved ones who died in the fire.

By 1900 industrial accidents in the United States killed thirty-five thousand workers each year and maimed five hundred thousand others. Most of the accidents failed to attract the attention of the American public. The Triangle fire, however, was regarded as one of the worst industrial tragedies in the country's history, and it motivated citizens to take action and demand reform. The New York state legislature appointed investigative commissions to examine factories statewide, and thirty laws in New York City were passed to enforce fire prevention measures.

Though Pauline Newman had left the company the year before the fire, many among the dead had been her friends. She knew that if she had not taken a position with ILGWU, she could

A burned workroom after the Triangle Shirtwaist Fire. *(AP/Wide World Photos. Reproduced by permission.)*

easily have died that day as well. She worked for the improvement of labor conditions, particularly those relating to health and safety, for the rest of her life. One of her many accomplishments was the founding of the ILGWU's Health Center, where she served as director of health education from 1918 to 1980. She was also an adviser to the United States Department of Labor in the 1930s and 1940s and served on the board of directors for the Bryn Mawr Summer School for Women Workers.

Did you know . . .

- Frances Perkins (1880–1965), later secretary of labor under President Franklin Delano Roosevelt (1888–1945; served 1933–45), stood by helplessly and watched the Triangle fire on March 25, 1911. Viewing the Triangle workers leaping to their deaths from the burning building influenced her to become a lifelong advocate for industrial workers.

- American sweatshops continued to exist after Newman's time, although garment factories in the country in the early twenty-first century employed mainly Hispanic and Asian immigrants rather than the Eastern Europeans and Italians of previous decades. U.S. Department of Labor studies in 2000 revealed that 67 percent of Los Angeles garment factories and 63 percent of New York garment factories violated minimum wage and overtime laws. Seventy-five percent of Los Angeles factories also violated health and safety regulations.

Consider the following . . .

- Pauline Newman's tone when she described the working conditions at Triangle and her employers there was angry, even forty years after she had worked there. What was it about working there that made her so displeased?

- If you were forced to work in Newman's job at Triangle, name the five things that would bother you most about the job as she describes it.

For More Information

Books

Orleck, Annelise. *Common Sense and a Little Fire: Women and Working-Class Politics in the United States, 1900–1965.* Chapel Hill: University of North Carolina, 1995.

Schofield, Ann. *To Do and To Be: Portraits of Four Women Activists, 1893–1986: Gertrude Barnum, Mary Dreier, Pauline Newman, Rose Pesotta.* Boston, MA: Northeastern University Press, 1997.

Von Drehle, David. *Triangle: The Fire That Changed America.* Boston, MA: Atlantic Monthly Press, 2003.

Web Sites

Newman, Pauline M. "Letters to Michael and Hugh [Owens] from P. M. Newman," May 1951. Document Number 6036/008, International Ladies' Garment Workers' Union Archives, Cornell University, Kheel Center for Labor-Management Documentation and Archives, Ithaca, NY. http://www.ilr.cornell.edu/trianglefire/texts/letters/newman_letter.html (accessed on July 6, 2005).

Sachar, Howard M. "The International Ladies Garment Worker's Union and the Great Revolt of 1909." *My Jewish Learning.com.* http://www.myjewishlearning.com/history_community/Modern/Overview_The_Story_17001914/Socialism/Socialism_in_America/GreatRevolt.htm (accessed on July 6, 2005).

Sherman, Pat. "If Not Now When: The Strike of 1909." *No Sweat Apparel.* http://nosweatapparel.com/news/article2.html (accessed on July 6, 2005).

Eight Hours

"Eight Hours"
Words by I. G. Blanchard; music by Rev. Jesse H. Jones
Originally published in 1878
Reprinted in *American Labor Songs of the Nineteenth Century*, 1975

"Eight hours for work, eight hours for rest, eight hours for what we will!"

Of the many job-related complaints of industrial workers in the late nineteenth century, the most widespread and passionate was over long working hours. In the early days of industrialization, many Americans had expected the new technology would make jobs easier, leaving more leisure time for all. However, in 1890 laborers in manufacturing companies worked an average of sixty hours per week, and it was not uncommon in some trades for workers to put in as many as 100 hours a week at their jobs. In 1900, 70 percent of the nation's industrial laborers worked ten hours or more each day. Some worked seven days a week. Laborers usually took jobs in their teens and continued working until they died or became too ill to continue. Because they spent so much of their lives at work, they were unable to enjoy time to relax with their families, participate in community activities, or express themselves through arts or other pastimes.

From the time the earliest U.S. factories were established, the issue of shorter working hours was one of the major points addressed by every labor movement. In the 1830s workers called for a ten-hour workday, and by the 1860s they were

Workers on strike for the eight-hour workday. *(© Corbis.)*

demanding an eight-hour day. In 1866 delegates from many unions nationwide formed the National Labor Union (NLU) to promote the eight-hour day, and two years later six states and several cities had passed legislation granting the appeal. Unfortunately, these gains were lost when the economy declined steeply in 1873. During this period many businesses collapsed and unemployment rose sharply. Labor leaders again called for shorter working days, but this time as a way to spread the existing jobs among more people.

By the early 1880s there were two national unions. The Noble Order of the Knights of Labor had been founded in 1869. Its platform called for the eight-hour day and workers' compensation (insurance that guaranteed workers injured on the job would receive financial support). The Knights of Labor leadership advocated educating the public as the proper means for workers to achieve their goals. They hoped to gradually create a more cooperative arrangement between the factory owners and laborers and believed workers should use boycotts (the refusal to buy or use something as a means of protest) rather than strikes to reach their goals. Another national union, the Federation of Organized Trades and Labor Unions, formed in 1881 from a combination of the skilled trade unions for carpenters, cigar makers, printers, merchant seamen, and steelworkers. It, too, sought the eight-hour day, but it did not oppose striking.

In 1884 the Federation of Organized Trades and Labor Unions passed a resolution stating that "8 hours shall constitute a legal day's work from and after May 1, 1886." The resolution energized workers in every U.S. industry, and excitement rose as the designated day approached.

The song "Eight Hours," written by I. G. Blanchard with music by Congregational minister Jesse Henry Jones (1836–1904), became the official song of the eight hours working day movement. The lyrics consider long working hours a violation of God's will, which requires that humans have time for personal reflection and communion with nature.

On May 1, 1886, hundreds of thousands of American workers nationwide went on strike, demanding an eight-hour workday. The strikers' slogan was, "Eight hours for work, eight hours for rest, eight hours for what we will!," the chorus of the song "Eight Hours." All work stopped for railroads and factories, and by the end of the day an estimated 150,000 workers had earned a guarantee of shorter working hours, including about thirty-five thousand meatpackers in Chicago who were granted an eight-hour day without loss of pay. The strike was a great victory for organized labor, but there was trouble ahead.

Well before May there had been an ongoing strike at Chicago's McCormick Harvester plant, a factory that produced machinery to harvest wheat. Fourteen hundred strikers demanding an eight-hour workday and daily wages of $2 had been replaced with nonunion workers by the company management. On May 3, 1886, two days after the nationwide strike, violence broke out at the Chicago plant and four strikers were killed by police. At a rally the following day at nearby

Haymarket Square, an unidentified person tossed a bomb at a group of policemen, killing seven and injuring sixty. Police fired their pistols into the crowd, killing ten people and injuring approximately fifty more.

Eight anarchist (people who advocated the use of force to overthrow all government) labor leaders were indicted for the death of the policemen killed at the square, although most of them had not even been at the rally. After an emotional trial, at which the accused were found guilty based on their political beliefs, seven were sentenced to death and the eighth to fifteen years in prison. In 1887 four of these labor leaders were hanged. Another committed suicide in prison shortly before his execution date. In 1893 the Illinois governor pardoned the three surviving labor leaders, saying there had not been sufficient evidence to convict them.

The Haymarket bombing incident increased antiunion sentiment in the United States. About one-third of the workers who had won the eight-hour day lost it in the month after the incident, and they began to seek leadership that could help regain the shortened hours. In 1888 the Federation of Organized Trades and Labor Unions reorganized as the American Federation of Labor (AFL). The new association pursued basic improvements in pay and working conditions in a practical way, steadily and with determination. Membership in the AFL grew, and the more radical political groups decreased in size.

Four labor leaders were hanged in 1887 after the Haymarket Square Riots. *(© Bettmann/Corbis.)*

At its founding convention, the AFL announced that May 1, 1890, would be International Labor Day. Workers throughout the world celebrated the day as a holiday to honor the strikers and labor leaders who died in the Haymarket incident and the achievements of the U.S. labor movement, in particular the struggle for the eight-hour workday.

Things to remember while reading "Eight Hours":

- The song "Eight Hours" was probably written in the late 1860s, during the early years of the national labor movement. The lyricist, Isaac G. Blanchard, was a printer and newspaper editor who lived and worked in Boston. The composer of the music, Jesse Henry Jones, participated in meetings of the Boston Eight Hour League, a society organized to fight for a shorter workday that was founded in 1863. Little else is known about the song's writers or origins.

- "Eight Hours" was published in 1878. It became one of the rallying songs of the great demonstrations of May 1, 1886, when hundreds of thousands of workers across the nation went on strike for the eight-hour workday.

"Eight Hours"

We mean to make things over, we are tired of toil for naught [nothing],
With but bare enough to live upon, and never an hour for thought;
We want to feel the sunshine, and we want to smell the flowers,
We are sure that God has will'd it, and we mean to have eight hours.
We're summoning our forces from the shipyard, shop and mill,

Chorus
Eight hours for work, eight hours for rest, eight hours for what we will!
Eight hours for work, eight hours for rest, eight hours for what we will!

The beasts that graze the hillside, and the birds that wander free,
In the life that God has meted [given] have a better lot than we.
Oh! hands and hearts are weary, and homes are heavy with dole [grief];
If our life's to be filled with drudgery, what need of a human soul!
Shout, shout the lusty rally from the shipyard, shop and mill,

Chorus

Eight hours for work, eight hours for rest, eight hours for what
*   we will!*
Eight hours for work, eight hours for rest, eight hours for what
*   we will!*

The voice of God within us is calling us to stand
Erect, as is becoming to the work of his right hand,
Should he, to whom the Maker his glorious image gave,
The meanest of his creatures crouch, a bread and butter slave!
Let the shout ring down the valleys and echo from ev'ry hill,

Chorus

Eight hours for work, eight hours for rest, eight hours for what
*   we will!*
Eight hours for work, eight hours for rest, eight hours for what
*   we will!*

Ye deem they're feeble voices that are raised in Labor's cause?
But bethink ye of the torrent [outpouring], and the wild torna-
*   do's laws!*
We say not Toil's uprising in terror's shape will come,
Yet the world were wise to listen to the monitory [warning]
*   hum,*
Soon, soon the deep-toned rally shall all the nations thrill,

Chorus

Eight hours for work, eight hours for rest, eight hours for what
*   we will!*
Eight hours for work, eight hours for rest, eight hours for what
*   we will!*

From factories and workshops, in long and weary lines,
From all the sweltering forges, and from out the sunless mines,
Wherever toil is wasting the force of life to live,
There the bent and battered armies come to claim what God
*   doth give,*
And the blazon [engraving] on their banner [flag] doth with
*   hope the nations fill,*

Chorus

Eight hours for work, eight hours for rest, eight hours for what
*   we will!*
Eight hours for work, eight hours for rest, eight hours for what
*   we will!*

Hurrah, hurrah, for Labor! for it shall arise in might;
It has filled the world with plenty, it shall fill the world with
*   light;*
Hurrah, hurrah, for Labor! it is mustering all its powers,
And shall march along to victory with the banner of Eight
*   Hours!*
Shout, shout the echoing rally till all the welkin [Heavens] thrill,

Chorus
Eight hours for work, eight hours for rest, eight hours for what
*   we will!*
Eight hours for work, eight hours for rest, eight hours for what
*   we will!*

What happened next . . .

The first federal action taken to shorten workdays was for the benefit of women industrial workers. By 1908 about twenty states had laws prohibiting employers from requiring women workers to work more than ten hours a day. An employer charged with violating the law in Oregon appealed, and the case went to the Supreme Court. Attorney Louis Brandeis (1856–1941) defended the state of Oregon in *Muller v. Oregon.* Brandeis's case rested on the idea that women were different than men and would be more severely damaged, both physically and mentally, by overwork. The Supreme Court upheld Oregon's law, marking the first time the court had been influenced by a presentation of sociological facts regarding workers.

In 1933, nearly fifty years after the strike on May 1, 1886, the first nationwide measure to establish maximum work hours was passed. The National Industrial Recovery Act was an emergency measure put into effect by President Franklin Delano Roosevelt (1882–1945; served 1933–45) during the major economic downturn known as the Great Depression (1929–39), when many Americans were unemployed. It was designed to improve standards of labor, promote competition, and reduce unemployment, and part of this was to be accomplished by imposing laws governing the wages, prices, and business practices of each industry. The act was ruled unconstitutional and overturned by the Supreme Court in May 1935 on the grounds that the act overstepped the legislative and commercial powers of the federal government. In 1938 Congress passed the Fair Labor Standards Act, which set the maximum workweek at forty-four hours. Employers were required to pay time-and-a-half (1.5 times the regular wages) to workers who worked more than that amount. In 1940 the maximum workweek was decreased to forty hours.

Attorney Louis D. Brandeis argued in *Muller v. Oregon* that women workers needed special protection. *(© Bettmann/Corbis.)*

Did you know . . .

- In 1930 the highly influential English economist John Maynard Keynes (1883–1946) predicted that by 2030 most people would be working a fifteen-hour workweek. Keynes was voicing a widespread belief that industrialization would relieve Americans from the majority of their work, allowing much more leisure time.

- The hundreds of thousands of workers who demonstrated on May 1, 1886, were led by a variety of labor leaders. Many of these leaders came from radical political groups that advocated major changes in the economic and/or political system in order to make the business owners and workers more equal. Middle- and upper-class Americans were frightened by these extreme politics, and U.S. courts, police forces, and businesses fought against them. Many American workers, fearing trouble and the loss of their jobs, turned to more moderate labor organizations like the AFL that sought specific goals and remained largely nonpolitical.

- After the first celebration of International Workers Day on May 1, 1890, May Day was observed as a labor holiday in many industrial nations such as Europe, Canada, South Africa, China, Japan, and Korea. The largest May Day turnouts were in the communist Soviet Union after the Russian Revolution began in 1917, and in Cuba, after its revolution and adoption of communism in 1959. Interestingly, although May Day began in the United States, it was not widely observed in the country by the early twenty-first century. In 1894 the United States initiated the far less controversial Labor Day holiday, which honored working Americans with parades and festivals on the first Monday of September.

Consider the following . . .

- After reading the lyrics of "Eight Hours," write a paragraph or two describing the complaints of the workers of the song.

- The song states that "the world were wise to listen to the monitory hum" of the workers. What is the warning in the song? Do you think the workers are threatening a revolution?

For More Information

Books

Arnesen, Eric. "American Workers and the Labor Movement in the Late Nineteenth Century." In *The Gilded Age: Essays on the Origins of Modern America.* Edited by Charles W. Calhoun. Wilmington, DE: Scholarly Resources, 1996.

Blanchard, I.G. "Eight Hours," (Lyrics only; music by Rev. Jesse H. Jones). In *American Labor Songs of the Nineteenth Century.* Edited by Philip S. Foner. Urbana: University of Illinois Press, 1975.

Smith, Page. *The Rise of Industrial America: A People's History of the Post-Reconstruction Era.* Vol. VI. New York: McGraw-Hill, 1984.

Summers, Mark Wahlgren. *The Gilded Age, or, the Hazard of New Functions.* Upper Saddle River, NJ: Prentice-Hall, 1997.

Web Sites

Criswell, Kim. "The Hand That Holds the Bread." *New World Records.* http://www.newworldrecords.org/linernotes/80267.pdf (accessed on July 6, 2005).

Whalen, Kelly. "How the Weekend Was Won." *Livelyhood: PBS.* http://www.pbs.org/livelyhood/workday/weekend/8hourday.html (accessed July 6, 2005).

Ragged Dick

Excerpts from **Ragged Dick, or, Street Life in New York with the Boot-Blacks**
By Horatio Alger
Published in 1868

During the Gilded Age (the era of industrialization from the early 1860s to the turn of the century in which a few wealthy individuals gained tremendous power and influence), many Americans became fascinated by the possible riches that could be made in the new economy. The American dream—the belief that anyone willing to work could live in middle-class comfort in the United States—was expanded to include rags-to-riches stories in which Americans born into poverty could overcome their circumstances and become millionaires. In fact, many real success stories occurred during this time. Oil industrialist John D. Rockefeller (1839–1937), steel businessman Andrew Carnegie (1835–1919), and railroad executive Cornelius Vanderbilt (1794–1877) had all been born in humble homes and yet went on to become some of the richest men in the nation. Novelist Horatio Alger Jr. (1834–1899) was one of the first writers to capture this rags-to-riches theme in fiction, and his dime novels for boys became so popular they were found in almost every American home in the late nineteenth century.

"'I really wish I could get somethin' else to do,' said Dick, soberly. 'I'd like to be a office boy, and learn business, and grow up 'spectable.'"

Cover of the *Ragged Dick* series. *(Courtesy of The Library of Congress.)*

A former Unitarian minister from Massachusetts, Alger left the church and made his way to New York City in 1866. (Unitarianism is a sect of Christianity that does not believe in the Trinity or the divinity of Christ, but believes that God is a single being.) At that time the city was run by a dishonest political machine, or an unelected governing system, headed by William Marcy "Boss" Tweed (1823–1878). Tweed stole millions from the city and placed his friends and supporters in important government positions in order to maintain his power.

In addition to its political problems, New York City was also experiencing a massive inflow of immigrants during the 1860s. The newcomers were arriving in such large numbers that terrible overcrowding resulted, and hastily constructed tenements (rundown apartments that barely meet minimum standards of safety, sanitation, and comfort) provided a very poor quality of life. While wealthy New Yorkers lived elegantly on Fifth Avenue and in other comfortable parts of the city, the areas in which the immigrants were crowded became increasingly filthy and dangerous.

When Alger arrived there were tens of thousands of homeless children in New York City. They were known as Street Arabs, since in those days many Americans associated Arabs with nomads, or wanderers. The children slept in boxes, old cars, or doorways. Many survived by begging, shining shoes, or selling newspapers or matches. There were a few institutions to provide these youths with a place to stay, among them the Young Men's Christian Association (YMCA) and several lodging houses built by the Children's Aid Society, where, for five or six cents a night they could get a bed and a meal. These establishments could only handle a tiny portion of the homeless children, however, and the rest had to survive on their own.

Alger wanted to help the poor children of the city. He began to interview them, studying their way of talking as they told him the sad stories of their short lives: broken homes; dead, drunken, or violent parents; and the abuse they encountered daily on the streets. Alger noted that, while most of the children he interviewed had little hope for the future, a few of them were eager to change. He believed the latter had a good chance of escaping the streets, and he decided to use his

Three homeless children, known as "Street Arabs," sleeping in a New York City alley. *(© Bettmann/Corbis.)*

fiction writing to try to focus public attention on their sad situation. He believed charitable help was good for the children, but he wanted New Yorkers to provide the means for them to work their own way out of poverty. He also hoped his stories would guide the homeless youth to actively pursue better lives as good, honest, and respectable citizens.

Alger's first New York City novel, often considered his best work, was *Ragged Dick, or, Street Life in New York with the Boot-Blacks* (1867). *Ragged Dick* first appeared in 1866 as a series in the young people's magazine *Student and Schoolmate*. The serial was an immediate success and was published in book form the following year. It presented a side of New York City that was unknown to the majority of Americans, for at that time few had written about the ugly facts of life for children on the street, and certainly not in popular fiction.

Though it revealed the brutal world the homeless children lived in, Alger's work on the whole was far from being harshly realistic. *Ragged Dick* presented a charming and heroic young bootblack (shoe-shiner), Dick, within a strongly moral tale. Dick and other Alger heroes conquered the many difficulties in their lives through hard work, self-reliance, education, and above all, honesty and good character. Oddly, it was generally not the boys' own efforts that got them out of the slums, but good luck. Good luck in an Alger novel only came to those who deserved it. In most Alger stories the young hero performed a brave or honest act that attracted the attention of a kind and rich older man who then helped the young hero escape poverty.

Horatio Alger. *(AP/Wide World Photos. Reproduced by permission.)*

Things to remember while reading the excerpts from *Ragged Dick*:

- In the first excerpt, Dick is introduced to the reader. He is seen going through his normal daily routine of waking up from his night's sleep on the city street and going off to shine shoes to pay for his food. The reader sees that Dick is charming, witty, honest, and outgoing, but has faults. If there is extra money from his day of shoe shining, Dick gambles it away or uses it to buy cigars or go to the theater. Because of this he starts each day as penniless and homeless as the day before.

- The second excerpt occurs very near the end of the novel, when Dick performs a heroic act and wins the gratitude of a wealthy gentleman. In between these two events Dick takes the steps necessary to become "spectable" (respectable) and also proves his good character.

- Early in the novel Dick offers to guide a wealthy boy, Frank, around the city while his uncle is at work. Frank gives Dick a set of presentable clothes and a place to clean up. The two boys become friends as they tour New York, and Frank tells Dick about the importance of getting an education. Dick resolves to stop going to the theater and gambling and to save his money so that some day he can be respectable. Frank's uncle gives him some money, and he rents a room. Though it is tiny, dirty, and in a very dangerous neighborhood, it is Dick's first home since his mother died when he was seven. Frank's belief in Dick has changed him forever.

- Later Dick encounters Henry Fosdick. Henry's father recently died, leaving him homeless. Henry is shy and small and doesn't get along well on the streets. Unlike the other street boys, however, he went to school and knows how to read, write, and do arithmetic. Dick invites the younger boy to live in his room with him rent-free in exchange for lessons in reading and writing. Dick is a good student and works hard at his studies, and Dick and Henry become close friends.

- Dick is popular with his customers and makes relatively good money shining shoes. He saves up his earnings, hoping he can make enough to one day take a job as a clerk. Though clerks receive less pay than bootblacks, the job is more respectable and more likely to lead to better things.

- Dick can see that Henry is not cut out for the streets or the shoe shining business. He uses the money he has saved to buy the boy a suit of clothes so that he can get a job as a clerk. Later in the story Dick uses some more of his money to help out another boy whose widowed mother is sick and cannot pay the rent.

- Not all the street children in Alger's novel are as charming or honest as Dick. One of Dick's friends, Johnny Nolan, is lazy and dull and does not try to improve his situation. Ragged Dick is constantly in conflict with Mickey Maguire, a bully who turns against Dick when he sees him in his new clothes. Mickey is hostile to anyone who strives for a better life and uses violence to attempt to bring Dick down to his level. Dick tries to avoid a fight, but when pushed he proves he can beat Mickey.

Excerpts from Ragged Dick, or, Street Life in New York with the Boot-Blacks

Chapter 1: Ragged Dick Is Introduced to the Reader

"Wake up there, youngster," said a rough voice.

Ragged Dick opened his eyes slowly, and stared stupidly in the face of the speaker, but did not offer to get up.

"Wake up, you young **vagabond!***" said the man a little impatiently; "I suppose you'd lay there all day, if I hadn't called you."*

"What time is it?" asked Dick.

"Seven o'clock."

"Seven o'clock! I oughter've been up an hour ago. I know what was made me so precious sleepy. I went to the **Old Bowery** *last night, and didn't turn in till past twelve."*

"You went to the Old Bowery? Where'd you get your money?" asked the man, who was a **porter** *in the employ of a firm doing business on Spruce Street.*

"Made it by shines, in course. My guardian don't allow me no money for theatres, so I have to earn it."

"Some boys get it easier than that," said the porter significantly.

"You don't catch me stealin', if that's what you mean," said Dick.

"Don't you ever steal, then?"

"No, and I wouldn't. Lots of boys does it, but I wouldn't."

"Well, I'm glad to hear you say that. I believe there's some good in you, Dick, after all."

"Oh, I'm a rough customer!" said Dick. "But I wouldn't steal. It's mean."

"I'm glad you think so, Dick," and the rough voice sounded gentler than at first. "Have you got any money to buy your breakfast?"

"No, but I'll soon get some."

While this conversation had been going on, Dick had got up. His bedchamber had been a wooden box half full of straw, on which the young bootblack had **reposed** *his weary limbs, and slept as soundly as if it had been a bed of* **down.** *He dumped down into the straw without taking the trouble of undressing.*

Vagabond: Wanderer.

Old Bowery: Rowdy popular theater in the Bowery District of New York City.

Porter: Person who carries parcels for a business.

Reposed: Rested.

Down: Soft feathers.

*Getting up too was an equally short process. He jumped out of the box, shook himself, picked out one or two straws that had found their way into **rents** in his clothes, and, drawing a well-worn cap over his uncombed locks, he was all ready for the business of the day.*

*Dick's appearance as he stood beside the box was rather peculiar. His pants were torn in several places, and had apparently belonged in the first instance to a boy two sizes larger than himself. He wore a vest, all the buttons of which were gone except two, out of which peeped a shirt which looked as if it had been worn a month. To complete his costume he wore a coat too long for him, dating back, if one might judge from its general appearance, to a **remote antiquity.***

Washing the face and hands is usually considered proper in commencing the day, but Dick was above such refinement. He had no particular dislike to dirt, and did not think it necessary to remove several dark streaks on his face and hands. But in spite of his dirt and rags there was something about Dick that was attractive. It was easy to see that if he had been clean and well dressed he would have been decidedly good-looking. Some of his companions were sly, and their faces inspired distrust; but Dick had a frank, straightforward manner that made him a favorite.

Dick's business hours had commenced. He had no office to open. His little blacking-box was ready for use, and he looked sharply in the faces of all who passed, addressing each with, "Shine yer boots, sir?"

"How much?" asked a gentleman on his way to his office.

"Ten cents," said Dick, dropping his box, and sinking upon his knees on the sidewalk, flourishing his brush with the air of one skilled in his profession.

"Ten cents! Isn't that a little steep?"

"Well, you know 'taint all clear profit," said Dick, who had already set to work. "There's the blacking costs something, and I have to get a new brush pretty often."

*"And you have a large rent too," said the gentleman **quizzically**, with a glance at a large hole in Dick's coat.*

*"Yes, sir," said Dick, always ready to joke; "I have to pay such a big rent for my manshun up on Fifth Avenoo, that I can't afford to take less than ten cents a shine. I'll give you a **bully** shine, sir."*

"Be quick about it, for I am in a hurry. So your house is on Fifth Avenue, is it?"

"It isn't anywhere else," said Dick, and Dick spoke the truth there.

*"What tailor do you **patronize?**" asked the gentleman, surveying Dick's attire.*

Rents: Holes or tears.

Remote antiquity: Ancient time.

Quizzically: In a puzzled manner.

Bully: Excellent.

Patronize: Do business with.

"Would you like to go to the same one?" asked Dick, shrewdly.

"Well, no; it strikes me that he didn't give you a very good fit."

*"This coat once belonged to **General Washington**," said Dick, comically. "He wore it all through **the Revolution,** and it got torn some, 'cause he fit [fought] so hard. When he died he told his wider [widow] to give it to some smart young feller that hadn't got none of his own; so she gave it to me. But if you'd like it, sir, to remember General Washington by, I'll let you have it reasonable.". . .*

Chapter 26: An Exciting Adventure

. . . On Wednesday afternoon Henry Fosdick was sent by his employer on an errand to that part of Brooklyn near Greenwood Cemetery. Dick hastily dressed himself in his best, and determined to accompany him. The two boys walked down to the South Ferry, and, paying their two cents each, entered the ferry boat.

*They remained at the stern, and stood by the railing, watching the great city, with its crowded **wharves,** receding from view. Beside them was a gentleman with two children—a girl of eight and a little boy of six. The children were talking gayly to their father. While he was pointing out some object of interest to the little girl, the boy managed to creep, unobserved, beneath the chain that extends across the boat, for the protection of passengers, and, stepping incautiously to the edge of the boat, fell over into the foaming water.*

At the child's scream, the father looked up, and, with a cry of horror, sprang to the edge of the boat. He would have plunged in, but, being unable to swim, would only have endangered his own life, without being able to save his child.

"My child!" he exclaimed in anguish, "Who will save my child? A thousand—ten thousand dollars to any one who will save him!"

There chanced to be but few passengers on board at the time, and nearly all these were either in the cabins or standing forward. Among the few who saw the child fall was our hero.

*Now Dick was an expert swimmer. It was an accomplishment which he had possessed for years, and he no sooner saw the boy fall than he resolved to rescue him. His determination was formed before he heard the liberal offer made by the boy's father. Indeed, I must do Dick the justice to say that, in the excitement of the moment, he did not hear it at all, nor would it have stimulated the **alacrity** with which he sprang to the rescue of the little boy.*

General Washington: George Washington (1732–1799), a general in the American Revolution and later the first president of the United States.

The Revolution: The American Revolution (1775–83) was the American colonists' fight for independence from England.

Wharves: Landing places or piers where ships load and unload.

Alacrity: Eagerness and promptness.

Treacherous: Dangerous.

Compass: Accomplish.

Little Johnny had already risen once, and gone under for the second time, when our hero plunged in. He was obliged to strike out for the boy, and this took time. He reached him none too soon. Just as he was sinking for the third and last time, he caught him by the jacket. Dick was stout and strong, but Johnny clung to him so tightly, that it was with great difficulty he was able to sustain himself.

"Put your arms round my neck," said Dick.

The little boy mechanically obeyed, and clung with a grasp strengthened by his terror. In this position Dick could bear his weight better. But the ferry-boat was receding fast. It was quite impossible to reach it. The father, his face pale with terror and anguish, and his hands clasped in suspense, saw the brave boy's struggles, and prayed with agonizing fervor that he might be successful. But it is probable, for they were now midway of the river, that both Dick and the little boy whom he had bravely undertaken to rescue would have been drowned, had not a row-boat been fortunately near. The two men who were in it witnessed the accident, and hastened to the rescue of our hero.

"Keep up a little longer," they shouted, bending to their oars, "and we will save you."

*Dick heard the shout, and it put fresh strength into him. He battled manfully with the **treacherous** sea, his eyes fixed longingly upon the approaching boat.*

"Hold on tight, little boy," he said. "There's a boat coming."

The little boy did not see the boat. His eyes were closed to shut out the fearful water, but he clung the closer to his young preserver. Six long, steady strokes, and the boat dashed along side. Strong hands seized Dick and his youthful burden, and drew them into the boat, both dripping with water.

*"God be thanked!" exclaimed the father, as from the steamer he saw the child's rescue. "That brave boy shall be rewarded, if I sacrifice my whole fortune to **compass** it."* . . .

What happened next . . .

At the novel's end, the father of the rescued boy does not give Dick (who has by then taken the name Dick Hunter) $10,000. Instead he hires Dick as a clerk in his large business, with promise of promotion if Dick applies himself and does a good job. Dick reappears as a wealthy man in later volumes by Alger.

Alger wrote well over one hundred books for boys. Critics did not like most of his novels, but the public—adults as well as children—loved them. Many well-known writers, politicians, and other influential people of later years admitted to having eagerly read Horatio Alger's books as children. In all, more than 200 million copies of his books were sold, an extremely large number for that time.

The public's literary tastes gradually changed. By the time of Alger's death in 1899, his books were often ridiculed for their simplistic moralizing and their similar plots. Most of his works went out of print (were no longer being published) by the early twentieth century.

In 1947 the Horatio Alger Association of Distinguished Americans was formed to honor Americans who had risen from poverty to success. It gives out millions of dollars annually in scholarships to promising young people from poor backgrounds. The association promotes free enterprise and industry using Horatio Alger's writings as its basis. The association's Web site said of the novelist: "Through his body of work, Horatio Alger, Jr., captured the spirit of a nation and helped to clarify that spirit."

Did you know . . .

- In one scene in *Ragged Dick*, the character Johnny Nolan hides in fear when he sees a gentleman approaching, telling Dick that the man had once sent him to live with a farming family in the western United States. This was a reference to the so-called orphan trains of the Children's Aid Society of New York City, which was founded in 1852 by Methodist minister Charles Loring Brace (1826–1890). The Children's Aid Society began helping New York's homeless children by providing cheap lodging houses, trade schools, and night schools for them. Loring eventually grew dissatisfied with the society's methods, however, noting that the children needed family care. He then began running the orphan trains, sending the children to places in the West where they were raised by farm families. These trains continued operating well into the 1920s, transporting hundreds of thousands of homeless children to farms across the nation. Though some children were saved from a harsh life in the slums by this practice, there were problems. Some of the families were only interested in getting free laborers to work on their farms and treated the children as servants or slaves. Other children were physically and mentally abused by their assigned families. Another problem arose as a result of the lack of respect for the Catholic religion held by Brace and his Methodist associates. They removed the children of poor immigrant Catholics and placed them with Protestant farming families so the children could be raised Protestant. This enraged many Catholics, and the Catholic church responded by building its own institutions for orphaned or runaway children.

- The lack of aid for homeless and mistreated children became front page news in 1874. That year social worker Etta Angel Wheeler found a ten-year-old girl in New York City who had been severely beaten and abused by her caretaker. At that time there were no laws to protect children from abuse. Though many of the girls' neighbors were shocked by what they saw and heard, no one knew how to remove her from the custody of the abusive caretaker. Finally Wheeler convinced the Society for the Prevention of Cruelty to Animals to intervene on the child's behalf. They did, and the little girl was removed from the abuser's home and raised by Wheeler's sister. Because of this incident, in 1875 the New York Society for the Prevention of Cruelty to Children was established. Soon other states created similar agencies to protect children from abuse and neglect.

Consider the following . . .

- What signs do you see in the excerpts that Dick is smart and headed for success?

- Can you think of some of the reasons that critics of later decades called Horatio Alger's recurring rags-to-riches theme overly simplistic?

For More Information

Books

Cashman, Sean Dennis. *America in the Gilded Age: From the Death of Lincoln to the Rise of Theodore Roosevelt.* New York and London: New York University Press, 1984.

Scharnhorst, Gary, and Jack Bales. *The Lost Life of Horatio Alger, Jr.* Bloomington: Indiana University Press, 1985.

Smith, Page. *The Rise of Industrial America: A People's History of the Post-Reconstruction Era.* Vol. VI. New York: McGraw-Hill, 1984.

Periodicals

Kanfer, Stefan. "Horatio Alger: The Moral of the Story." *City Journal* (autumn 2000). This article can also be found online at http://www.city-journal.org/html/10_4_urbanities-the_moral.html (accessed on July 6, 2005).

Web Sites

Alger, Horatio. "Ragged Dick, or, Street Life in New York With the Boot-Blacks." *Authorama.* http://www.authorama.com/ragged-dick-1.html (accessed on July 6, 2005).

Geck, John A. "The Novels of Horatio Alger, Jr." *University of Rochester Libraries.* http://www.lib.rochester.edu/camelot/cinder/Horatiomain.htm (accessed on July 6, 2005).

Seaburg, Alan. "Horatio Alger." *Unitarian Universalist Historical Society.* http://www.uua.org/uuhs/duub/articles/horatioalgerjr.html (accessed on July 6, 2005).

18

The Rise of Silas Lapham

Excerpts from **The Rise of Silas Lapham**
By William Dean Howells
Originally published in 1885
Reprinted by Signet Classic in 2002

"But there's no doubt but money is to the fore now. It is the romance, the poetry of our age. It's the thing that chiefly strikes the imagination."

William Dean Howells (1837–1920) was a journalist, a well-known literary critic, and a popular writer of novels, poetry, travel essays, plays, and short stories. His most famous book, *The Rise of Silas Lapham* (1885), captured the changes taking place in the social world of Boston in the 1880s, when the "new rich"—people from humble backgrounds who had made a fortune in the industrial era—were entering the once-exclusive circles of the city's old ruling class of wealthy and elite. The novel presents Howells's vision of a more democratic and tolerant, if less cultured, American society of the future and introduced business and industry as an essential subject in fiction writing during the industrial age.

Howells was born in Martin's Ferry, Ohio, and was the second child in a family of eight. His father, William Cooper Howells, was a printer for several small Ohio newspapers. When William Dean was three, the family moved to Hamilton, Ohio, where his father was the editor of a weekly journal. According to his memoirs, Howells learned to set newspaper type before he could read. (In the nineteenth century typesetting, or preparing text for print, was done with small pieces of metal that had been formed into the shapes of letters, punctuation marks, and spaces. Workers would use these shapes to form the lines of text on the page.) Howells's parents soon purchased a tri-weekly newspaper (a paper published three times a week) in Dayton, Ohio, with the intention of turning it into a daily paper. The project proved more difficult than anticipated, and the entire family was required to labor long hours. Therefore Howells dropped out of school at a young age in order to work, frequently setting type until midnight only to arise four hours later to deliver papers. This prevented him from getting a high school or college education, but he was very successful at instructing himself with the few books the family owned. He preferred literature and languages to other studies and taught himself Greek, German, French, Spanish, Italian, and some Latin.

In 1851 the Howells family moved to Columbus, Ohio. William Dean proved to his employer, the *Ohio State Journal,* that he was as skilled at journalism as he was at typesetting. Between 1856 and 1861, he served as reporter, editor, and editorial writer. His goal, however, was to become an accomplished poet, and at twenty-two he succeeded in publishing a collection of poems with a friend. Several of his other poems were then published in the *Atlantic Monthly,* a new literary journal based in Boston. Howells traveled to Boston to meet the famous founders of the magazine. The founders included poet James Russell Lowell (1819–1891), poet and essayist Ralph Waldo Emerson (1803–1882), essayist Henry David Thoreau (1817–1862), novelist and essayist Nathaniel Hawthorne (1804–1864), poet Walt Whitman (1819–1892), and legal scholar, essayist, and future justice of the U.S. Supreme Court Oliver Wendell Holmes (1841–1935). As well as being successful writers, all were Boston Brahmans, a term used to describe a class of wealthy, educated, elite members of Boston society in the nineteenth century.

Howells accepted an assistant editorship at the *Atlantic Monthly* in 1866. He became the magazine's editor in chief by the age of twenty-nine and transformed the magazine from a regional New England journal into a national one. Howells remained a prominent literary magazine editor for more than

James Russell Lowell was one of the founders of *Atlantic Monthly.* *(© Bettmann/Corbis.)*

forty years, during which time he advanced the early careers of many major American writers, such as novelists Stephen Crane (1871–1900), Frank Norris (1870–1902), Henry James (1843–1916), and Mark Twain (Samuel L. Clemens; 1835–1910).

Howells was passionately devoted to American literature. As he became well respected among American literary critics and editors, his career as a novelist was also blossoming. Howells believed that modern literature was moving toward realism, which he defined simply as depicting one's subjects honestly, without making them overly sentimental or romantic. To Howells, every detail of daily life and human interaction was important. His novels were often called novels of manners because he focused on the habits, tastes, and conversations of his characters, particularly when different social groups came into contact with each other. Henry James described Howells's writing in a *Harper's Weekly* article in 1886: "He is animated by a love of the common, the immediate, the familiar and vulgar elements of life.... He adores the real, the natural, the colloquial [in the style of informal conversation], the moderate, the optimistic, the domestic, and the democratic."

As he had progressed from his humble origins in the American West to rise to the top of the Boston elite, Howells had a rare personal understanding of some of the different social elements of the rapidly industrializing nation. James W. Tuttleton, in his 1972 book *The Novel of Manners in America,* remarked:

> *Few men of his time were more capable than Howells of representing accurately in fiction the social contradictions that characterized American life in the last quarter of the nineteenth century. He saw the spectacle of simple*

Westerners like himself thrown up against hyper-civilized Boston snobs, of provincial country folk deracinated [uprooted] and struggling to find themselves in the developing cities, of the underworld of the laboring poor, and of the newly rich millionaires trying to crash polite society.

In novels such as *The Rise of Silas Lapham,* Howells brought together some of the many opposing groups of the United States—urban/rural, aristocrat/working class, Northeasterns/Westerners, and older generation/younger generation. His literary portrait of the country showed its flaws and weaknesses, but it also showed the goodness and humanity in its citizens.

The Rise of Silas Lapham reflected Howells's optimism about life in the United States. The businessmen in the story valued morality over riches, the aristocrats tolerated change, and the younger generation was principled and wisely realistic. In an essay written in the early 1880s (collected in *Criticism and Fiction* [1891]), Howells argued that circumstances in the United States were usually pleasant and comfortable compared with other nations: "Very few American novelists have been led out to be shot, or finally exiled to the rigors of a winter at Duluth [a city in Minnesota that was very cold in winter]; and ... the sum of hunger and cold is comparatively small, and the wrong from class to class has been almost inappreciable [too small to be perceived], though all this is changing for the worse." He believed that writers should present the "smiling aspects of life" in America in order to present an honest picture of the country. His views, however, soon changed after the publication of *The Rise of Silas Lapham.*

Things to remember while reading the excerpts from *The Rise of Silas Lapham*:

- By the time *The Rise of Silas Lapham* was published, Howells had become the most well-known novelist of his day and had a large following. The novel was first published as a series in the *Century Illustrated Monthly Magazine* from October 1884 to May 1885. An estimated one million readers eagerly followed the novel's installments. It was published in book form in 1885.

William Dean Howells. (© Corbis.)

- The title character of the novel, Silas Lapham, is from a rural Vermont background and has had little education. He served nobly as a colonel for the Union army in the American Civil War (1861–65; a war between the Union [the North], who were opposed to slavery, and the Confederacy [the South], who were in favor of slavery). After achieving modest success in several businesses, Lapham discovers an important mineral used to make paint on his family farm in Vermont. He experiments with making paint and then establishes a large paint manufacturing business. The business does well, and Lapham finds himself a very wealthy man operating a large industry. He is initially very good at taking care of his business and often brags about his success and the profits he makes.

- Lapham's experiences echo the life stories of some of the real-life industrialists of the era, such as oil businessman John D. Rockefeller (1839–1937) and railroad owner Cornelius Vanderbilt (1794–1877). Unlike these men, however, Lapham is extremely honest and conscientious in his business dealings.

- Lapham and his wife and two daughters move to Boston, where they are unable to find a social circle they feel comfortable in. The Laphams do not want to mingle with the upper-class society in the city, but they do wish to find husbands for their two daughters. Silas Lapham is building a home in an exclusive area in the hopes of making new acquaintances there.

- Tom Corey, a young man from a wealthy Boston family, meets the Laphams and begins to court one of their daughters. Tom's father, Bromfield, is from the old aristocracy.

A talented artist and a brilliant conversationalist, he spent years entertaining himself in Italy and lost most of his family fortune, which he has no intention of going to work to replace. A man of the greatest refinement, wit, and taste, Bromfield Corey's idleness and snobbery are offset by basic charm and honesty.

- Tom Corey, unlike his father, wants to work and to find a role for himself in the new industrial society. He understands that successful industrialists like Silas Lapham are the key to the nation's economic future. Over the objections of his parents he goes to work in Lapham's paint manufacturing industry.

- During the course of the novel Lapham encounters problems with his business. He struggles with unprincipled men who seek to gain control over the entire paint industry. Lapham tries to maintain his own moral standards and deal honestly with the dishonest people. In the end his honesty results in the collapse of his business, but this failure brings about Lapham's spiritual and moral rise. In losing his money and the trappings of wealth, Lapham finds peace and comfort in the things that have always mattered most to him, his family and his conscience.

- Two excerpts from the novel are included here. Excerpt 1 is from the first chapter and serves as an introduction to the boastful earnestness of Silas Lapham as he relates the story of his rise to success. The second excerpt is a conversation between Tom Corey and his father, Bromfield, about the changing social world in the industrial era.

Excerpts from The Rise of Silas Lapham

[Excerpt 1]

[As the novel begins, Lapham is being interviewed by a journalist for a series on Boston's eminent and wealthy men. In this excerpt Lapham is in the midst of an overly long and detailed history of his favorite subject: himself.] "Mother," he added gently, "died that winter, and I stayed on with father. I buried him in the spring; and then I came down to a little

place called Lumberville, and picked up what jobs I could get. I worked round at the saw-mills, and I was **ostler** a while at the hotel—I always DID like a good horse. Well, I WA'N'T exactly a college graduate, and I went to school odd times. I got to driving the stage after while, and by and by I BOUGHT the stage and run the business myself. Then I hired the **tavern-stand,** and—well to make a long story short, then I got married. Yes," said Lapham, with pride, "I married the school-teacher. We did pretty well with the hotel, and my wife she was always at me to paint up. Well, I put it off, and PUT it off, as a man will, till one day I give in, and says I, 'Well, let's paint up. Why, Pert,'—m'wife's name's Persis,—' I've got a whole paint-mine out on the farm. Let's go out and look at it.' So we drove out. I'd let the place for seventy-five dollars a year to a shif'less kind of a **Kanuck** that had come down that way; and I'd hated to see the house with him in it; but we drove out one Saturday afternoon, and we brought back about a bushel of the stuff in the buggy-seat, and I tried it **crude,** and I tried it burnt; and I liked it. M'wife she liked it too. There wa'n't any painter by trade in the village, and I mixed it myself. Well, sir, that tavern's got that coat of paint on it yet, and it hain't ever had any other, and I don't know's it ever will. Well, you know, I felt as if it was a kind of **harum-scarum** experiment, all the while; and I presume I shouldn't have tried it but I kind of liked to do it because father'd always set so much store by his paint-mine. And when I'd got the first coat on," —Lapham called it CUT,—"I presume I must have set as much as half an hour; looking at it and thinking how he would have enjoyed it. I've had my share of luck in this world, and I ain't a-going to complain on my OWN account, but I've noticed that most things get along too late for most people. It made me feel bad, and it took all the pride out my success with the paint, thinking of father. Seemed to me I might 'a taken more interest in it when he was by to see; but we've got to live and learn. Well, I called my wife out,—I'd tried it on the back of the house, you know,—and she left her dishes,—I can remember she came out with her sleeves rolled up and set down alongside of me on the **trestle,**—and says I, 'What do you think, Persis?' And says she, 'Well, you hain't got a paint-mine, Silas Lapham; you've got a GOLD-mine.' She always was just so enthusiastic about things. Well, it was just after two or three boats had burnt up out West, and a lot of lives lost, and there was a great cry about non-inflammable paint, and I guess that was what was in her mind. 'Well, I guess it ain't any gold-mine, Persis,' says I; 'but I guess it IS a paint-mine. I'm going to have it analysed, and if it turns out what I think it is, I'm going to work it....'"

"I set to work and I got a man down from Boston; and I carried him out to the farm, and he analysed it—made a regular Job of it. Well, sir,

Ostler: Also hostler; someone who tends horses.

Tavern-stand: An inn, usually with a bar/eatery and rooms to rent by the night.

Kanuck: Impolite term for a Canadian.

Crude: In the state in which it came from the ground; unrefined.

Harum-scarum: Reckless.

Trestle: Metal framework perhaps being used as a scaffold to paint from.

*we built a **kiln**, and we kept a lot of that paint-ore red-hot for forty-eight hours; kept the Kanuck and his family up, firing. The presence of iron in the ore showed with the magnet from the start; and when he came to test it, he found out that it contained about seventy-five percent of the **peroxide** of iron."*

Lapham pronounced the scientific phrases with a sort of reverent satisfaction, as if awed through his pride by a little lingering uncertainty as to what peroxide was. He accented it as if it were purr-ox-EYED; and Bartley had to get him to spell it.

"Well, and what then?" he asked, when he had made a note of the percentage.

*"What then?" echoed Lapham. "Well, then, the fellow set down and told me, 'You've got a paint here,' says he, 'that's going to drive every other mineral paint out of the market. Why'' says he, 'it'll drive 'em right into the **Back Bay!**' Of course, I didn't know what the Back Bay was then, but I begun to open my eyes; thought I'd had 'em open before, but I guess I hadn't."*

[Excerpt 2]

[Bromfield Corey and his son Tom are talking in their home. The dialogue begins with Bromfield.] ". . . But the suddenly rich are on a level with any of us nowadays. Money buys position at once. I don't say that it isn't all right. The world generally knows what it's about, and knows how to drive a bargain. I dare say it makes the new rich pay too much. But there's no doubt but money is to the fore now. It is the romance, the poetry of our age. It's the thing that chiefly strikes the imagination. The Englishmen who come here are more curious about the great new millionaires than about any one else, and they respect them more. It's all very well. I don't complain of it."

"And you would like a rich daughter-in-law, quite regardless, then?"

*"Oh, not quite so bad as that, Tom," said his father. "A little youth, a little beauty, a little good sense and pretty behaviour—one mustn't object to those things; and they go just as often with money as without it. And I suppose I should like her people to be rather **grammatical.**"*

*"It seems to me that you're **exacting**, sir," said the son. "How can you expect people who have been strictly devoted to business to be grammatical? Isn't that rather too much?"*

"Perhaps it is. Perhaps you're right. But I understood your mother to say that those benefactors of hers, whom you met last summer, were very passably grammatical."

Kiln: Oven.

Peroxide: Compound in which two parts of oxygen are joined.

Back Bay: Once a bay in the city of Boston, the waters of the Back Bay were filled in with dirt over a period of forty years between the 1840s and 1880s, and the area became one of the city's elegant neighborhoods.

Grammatical: Conforming to the rules of grammar.

Exacting: Making heavy demands.

"The father isn't. . . . But do you know that in spite of his **syntax** I rather liked him?"

The father looked **keenly** at the son; but unless the boy's full confidence was offered, Corey was not the man to ask it. "Well?" was all that he said.

"I suppose that in a new country one gets to looking at people a little out of our tradition; and I dare say that if I hadn't passed a winter in Texas I might have found Colonel Lapham rather too much."

"You mean that there are worse things in Texas?"

"Not that exactly. I mean that I saw it wouldn't be quite fair to test him by our standards."

"This comes of the error which I have often deprecated [disapproved of]," said the elder Corey. "In fact I am always saying that the Bostonian ought never to leave Boston. Then he knows—and then only—that there can BE no standard but ours. But we are constantly going away, and coming back with our **convictions** shaken to their foundations. One man goes to England, and returns with the conception of a grander social life; another comes home from Germany with the notion of a more searching intellectual activity; a fellow just back from Paris has the absurdest ideas of art and literature; and you **revert** to us from the cowboys of Texas, and tell us to our faces that we ought to try Papa Lapham by a jury of his peers. It ought to be stopped—it ought, really. The Bostonian who leaves Boston ought to be **condemned to perpetual exile.**"

The son **suffered** the father to reach his climax with smiling patience. When he asked finally, "What are the characteristics of Papa Lapham that place him beyond our **jurisdiction?**" the younger Corey crossed his long legs, and leaned forward to take one of his knees between his hands.

"Well, sir, he bragged, rather."

"Oh, I don't know that bragging should **exempt** him from the ordinary processes. I've heard other people brag in Boston."

"Ah, not just in that personal way—not about money."

"No, that was certainly different."

"I don't mean," said the young fellow, with the **scrupulosity** which people could not help observing and liking in him, "that it was more than an indirect expression of satisfaction in the ability to spend."

"No. I should be glad to express something of the kind myself, if the facts would justify me."

Syntax: The way words are put together to form sentences.

Keenly: Intensely.

Convictions: Beliefs.

Revert: Return.

Condemned to perpetual exile: Banished from his home forever.

Suffered: Endured; put up with.

Jurisdiction: Authority to apply law; meaning in this case the standards used in Boston society.

Exempt: Excuse from duty or requirement.

Scrupulosity: Strict regard for what is right.

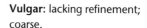

*The son smiled tolerantly again. "But if he was enjoying his money in that way, I didn't see why he shouldn't show his pleasure in it. It might have been **vulgar**, but it wasn't **sordid**. And I don't know that it was vulgar. Perhaps his successful strokes of business were the romance of his life. . . ."*

"I don't believe," added the young fellow, "that I can make you see Colonel Lapham just as I did. He struck me as very simple-hearted and rather wholesome. Of course he could be tiresome; we all can; and I suppose his range of ideas is limited. But he is a force, and not a bad one. . . ."

*"Oh, one could make out a case. I suppose you know what you are about, Tom. But remember that we are Essex County people, and that in **savor** we are just a little beyond the **salt of the earth**. I will tell you plainly that I don't like the notion of a man who has rivaled the hues of nature in her wildest haunts with the tints of his mineral paint; but I don't say there are not worse men. He isn't to my taste, though he might be ever so much to my conscience."*

Vulgar: lacking refinement; coarse.

Sordid: Vile or degrading.

Savor: Experience or taste.

Salt of the earth: The best or noblest part of society.

What happened next . . .

On May 3, 1886, there was trouble at the McCormick Harvester plant in Chicago, Illinois, a factory that produced machinery for harvesting wheat. A strike for better working conditions and a shorter workday had been going on there for several months when, in May, the factory owners decided to replace fourteen hundred of the laborers at the plant who were on strike with nonunion workers. Violence broke out between the two groups, resulting in the deaths of four strikers at the hands of the police. At a rally for labor groups the following day at nearby Haymarket Square, an unidentified person tossed a bomb at a group of policemen, killing seven people and injuring sixty. Police fired their pistols into the crowd. In the resulting disorder, ten people were killed and approximately fifty wounded. Eight anarchist (people who advocated the use of force to overthrow all government) labor leaders, most of whom had not even been at the rally, were charged with the deaths of the policemen. The labor leaders were determined guilty because of their political beliefs. Seven were sentenced to death and the eighth to fifteen years in prison.

Author Mark Twain was a long-time friend of Howells.

(AP/Wide World Photos. Reproduced by permission.)

Howells was shocked by the unfairness of the trial. He was one of a small number of prominent Americans who publicly sought justice for the unpopular anarchists. Nevertheless, in 1887 four of the labor leaders were hanged, and another committed suicide in prison shortly before his execution date. Howells was outraged and became more involved in politics after the Haymarket incident. He was disappointed with the capitalist system (an economic system in which the means of production and distribution are privately owned by individuals or groups and competition for business establishes the price of goods and services) and spoke out against the concentration of money in the hands of the few. He began to take up the principles of socialism, an economic system in which the means of production and distribution is owned collectively by all the workers and there is no private property or social classes. These ideas were reflected in his later novels.

Did you know . . .

- William Dean Howells and Mark Twain were close friends for over forty years. In an article that can be found online at The Literature Network, Twain wrote of Howells: "For forty years his English has been to me a continual delight and astonishment. In the sustained exhibition of certain great qualities—clearness, compression, verbal exactness, and unforced and seemingly unconscious felicity [pleasing manner] of phrasing—he is, in my belief, without his peer in the English-writing world."

Consider the following . . .

- Read over the first excerpt and make a list of the good characteristics and another list of the bad characteristics of Silas Lapham that are revealed in it.

- In reading the second excerpt, what characteristics do you notice about Bromfield Corey? Make a list of his good and bad characteristics, and compare the characteristics of Silas Lapham to those of Bromfield Corey. Which man do you like better and why?

- Read the excerpts from Horatio Alger's rags-to-riches novel *Ragged Dick* in Chapter 17. Compare and contrast the characters of Ragged Dick and Silas Lapham.

For More Information

Books

Howells, William Dean. *Criticism and Fiction, and Other Essays*. Edited by C. M. Kirk and R. Kirk. New York: New York University Press, 1959.

Howells, William Dean. *The Rise of Silas Lapham*. New York: Signet Classic, 2002.

Tuttleton, James W. *The Novel of Manners in America*. Chapel Hill: University of North Carolina Press, 1972.

Van Doren, Carl. *The American Novel*. New York: Macmillan, 1921.

Periodicals

James, Henry. "William Dean Howells." *Harper's Weekly*, 30 (June 19, 1886): pp. 394-95. This article can also be found online at http://www.wsu.edu/~campbelld/amlit/howjames.htm (accessed on July 6, 2005).

Web Sites

"A History of the Atlantic Monthly." From a presentation given in 1994 by Cullen Murphy, managing editor. *The Atlantic Online*. http://www.theatlantic.com/about/atlhistf.htm (accessed on July 6, 2005).

Twain, Mark. "William Dean Howells." *The Literature Network*. http://www.online-literature.com/twain/1325/ (accessed on July 6, 2005).

Where to Learn More

Books

Bagley, Katie. *The Early American Industrial Revolution, 1793–1850.* Bridgestone Books, Mankato, MN: 2003.

Calhoun, Charles W., ed. *The Gilded Age: Essays on the Origins of Modern America.* Wilmington, DE: Scholarly Resources, 1996.

Cashman, Sean Dennis. *America in the Gilded Age: From the Death of Lincoln to the Rise of Theodore Roosevelt.* New York and London: New York University Press, 1984.

Clare, John. D. *Industrial Revolution.* San Diego: Harcourt Brace & Co., 1994.

Faler, Paul. *Mechanics and Manufacturers in the Early Industrial Revolution: Lynn, Massachusetts, 1780–1860.* Albany: State University of New York Press, 1981.

Foner, Philip S., ed.*The Factory Girls.* Urbana, IL: University of Illinois Press, 1977.

Hindle, Brooke, and Steven Lubar. *Engines of Change: The American Industrial Revolution, 1790–1860.* Washington, D.C. and London: Smithsonian Institution Press, 1986.

Kornblith, Gary J., ed. *The Industrial Revolution in America.* Boston, MA: Houghton Mifflin, 1998.

McCormick, Anita Louise. *The Industrial Revolution in American History.* Berkeley Heights, NJ: Enslow Publishers, 1998.

Olson, James S. *Encyclopedia of the Industrial Revolution in the U.S.* Westport, CT: Greenwood Press, 2002.

Orleck, Annelise. *Common Sense and a Little Fire: Women and Working-Class Politics in the United States, 1900–1965.* Chapel Hill: University of North Carolina, 1995.

Rivard, Paul E. *A New Order of Things: How the Textile Industry Transformed New England.* Hanover, NH: University Press of New England, 2002.

Ruggoff, Milton. *America's Gilded Age: Intimate Portraits from an Era of Extravagance and Change, 1850–1890.* New York: Henry Holt and Company, 1989.

Smith, Page. *The Rise of Industrial America: A People's History of the Post-Reconstruction Era.* Vol. 6. New York: McGraw-Hill, 1984.

Summers, Mark Wahlgren. *The Gilded Age, or, the Hazard of New Functions.* Upper Saddle River, NJ: Prentice-Hall, 1997.

Web Sites

"The Industrial Revolution." http://www.bergen.org/technology/indust.html (accessed on July 8, 2005).

"Rise of Industrial America, 1876–1900." *The Learning Page.* http://memory.loc.gov/learn/features/timeline/riseind/riseof.html (accessed on July 8, 2005).

"Technology in 1900." *Way Back: U.S. History for Kids.* http://pbskids.org/wayback/tech1900/ (accessed on July 8, 2005).

"Transcontinental Railroad." *American Experience: PBS.* http://www.pbs.org/wgbh/amex/tcrr/index.html (accessed on July 8, 2005).

"Wake Up, America." Webisode 4 of "Freedom: A History of US." http://www.pbs.org/wnet/historyofus/web04/ (accessed on July 8, 2005).

Index

Bold type indicates major
entries.
Illustrations are marked
by (ill.).

Mulberry Bend Park, 106
Muller v. *Oregon,* 178
Munn v. *Illinois,* 153
Museum of the City of
New York, 106
Muskets, manufacture of, 26–27

N

Nast, Thomas, political cartoons
by, 137, 145
Nation (newspaper), 62–63
National Industrial Recovery Act
(1933), 178–79
Natural selection, 89
Naturalization Act (1790), 82
Netscape, 159
New England Workingmen's
Association, 47
New York City
Children's Aid Society in, 191–92
garment industry in, 162–64,
162 (ill.)
homeless children in, 183,
184 (ill.)
immigrants in, 101, 102,
161–62, 183
population of, 101
sweatshops in, 163–64
tenements in, 101–2, 161–62
New York Society for the
Prevention of Cruelty to
Children, 192
New York Sun, Riis as reporter for,
99–100
New York Tribune, Riis as reporter
for, 98–99
Newman, Pauline M., 161–70
early life of, 161
employment of, at Triangle
Shirtwaist Factory, 161
excerpt from *Letters to Michael
and Hugh [Owens] from P. M.
Newman* by, 165–67
position with International
Ladies' Garment Workers
Union (ILGWU), 168–69
as speaker at Triangle
strikes, 165
Niagara Falls, 53
Noble Order of the Knights of
Labor, 173–74
Norris, Frank, 196

North American Review, Adams as
editor of, 63
Northern Securities Co. v. *U.S.,* 158
Notes on the State of Virginia, 1–9
excerpt from *Notes on the State of
Virginia* (Jefferson), 5–6
questions posed in, 3–4
The Novel of Manners in America
(Tuttleton), 196–97

O

Ohio, antitrust legislation in, 152
Ohio State Journal, 195
Ohio v. *Standard Oil Co. Ohio,* 142
Old Northwest, 49
Orphan trains, 191–92

P

Packet-boats, 52 (ill.), 53–54
Paris Exhibition of 1900, 64
Patent Act (1790), 25
Patent Office, U.S., 28
creation of, 25
Patents
infringement of, 24
process for receiving, 23
provision for, in Constitution,
24–25
renewal of, 24
Pennsylvania Gazette (newspaper),
137
Pennsylvania Railroad, 138
Pennsylvania Society for the
Encouragement of
Manufactures and the Useful
Arts, 13
Perkins, Frances, labor movement
and, 169
Photography, developments in, 106
Pittsburgh, Pennsylvania,
immigrant populations in, 101
Political cartoons, 137
Carnegie, Andrew as subject of,
137–38, 142, 143 (ill.)
of Franklin, Benjamin, 137
of Nast, Thomas, 137, 145
Rockefeller, John D. as subject of,
110, 137–38, 142, 144 (ill.)
trusts as targets of, 137–38
Pools, 151

3/06 $55.00

LONGWOOD PUBLIC LIBRARY
Middle Country Road
Middle Island, NY 11953
(631) 924-6400

LIBRARY HOURS

Monday-Friday	9:30 a.m. - 9:00 p.m.
Saturday	9:30 a.m. - 5:00 p.m.
Sunday (Sept-June)	1:00 p.m. - 5:00 p.m.